ASPECTS OF GREEK AND ROMAN LIFE

General Editor: H. H. Scullard

* * *

ROMAN COLONIZATION UNDER THE REPUBLIC

E. T. Salmon

ROMAN COLONIZATION UNDER THE REPUBLIC

E. T. Salmon

CORNELL UNIVERSITY PRESS
ITHACA, NEW YORK

First published 1970

Standard Book Number: 8014–0547–5

Library of Congress Catalog Card Number: 72–87009

PRINTED IN ENGLAND

CONTENTS

LIST OF ILLUSTRATIONS

PLATES

FIGURES

PREFACE

THE MAJOR ROLE that the *coloniae* of Rome played in helping her to win and hold an empire is one of the important facts of history, and one about which many authors have waxed eloquent. Niccolò Machiavelli, for instance, long ago made the colonies a subject for enthusiastic eulogy; and Machiavelli, even if unique in the degree of his distinction, is far from being alone in his praises. So much has been said about this great Roman institution in the past that anyone who writes about it today is hardly likely to shed a blinding new light on it, much less to revolutionize traditional conceptions of it. He can, however, seek to collate what is known or guessed about the colonies, provide an up-to-date synthesis, describe their vicissitudes and men's changing attitudes towards them, appraise their varying purpose and importance, and perhaps suggest some new approaches to several old problems. Such is the intended scope of the present work.

The colonies, in my opinion, were of greater significance in the days before the Social War than in any later period. Indeed such was their impact before 91 BC that to describe them then comes close to writing a chronicle of the spread of Rome's power over Italy. For that reason the bulk of this book is devoted to the Roman Republic, although an account, much less detailed, of colonization under the Roman Empire has been included to round out the story.

Dates throughout are BC, unless described otherwise. The notes make no effort to document well-known events that hardly need their sources to be listed. On the other hand, care has been taken to cite the evidence whenever details are singled out for emphasis or controversial views put forward.

To study and write about Roman history is always stimulating, and it is made still more pleasant by the advice and kind helpfulness that one obtains from others. This book has been produced with aid from a great many people. I wish especially to thank Professor Scullard for help and encouragement that far exceeded what any author could reasonably expect from his editor. The hospitable librarians of the Institute of Classical Studies in London, of the American Academy, British School and German Archaeological Institute in Rome, and above all Professor Ready and his obliging assistants in Mills Memorial Library at McMaster University responded to all requests with the generosity and courtesy characteristic of their profession. For the illustrations I am greatly indebted to Dr Bonacina and Miss Dentamaro of the Centri Didattici in Rome, to Dr Nash of the Fototeca Unione, also in Rome, to Dr La Regina of the Soprintendenza alle Antichità at Chieti and to Dr Carson of the Coins and Medals Department at the British Museum. Finally, I very much wish to record my appreciation of the alert and competent team at the publishing house of Thames and Hudson.

McMaster University, E. T. Salmon
Hamilton, Ontario
May 1969

CHAPTER I

INTRODUCTION

THE PURPOSE AND PRACTICE OF ROMAN COLONIZATION

THE WORD 'COLONY' obviously derives from the Latin *colonia*, and to people living in modern times this conveys a notion of imperialism, since it is commonly applied to a portion, usually a large and undeveloped, and usually too an overseas portion, of a large dependent empire. For this modern usage there is only partial historical justification, since in Latin *colonia* did not mean a big subject territory, much less one that was separated by sea from peninsular Italy.[1] Nevertheless it was not entirely unconnected with the idea of conquest and what would today be called imperialism, since the *colonia* was one of the Romans' principal instruments for expanding their national territory, the Ager Romanus.

Realizing that permanent consolidation within Italy was best achieved by establishing settlers of their own on any conquered region, they regularly annexed territory from any enemies they defeated there and peopled it with colonists. With them colonization was always an official act of the state and not something left, as colonization has often been left in modern states, to the haphazard enterprise of private individuals.

If, for one reason or another, settlers were not immediately available, the annexed land remained under public ownership as state domain (*ager publicus*), and as such it might be leased for farming or stockbreeding purposes and thereby make a profit for the Roman state as well as for those who leased it.[2]

Most of it, however, was distributed to settlers (*coloni*) whose private property and domicile it then became. There were two distinct and differing ways of doing this. Under the one system, known as viritane distribution (or *assignatio*, to use the Roman term), individual Romans received parcels of land, but were not organized on their new holdings into self-administering communities: they continued to be not only under the jurisdiction of, but actually administered directly from, Rome itself, even though they might now be residing at quite some distance from the city.[3] Under the other system also (and this was colonization in the technical Roman sense), the settlers likewise received parcels of land in private ownership; but from the very outset they were organized as self-governing communities with their own civic centres and apparatus of administration.[4]

The decision whether to establish a colony or carry out a viritane distribution on a piece of annexed territory depended partly no doubt on the number of existing acklands, but above all on the prevailing military circumstances. A region that had been only partially or imperfectly subjugated or that was exposed to nearby enemies was unsuitable for viritane distribution, since the individual settlers would be scattered over it in sporadic pockets and, lacking a strongly fortified town to serve as a refuge, would be unable to defend it; nor would it be very feasible for the authorities far away in Rome to mobilize them swiftly and lead them efficiently in times of danger. Accordingly, whenever there seemed much likelihood of the settlers encountering armed hostilities in their new homes, the Romans thought it prudent to establish them as a compact and organized new community, or *colonia*, with their own heavily walled urban centre. Even in such a stronghold a successful defence depended on the immediate mobilization and skilful direction of the community's fighting men, and this could be effected only by officials on the spot: in other words, the community had to have its own administration and be self-governing. For this reason a *colonia* was a city-state.[5] It was not a geographical region or administrative subdivision of the Roman state but an urban commonwealth with its immediately surrounding territory (*territorium*).[6] In the early days of Roman history this meant an urban centre in Italy, since it was not until the late second century that the Romans began seriously to think of establishing colonies overseas, and even then they continued to envisage them as city-states.[7] From what has been said, it follows that colonization often preceded viritane distribution in a given region or, more accurately perhaps, that the land distributed on a viritane basis was often to be found in between a *colonia* and Rome.

Strictly *colonia* was a collective noun meaning a body of *coloni* (= 'tillers of the soil', 'peasants': from *colere*, 'to cultivate'), but when used technically the word had a precise significance. It denoted a group of settlers established by the Roman state, collectively and with formal ceremony, in a specified locality to form a self-administering civic community: the formal act of colonization was called *deductio*. The locality might be in virgin territory, but frequently it was a place of earlier settlement whose former inhabitants had had to make way for the incoming *coloni*. Appian succinctly describes the Roman practice: 'As the Romans subjugated the peoples of Italy successively, it was their habit to confiscate a portion of land and establish towns on it or enrol colonists of their own in the towns already on it. They intended these for strongholds.'[8]

Rome was able thus to rid herself of some landless poor, but that was not the main aim. The chief purpose of colonies was strategic, 'either to hold the earlier inhabitants in subjection or to repel enemy inroads'. It was not until the second century that economic ends came to the fore. Before then colonies were founded in order to make the Roman state more secure. There may have been the incidental benefit that some paupers were removed from the ranks of the indigent Roman proletariat and made eligible for military service, but the chief consideration was the defence of Roman soil and the establishment of future bases for military operations.[9]

In the great days of the Roman Republic, in the fourth, third and second centuries, the colonies sent out by the Romans were of two kinds. The one kind, the so-called Latin colonies (*coloniae Latinae*), were peopled by settlers who did not possess the Roman citizenship; the other kind, the so-called Citizen colonies (*coloniae civium Romanorum*), were peopled by settlers who did. Since both kinds of colonies were authorized and established by the Roman state, it may well be asked what determined the choice of one type rather than the other on any given occasion.[10]

Until after the Second Punic War the preference was clearly for Latin colonies. Colonies of this type were far more numerous and ubiquitous; they were also very much larger and the settlers in them received much bigger land-grants. The nature of the Roman state accounts for this. At the time of its foundation a *colonia* might well be physically separated from Roman territory, and in any case it could hardly discharge its intended military function without officials of its own. Clearly it was also desirable for it to be a large, as well as a self-governing, community since otherwise its military usefulness was limited. In early Italy, where citizenship was identified with domicile, it was the Latin colony that best satisfied these requirements. The Citizen colony was not fully suitable, since it was unthinkable that a fraction of the Roman citizen body should reside in an area isolated from the main body of its fellow citizens by an intervening stretch of foreign territory. Indeed it was regarded as barely within the bounds of administrative possibility for a group of citizens to reside in an area which, even though not separated from the rest of the state territory, was awkwardly distant from the main civic centre where citizen rights were exercised. Nor had anyone at the beginning of the fourth century hit upon the notion that a fraction of the citizen body might have a local sub-government of its own distinct from that of the citizen body as a whole: the problems arising from such a dual administration would have seemed insuperable. Considerations such as these led the Romans to use Latin colonies, wherever possible, down to the end of the Second Punic War.

The Citizen colonies, on the other hand, are clearly anomalous, since they could be distant from Rome and could also have at least some local officials. Before the Second Punic War, however, the Romans tried to keep the anomaly down to negligible proportions by founding Citizen colonies only rarely, by making them small and by placing them on the central, unbroken body of Roman territory. The Citizen colonies were in fact a species of emergency establishment, envisaged not as viable agrarian communities, but as sentinel garrisons on the sea coast, whose only *raison d'être* was to spare Rome the necessity of maintaining fleets. They obviously invalidate the statement that a fraction of the citizen body could not have its own administrative apparatus distinct from the main organs of the state, but only to a slight extent. The local administration allowed them before *c.* 185 was the irreducible minimum of a routine sort needed by tiny hamlets, and it is to be noted that the Romans had not brought themselves to countenance even this much until 338, when they became reconciled to the idea as a result of their own ingenuity in devising the *municipium*, an annexed foreign community which after incorporation into the Roman citizen body was allowed to retain its own earlier instruments of government. Down to the Second Punic War the Romans used Citizen colonies only for small garrisons on the littoral, directly linked to Rome and, apart from their sea front, entirely surrounded by Roman territory.

Both the Latin and the Citizen colonies played a significant role in the Roman conquest and organization of Italy, so much so in fact that Velleius Paterculus, writing in AD 30, thought it worth while to list their names and the dates when they were founded, since they had contributed so markedly to 'the spread of the Roman name'. The parlous state of Velleius' text makes his information very unreliable, but the fact that he was prepared to insert an excursus on *coloniae* into his short compendium of Roman history is an indication that he regarded them as one of the most important of Roman political institutions. Velleius, however, is a source of secondary importance. Other writers are both more trustworthy and more informative. The occasions when colonies were founded before the Gracchi are described by Livy, and in such a way as to suggest that his information was taken from official records: inscriptions confirm some of the details he gives and for the period before 300 meagre notices in Diodorus lend him additional support. Our knowledge about colonies in the last century of the Republic is not provided in a continuous narrative in the same way, but has to be pieced together from occasional scraps of information or inferred from casual allusions. Much uncertainty is the inevitable result: it is, for instance, impossible to compile a definitive list of Sulla's *coloniae*. On the other hand, the wealth of constitutional, historical and antiquarian information about colonies in the works of Cicero enables one to visualize the practices of the Roman Republic with some degree of confidence. For the Empire the material is abundant, though here too it is scattered. Augustus' generalized remarks about his own colonizing activity can be supplemented, even though not in full detail, from the frequent references to colonies in Strabo and in the geographical sections of the Elder Pliny's *Natural History*. The corpus of writings on the subdivision and allocation of land known as the Gromatici Veteres is a most useful mine of information: some of it is untrustworthy and occasionally even unintelligible, yet it does describe with accuracy the surveying practices in use at the end of the first century AD. Above all, there is the evidence from inscriptions: these are very numerous and quite valuable, revealing many an otherwise unidentified *colonia* or unrecorded detail[11] (*Pls. 1–5*).

According to Aulus Gellius the *coloniae* 'have the appearance of miniatures, and are reproductions of Rome herself', and although Gellius was referring to colonies of his own day (AD 169), his description is valid to a great extent also for those of the Republic.[12] Nevertheless, despite their uniform tendency to imitate Rome and her institutions, *coloniae* might still differ from one another in a number of ways. Thus, although the total of settlers was always carefully specified and even standardized for given periods, it varied from one type of colony to another. There was also variety in the area of their urban centres, in the size of their land allotments, and in the extent of their dependent territories, the differences being largely due to the type of colony (whether Latin or Citizen), its site and the kind of terrain surrounding it, its distance from Rome, its purpose, the availability of settlers, and the period of the foundation (whether in the middle or late Republic or in the early or middle Empire). Some *coloniae* had as few as three hundred *coloni*, yet one is said, quite incredibly, to have had as many as twenty thousand. Archaeological exploration has revealed enormous disparities in the sizes of the actual towns: early Ostia covered little more than 5 acres, imperial Nemausus almost 800. The allotments of the settlers might be as small as 2 *iugera* (= $1\frac{1}{4}$ acres) or as large as 100 *iugera* (= $62\frac{1}{2}$ acres) and more. The dependent *territoria*, out of which these allotments were carved, were 50 square miles or less in republican Latium, but might be hundreds of square miles in the imperial provinces.[13]

Naturally the foundation of a colony, whether Latin or Citizen, required detailed and meticulous planning, followed by careful surveying and purposeful supervision. The same holds true, of course, for a viritane distribution. But a colony called for exceptional measures since it had to be established as a fully organized, self-governing community and needed an elaborate urban centre and a functioning administrative apparatus for its corporate existence.

The decision when to found a colony and where, and with how many settlers, belonged technically to the Roman People, and for that reason a colonization, in republican times anyway, was preceded by a law (*lex coloniae*) passed by the Plebeian Assembly (*concilium plebis*).[14] In actual practice the real responsibility for foundations lay elsewhere: before 200 with the Roman Senate, in the second century with plebeian tribunes, in the first century with military dictators, and under the Empire with the Roman emperors[15] (*Pl. 11*).

Once the decision to plant a colony had been taken, commissioners were appointed to supervise all aspects of the foundation. They were normally three in number and might include ex-consuls, and down to the time of Sulla they were elected in the Tribal Assembly (*comitia tributa*) to serve for a stipulated period, usually three years. From the time of Sulla onwards they were nominees of the master of the state, whether military dictator or emperor. Cicero implies that one of the three served as the head of the founding commission, but does not say how he was selected.[16]

The three-man commission delimited the boundaries of the territory of the colony, assigned allotments to its settlers, adjudicated any disputes that broke out between them, or between them and the nearby natives, laid down the constitution for the new community, and appointed its first office-holders and priests. To enable them to discharge these duties efficiently the commissioners were invested with *imperium*, the power to act at their own discretion in the name of the Roman People. They were also provided with supporting staffs, equipment, transportation, clothing and funds.[17]

The task of founding commissioner was anything but a sinecure. The preliminary preparations alone were so demanding as to require considerable time and energy; and, after them, came the work at the actual site. As this was normally in recently subjugated and in some cases still hostile territory, there was a very real possibility of physical danger: the commissioners founding Placentia in 218 were actually captured by the Gauls and subsequently handed over to Hannibal.[18]

Exactly how the commissioners carried out their duties in the early Republic we are not told. But descriptions of their operations from the time of Augustus, and for some details from even earlier, survive, and one is left with the impression that their methods remained basically unchanged for centuries.[19]

Before any *coloni* could be actually settled on their allotments, the *territorium* of the colony had to be surveyed and subdivided into sections from which the land parcels could be carved for the individual recipients. This task was accomplished with the aid of an instrument called a *groma*. Surviving specimens reveal it to

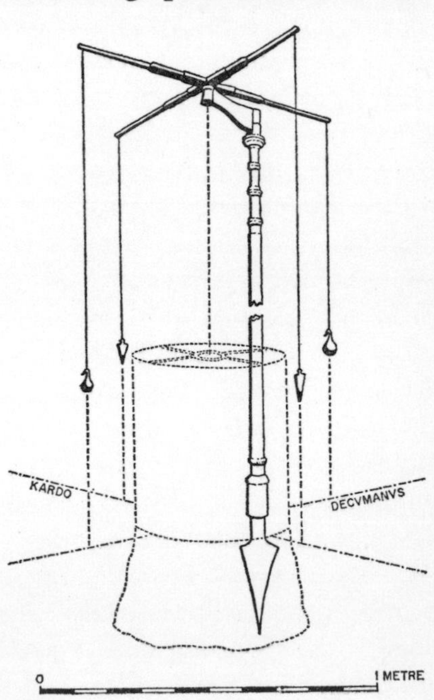

Fig. 1 Reconstruction of a groma

have been essentially a vertical shaft with a curved bracket attached to its upper end. This bracket supported a horizontal cross, the four arms of which were at right angles to one another and of the same length. The vertical shaft was stuck into the ground, care being taken to have the centre of the cross precisely above the exact centre of the area to be subdivided. Plummets were then let down on plumb-lines from the four ends of the cross and, by means of these, sights could be taken in all four directions. The method sounds crude, but right angles could be surveyed by it with considerable accuracy, especially on still days. Moreover the surveyors could verify their results continuously by taking bearings on adjacent fixed points (Fig. 1).

The process of surveying and subdividing the land was called *limitatio*, a word that for obvious semantic reasons can hardly be used for it in English. In its place English employs another Latin word, centuriation, from *centuria*, meaning a square of land covering 200 *iugera* (= 125 acres).[20] Centuriation meant the application to the countryside of a checkerboard layout similar to that commonly used for the ground plan of a city. Hence, seen from the air, a centuriated territory presents the appearance of a grid. Ideally it was a grid of *centuriae*, that is squares, each of which contained one hundred 2-*iugera* plots, the 2-*iugera* plot being the traditional, hereditary land parcel (*heredium*) of a Roman citizen.[21] The *centuriae* were separated from one another by field boundaries (*limites*), running at right angles to each other. These boundaries might be baulks, but they often took the form of roads called *decumani* and *kardines*, the two that intersected at the centre of the grid being the *decumanus maximus* and the *kardo maximus*.[22] All the *decumani* were parallel to and numbered serially from the *decumanus maximus*, and every fifth one resembles it in being somewhat wider than the others. The *kardines* were related to the *kardo maximus* in the same way. Any orientation seems to have been permissible, but it was common for the *decumani* to run east-west and the *kardines* north-south. At a corner of each *centuria* an inscribed boundary stone was set up, stating exactly where that particular *centuria* was located in relation to the intersection of the principal *decumanus* and *kardo* (Fig 2).

Ideally then centuriation was based on the traditional 2-*iugera* hereditary plot of the Roman citizen and was therefore particularly suitable for extensions of the citizen body, in other words for Citizen colonies. The early Latin colonies, being technically independent commonwealths and not parts of the Roman state, did not need to take any account of the ancestral Roman 2-*iugera* plot. Consequently their territories might be, and sometime, were, subdivided differently, either into strips, or into rectangles, or into squares of non-standard size: thus the word centuriation ought not, strictly, to be applied to them. Nevertheless it is now regularly used with generic meaning for the land subdivision in any type of colony, and this usage is justified partly because it is convenient and partly because division into *centuriae* became the regular practice from shortly before 200, after which time practically all new colonies were Citizen.[23]

The town site, no less than the dependent territory, was also often divided into a grid; and even though it was more usual for the centuriation of the colony to begin at the foot of the town wall, it might include the town, since the intersection of *decumanus* and *kardo maximus* was in theory supposed to be at the dead centre of the *colonia*. But even in towns with a grid layout it cannot be proved that the streets were called *decumani* and *kardines*, and sometimes, at Cosa for instance, these town streets were not aligned with the *limites* of the centuriated *territorium*. Naturally a colony that took over a hilltop or other non-arable area would have the intersection of its *decumanus* and *kardo maximus* outside the town proper at a spot carefully chosen with reference to the land that was going to be distributed to the *coloni*.

The *territorium* was not centuriated in its entirety, since in some cases it extended for hundreds of square miles. The surveyors subdivided just enough to provide for the settlers' allotments and sometimes not enough for all of these: settlers could receive uncenturiated land. The remnants of arable *territorium* that were surplus after all the *coloni* had been provided for, or that for some other reason were not centuriated, parcels for example that were too small or too irregular to form a *centuria*, were called *subseciva* ('remainders').[24]

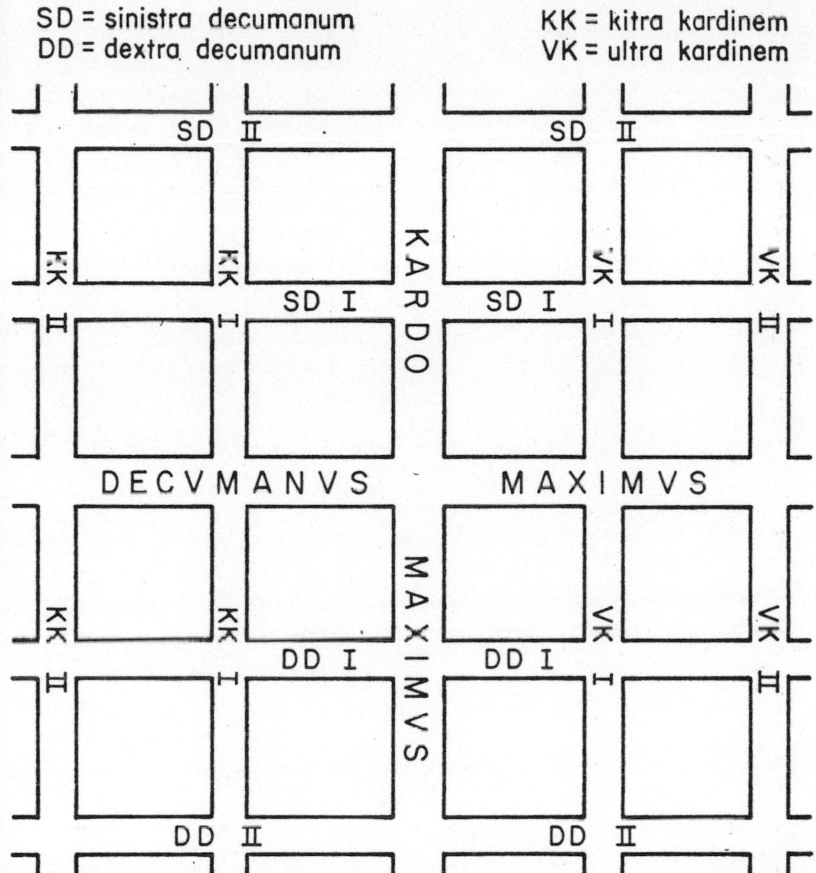

Fig. 2 Plan of a centuriation grid

Examples of centuriation have been clearly revealed by air photography in various parts of the Roman Empire, above all in the Po valley and in Tunisia, and they graphically illustrate Roman land settlement. Since centuriation was used also for viritane distribution, these are not always the relics of colonies. But traces of centuriation can still be discerned at the sites of many of the early colonies in Italy: Luceria, Cosa, Paestum, Ariminum, Beneventum, Brundisium, Spoletium, Cremona, Placentia, Vibo, Bononia (all Latin), Antium, Tarracina, Puteoli, Salernum,

Pisaurum, Parma, Mutina, Auximum (all Citizen). Unfortunately the centuriation as a rule cannot be dated, but some specimens of it probably go back to the original colonization.[25]

Once the site had been surveyed and centuriated, it was ready for allocation to the *coloni*. These latter had been enrolled by the founding commissioners who could apparently resort to conscription to get recruits for Citizen colonies. They could not, however, conscript settlers for Latin colonies;[26] and it may also be doubted whether in actual fact they did so for Citizen colonies either, since the evidence suggests that, until Gracchan times at any rate, they could enrol non-Romans for either type of colony when not enough Roman citizens volunteered. In some Latin colonies, especially in the handful founded after the Second Punic War, the non-Romans may have been quite numerous.

Once enrolled the *coloni* were marched to the colony-site in military formation under a banner (*vexillum*). After their arrival auspices were taken and sacrifices made to win the favour of the gods for the new foundation, and the burnt offerings were deposited in a ritual pit. If the town site was a virgin one, the chief commissioner, clad in ritual dress (*cinctus Gabinus*) with his toga pulled up over his head, marked the line of the town wall by drawing a ritual furrow (*sulcus primigenius*) with a bronze plough drawn by a white steer on the right and a white heifer on the left. At the points, traditionally three in number, where the town gates were going to be, the bronze plough was lifted clear of the ground. The ploughing ritual was prescribed by the *Etrusca disciplina* and is presumably a survival from the primitive period when there was a taboo on iron: hence the plough of bronze. Yet the ceremony seems to have little changed for centuries: it was certainly in use in the days of the Roman Empire[27] (*Pls. 8–10*).

The parcels of land were assigned to the *coloni* by lot, and for that reason were often called *sortes*. The amount of land a settler got varied from colony to colony and from age to age. In republican times allotments in Latin colonies were regularly larger than those in Citizen. The reason for this territorial discrimination is nowhere recorded, but it has been plausibly suggested that land grants in Citizen colonies were deliberately kept to a small size in order to prevent their recipients from qualifying for a higher class in the Centuriate Assembly and thus endangering aristocratic control of that body. As Latin colonists were not Roman citizens, the size of their holdings would not affect Roman domestic politics in the same way, and there might be some advantage in making them fairly large, since Romans might then be attracted into them and enhance their prospective reliability: Romans could hardly be expected to surrender the birthright of their citizenship unless materially compensated for doing so. In any case, after the Second Punic War, the allotments got bigger. Whereas 2 *iugera* constituted the standard allotment in the early Citizen colonies, 200 might be given in imperial times. After the Second Punic War, also, it became normal for the size of the allotments in Latin colonies to depend on the recipient's status, centurions and troopers obtaining far more land than the other colonists. The purpose of favouring some settlers in this way may have been to ensure that there was a local aristocracy which might serve as the administrative class in the colony: Roman preference for the well-to-do in this capacity is well known. Ultimately the system was extended to the Citizen colonies as well, and in the time of the Empire when the *coloni* were usually retired professional soldiers the size of an allotment depended partly on the quality of the soil, but especially on the beneficiary's military record and rank.

The earliest months of a colony must have often been precarious. The risk of attack by neighbouring and hostile natives meant that the defences of the settlement had to be placed in some state of readiness right from the outset. Measures were also surely necessary for tiding the settlers over until they could harvest their first crops: perhaps they received aid for the critical period from Rome.[28]

When the colonists were settled in already existing towns there was an immediate problem of adjustment with the natives. These might be simply expelled *en masse*; or some, and perhaps even all, of them might be admitted to the *colonia* with burgess rights therein (this happened in the earliest Citizen colony and was not unknown much later); or they might be permitted to remain as inferior inhabitants of the colony without burgess rights (the *incolae* mentioned in inscriptions as residents, but not citizens, of colonies almost certainly include some of these); or they might be allowed to maintain their political existence in a separate community of their own (instances of 'double communities', sometimes physically separated by a wall, are found under both the Republic and Empire).[29]

Boundary stones indicated where the *territorium* of a *colonia* began and ended; and, so that an official record and land registers might be kept, a *forma*, that is a plan, of the colony was engraved on bronze, meticulously showing the centuriation and allotments. No actual specimen of a *forma* survives, but fragments of copies of *formae* in marble and on papyrus have been found. Moreover illustrations in the MSS of the Gromatici Veteres resembling *formae* give some idea of what they were like[30] (*Pl. 12*).

The *forma* was set up in the forum of the colony together with a copy of the *lex colonica* and simultaneously the *groma* was ceremoniously removed. These formalities terminated the colonization procedures. The founding commissioners had now completed their task, and the *colonia* dated officially from that moment: the actual 'birthdays' of several of the colonies are known. The colony could, however, be renewed or enlarged, either by re-assigning allotments that for some reason or other had fallen vacant, or by subdividing yet more of the *territorium*.[31]

After the foundation formalities were finished, the work of building still went on. The colonization of a virgin site obviously called for a great deal of construction, and even one at an already existing town must have entailed some. The settlers themselves must have supplied the labour. Presumably they started building even before the surveyors had finished the task of centuriation, and they were still at it long after the founding commissioners had departed. Some town walls are so massive that they must have taken years to complete.

The periodical changes in their purpose and function affected the siting of colonies, their size, their composition, their constitution, and even their outward aspect. Excavations at Ostia, Minturnae and Pyrgi suggest that the small Citizen colonies of the fourth and third centuries looked like Roman army camps, which in effect is what they were: they were rectangular, had a gate in each wall, a peripheral road, and a checkerboard plan[32] (*Pls. 13, 14*).

Far more important and interesting are the Latin and later Citizen colonies. Throughout the half millennium and more during which these settlements were founded, they were as a rule typically Roman in appearance.[33] Locations might be either plains or hilltops; materials might change, town-planning become more sophisticated and buildings more monumental; moreover the checkerboard plan theoretically expected from centuriation sometimes failed to materialize owing to pre-existing buildings or other obstructions at the site. Nevertheless, with all the shifts of fashion and theory, the general plan and layout of the *coloniae* remained recognizably similar for centuries, a state of affairs to which the traditional founding formalities, essentially unchanging, undoubtedly contributed. At some of the sites, especially those of later colonies such as Augusta Praetoria, Augusta Taurinorum, Sarmizegethusa and Thamugadi, the symmetry of the grid is quite remarkable. In earlier colonies, such as Alba Fucens, Cosa and Ariminum, rectangular city-blocks rather than square are the rule and the town walls follow the contours of the land: but even in them symmetry is anything but absent (Figs. 10, 11; *Pl. 18*).

It was normal for the urban centre to have a protective ring wall, of stone in early republican times and of brick veneer in imperial, to equip it for the military role it might have to assume. Just inside it there was a pomerial road, and near the heart of the town, sometimes at its very centre, there was a forum. The shape of this in the early Republic may have been irregular to conform with the topographical exigencies of the site, but from the third century onwards it was normally rectangular. Hard by the forum, if not actually adjoining it, and axially aligned with it, would be appropriate public buildings of Roman type: a temple, a curia (where the local senate [*ordo*] met), and a basilica, presenting its long side to the forum and serving as law court and commercial centre. Sometimes, especially after 100, a portico might surround part, or even all, of the forum, and well before 100 there is at least one colony where entrance to the forum was gained by way of an arch. Other public structures of the *colonia*, particularly in the days of the Empire, might include triumphal arches, baths, theatres and, usually outside the town wall, amphitheatres. In such details as terracotta ornaments, cornice mouldings and the like the buildings might show the effects of local influences. But in general the colonies, Latin and later Citizen alike, must have displayed a consistently Roman aspect. Ariminum, Beneventum and Cales under the Republic and Pisidian Antioch under the Empire even used the names of Roman wards for those in their own cities; and Corinth, and perhaps Minturnae as well, actually had symbolical representations in public places of some of the seven hills of Rome[34] (*Pls. 16–23*).

The public structures occupied a large proportion of the area within the town wall, and this, especially in the smaller colonies, left none too much for the habitations of the settlers and their families. Those with the nearest allotments presumably lived inside the town, but those whose holdings lay farther afield often lived either on them or in the hamlets scattered over the *territorium* of the colony. In Livy there is a vivid picture of Hannibal in the fields of Sinuessa burning the dwellings of the *coloni* who had themselves evidently sought asylum inside the walls of the town.[35] The town-centre of a *colonia* was in the first instance its centre of administration. It did not necessarily provide homes for all its *coloni*. It was also a market place and a place of worship, especially of Roman divinities. Above all, if forethought had been given to its water supply and stores of food, it could serve as a place of refuge, as the burgesses of Sinuessa evidently demonstrated in 217.

APPENDIX

Cosa: a typical Latin colony

Remains of Roman *coloniae* survive in many parts of Europe and the Mediterranean world, but perhaps none convey so clear a picture of Roman colonization in the heyday of the Latin colonies as do the ruins at Cosa, or Ansedonia to give the place its mediaeval name. This site on the coast of central Etruria, about 85 miles north-west of Rome, was the scene of but little human habitation either before its colonization under the Republic or after its abandonment under the Empire;[36] and the careful excavations that have been conducted there under skilled American direction since the Second World War indicate that, even during the life of the town, major and radical changes to the original layout and buildings were few. Today's visitor can say, as Rutilius said over fifteen hundred years ago: 'We see the ancient ruins and crumbling walls of desolate Cosa, its defenders gone.' Such a favourable combination of circumstances, found at no other colonial site, has made of Cosa 'the very paradigm of a Latin colony'. There one can learn what the defences, the street plan, public buildings and housing arrangements of a Latin colony were like. Accordingly a short description will not be out of place (Figs. 3, 4).

The territory of Cosa had belonged to the Etruscan city-state of Vulci, which ceded it to Rome after being defeated by the Roman general Tiberius Coruncanius in 280. Like Paestum, the Latin colony that was planted at exactly the same time but much farther south, Cosa lies on the sea coast. It is not, however, on the beach. Like many another early Latin colony—Signia, Norba, Setia, Narnia, Hadria, Firmum—it was perched on a hill. Strabo describes it accurately: Cosa is 'a city somewhat above the sea; the cove ends in a lofty knoll on which stands the town.' Actually the

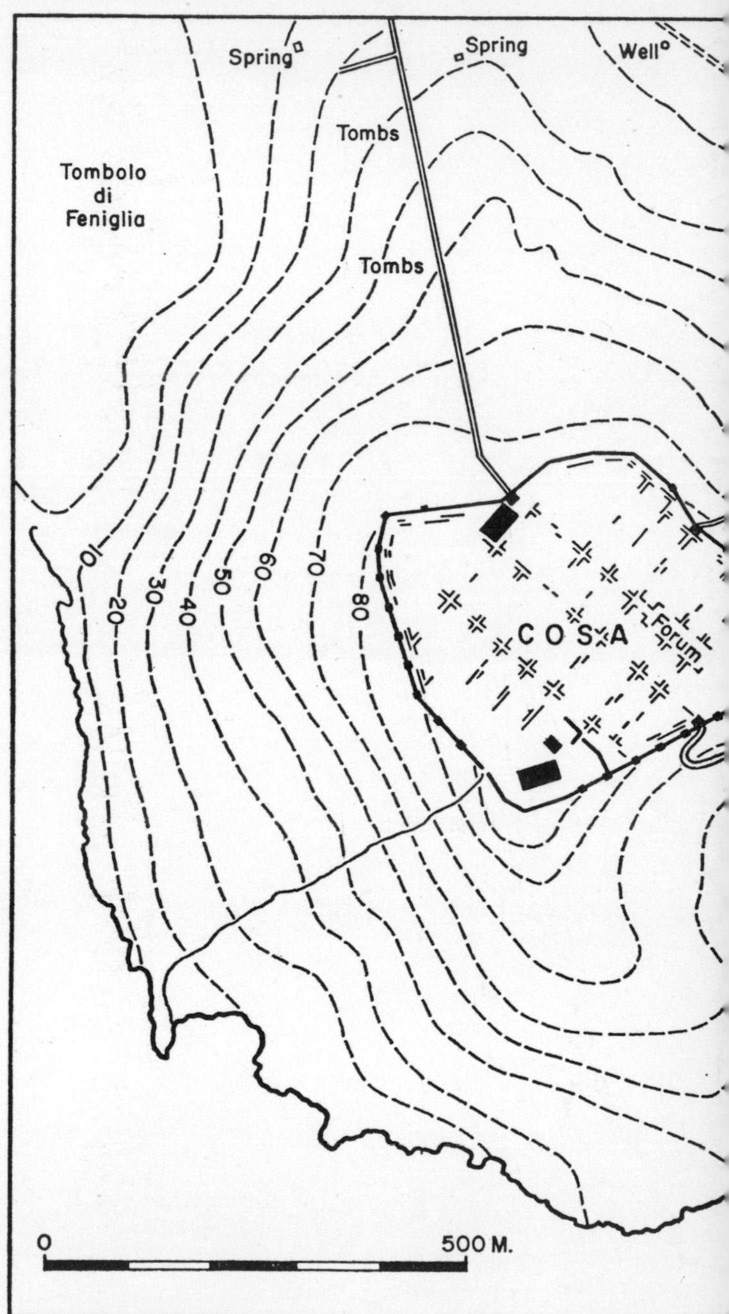

Fig. 3 Plan of the area of Cosa

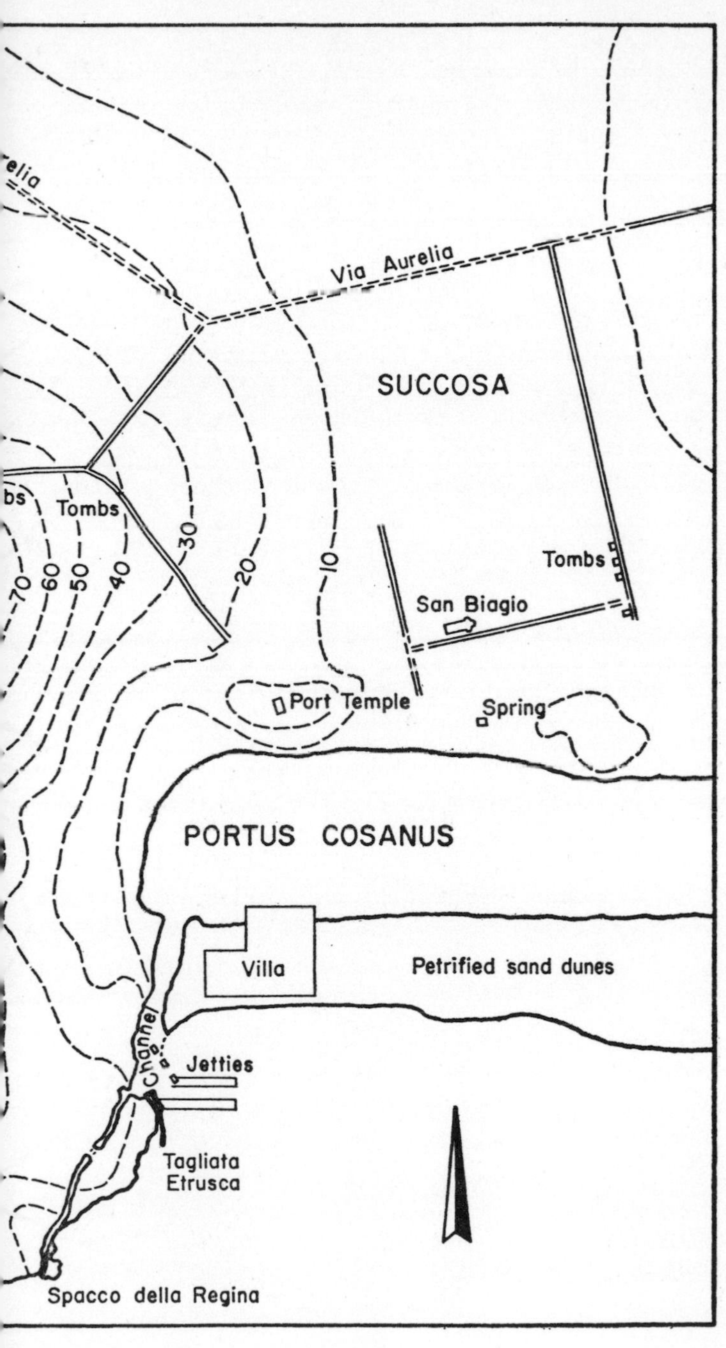

elia
Via Aurelia
SUCCOSA
bs
Tombs
70
60
50
40
30
20
10
Tombs
San Biagio
Port Temple
Spring
PORTUS COSANUS
Villa
Petrified sand dunes
Channel
Jetties
Tagliata
Etrusca
Spacco della Regina

knoll is a truncated hill some 350 feet high, low enough to be accessible, but lofty enough to be defensible. Tacitus labels it 'a promontory in Etruria', and this it is, although it is conceivable that the historian may have been thinking of that much more striking headland, Monte Argentario, the peninsula which lies out to sea from Cosa and is linked to the mainland by three spits of land on the middle one of which stands the town of Orbetello. Vergil says that Cosa helped Aeneas, but Pliny implies that the town began much later, with the *deductio* of the Latin colony. Archaeology seems to confirm Pliny, for although the site would serve admirably as the port town for Vulci, no remains of an organized settlement earlier than the colony have been found on the hill. The Etruscans must have used the harbour, which lies below and some 500 yards farther east, since with Portus Herculis on nearby Monte Argentario it provided the best anchorage on the Tyrrhenian coast between Gaeta and the Bay of Spezia. But Cosa and its harbour are both essentially Roman.[37]

The town wall, on the evidence of Etrusco-Campanian potsherds found buried in it, belongs to the period when the colony was founded, but it must have taken years to build. It is quite well preserved and is very impressive, its easternmost section still standing over 30 feet high. The circuit is about 1,500 yards and follows the contours of the hill in a manner that is very suitable for defence purposes. It encloses an area of approximately 33 acres, or between six and seven times the area of the *castrum* at the Citizen colonies of Ostia and Pyrgi. The wall has two faces with the interspace packed with rubble and is about 6 feet thick at the top and a third more than that at the bottom. Its original height varied with the terrain, but the outer face could not have been less than 20 feet anywhere. This outer face is everywhere higher than the inner, an arrangement that provided a protected rampart walk for sentries and defenders. Both faces consist of large polygonal blocks of the local limestone carefully fitted together without mortar or cement, and the outer one has been smoothed flat at enormous expenditure of time and toil.

This type of town wall is not Etruscan. It is, however, common enough in Roman colonies, whether of the Latin or Citizen variety. It can be seen, for example, at Signia, Norba, Alba Fucens (all Latin), Pyrgi and Saturnia (both Citizen). Quite uncommon, on the other hand, are the square towers built into the wall and projecting about 12 feet beyond its outer face and about 5 feet beyond its inner. Counterparts to these towers are not easily found elsewhere, although there is a round tower and bastion at Norba: the idea for them may have come from the hellenized south of Italy or Sicily. The towers are contemporary with the wall and made of the same material. There are eighteen of them and their sides are about 23 feet long on the average. They were as high as the wall and appear to have had a superstructure that overtopped it[38] (*Pls. 25–27*).

According to Strabo,[39] on this section of the Tyrrhenian coast more danger was to be apprehended from the sea than from the land, and consequently founders of settlements there threw defences forward towards the sea, in order not to be exposed as a ready prey to anyone sailing against them. Certainly at Cosa most of the towers face the Tyrrhenian, being in the western sections of the town wall. The defenders could enfilade attackers of this part of the wall with arrows from the towers. From the towers likewise they could look far out to sea and keep long stretches of the Tyrrhenian coast under observation in either direction.

In accordance with native Italic practice, there were three gateways in the town wall.[40] The best preserved, with beautifully fitted pentagonal blocks, is that on the north-east (Porta Romana); the one on the south-east (Porta Marina), which led to the port, was the most strongly fortified; the third, on the north-west (Porta Fiorentina), was the largest, but it is badly ruined. Each gateway consists of an outer gate which could be closed with a portcullis (the slots for the portcullis can still be seen), an inner gate which was closed by doors, and a court in between. The portcullis, also found at Alba Fucens, was an idea probably borrowed from Magna Graecia, one of the very few non-Italic features in an otherwise very Roman town, and a remarkably uniform republican town at that.[41]

Immediately inside the town wall was a pomerial road, as at Ariminum. It was 15 feet wide and it surrounded the built-up area of the town. No great Roman highway ran through Cosa to serve as its *decumanus maximus* in the way that the Via Appia did through Minturnae or the Via Valeria through Alba Fucens. In the year 273 the Via Aurelia was still in the future and, even after it came, it skirted the hill of Cosa without going over it. In fact there was no through street at all in Cosa: to get from one gateway to another, one had to make one or more right-angled turns. The streets were laid out in a grid pattern at right angles to one another and divided the town into long rectangular blocks, which approximated one another in size but were not identical. The same arrangement is found at Norba, Alba Fucens and Ariminum.[42]

The *decumani* at Cosa (see pp. 36–37) ran from north-west to south-east and the *kardines* from north-east to south-west, if use of the expressions *decumani* and *kardines* is allowable. There were three principal streets, each about 20 feet wide, two of them being *decumani*. One of these led directly from the north-west gateway, where a large temple stood, to the forum which was long and narrow (about 300 feet by 120) and was entered through a monumental triple arch, the earliest dateable one in Italy. To conform to the lie of the land, the forum was not at the centre of the town (a small public bath was there), but it was not far away, in the south-eastern quarter, and it was also reasonably close to the Porta Marina, almost as if to illustrate Vitruvius' dictum that, when a town is by the sea, a site very close to the port should be chosen for its forum. The forum, like the one at Alba Fucens, was flanked by a large rectangular basilica, complete with tribunal, which served as the legal and commercial centre.[43] Two small temples and what looks like an aerarium or town treasury also stood at the forum, and not far away there was the sanctuary for a mystery cult of Bacchus. Also close at hand was the comitium, or assembly-place of the burgesses, circular and stepped like those at Rome, Alba Fucens and Paestum; and behind this comitium, also as at Rome, was the curia or local senate-house. Along one side of the forum a row of stone-lined square pits has been unearthed; similar pits have been found at Alba Fucens and in the Roman forum, but their purpose is unknown: perhaps they served religious rituals in some way. One is left with the impression of a forum that resembled the one in third-century Rome (*Pls. 28–32*).

From the forum a principal *kardo* ran to the north-east gate, while a secondary *kardo* (15 feet wide) led south-west to the highest part of the town, the citadel (*arx*), a sacred precinct almost two acres in extent, dedicated to the gods 'under whose protection the community chiefly is', and marked off and kept separate from the rest of the town by its own polygonal precinct wall.[44] From an open gateway in this precinct wall a wide processional way (Via Sacra) ran to the summit of the citadel where, as at Signia, a Capitolium stood. It is an edifice of the early second century, occupying the site of the original dedication altar of the colony. It had three cellae, the side walls of which, made of limestone slabs set in mortar, still stand to a height of twenty feet or more. Its deep pronaos had two rows of columns and was approached by a broad flight of steps from a terraced forecourt. Underneath the pronaos there was a large vaulted cistern, lined with impervious *opus signinum*, for the storage of rainwater, one of scores which the waterlessness of the hill made necessary in the town[45] (*Pl. 33*).

At one time the citadel contained two other temples, both older but much smaller than the Capitolium: one of them was destroyed by fire in the first century and was apparently never rebuilt. A small atrium-type building, which probably belonged to some religious confraternity, also stood in the precinct.

From the Capitolium there is a magnificent panorama over Monte Argentario, with its lagoons and the town of Orbetello, and over the wide expanse of the Tyrrhenian, with the offshore islands of the Tuscan archipelago: Igilium (Giglio) and Dianium (Giannutri).

The public buildings of Cosa, apart from the structures in the *arx* precinct and from two large temples, were mostly concentrated around or close to the forum. In all they occupied at least twenty-five per cent of the area within the town wall. The streets used up another fifteen per cent. This left about sixty per cent for dwellings and it was covered with them, quite literally, for no space was left unused: houses clustered particularly thick in the north-western quarter. They seem to have been standardized,

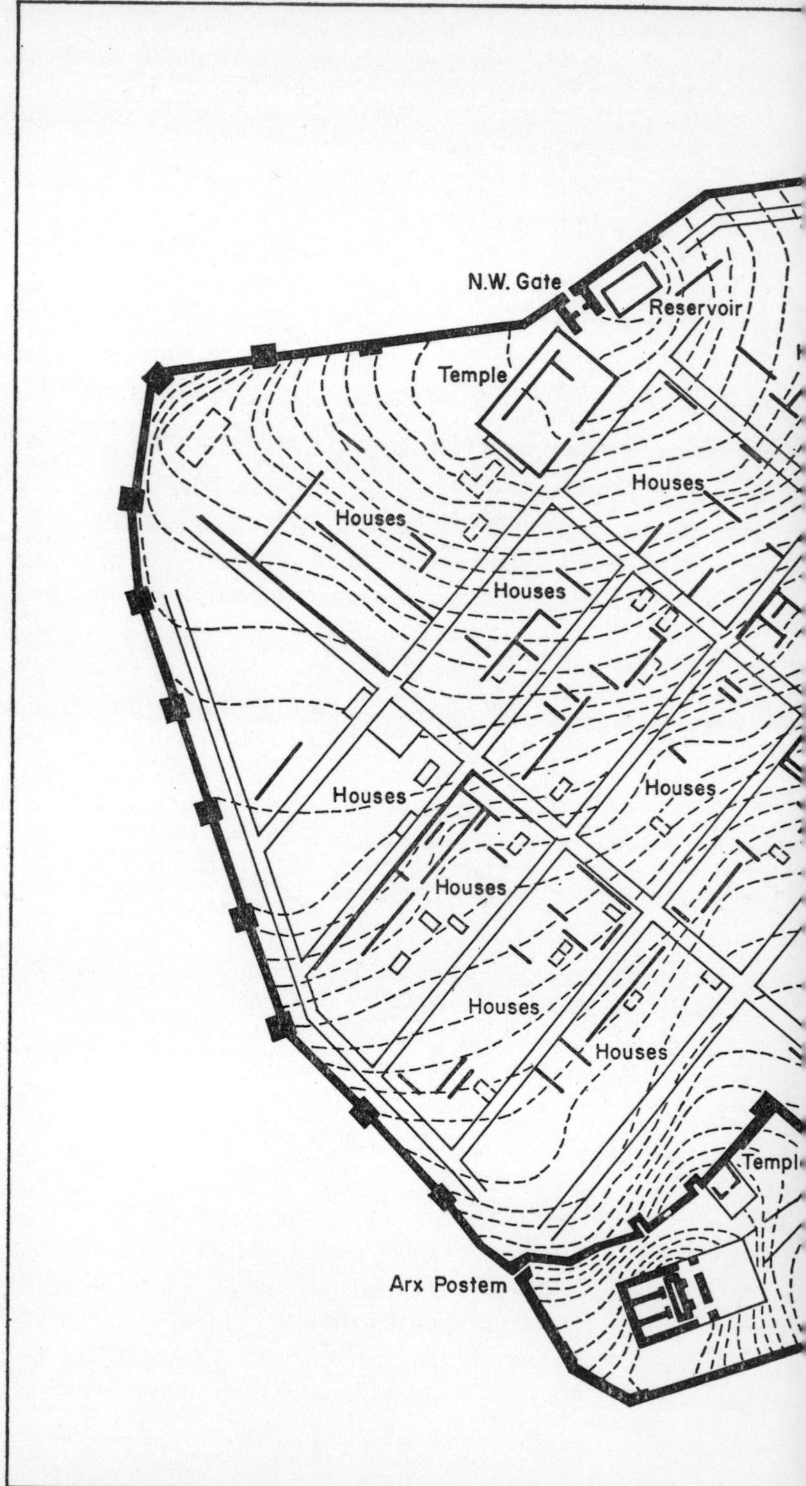

Fig. 4 Plan of Cosa

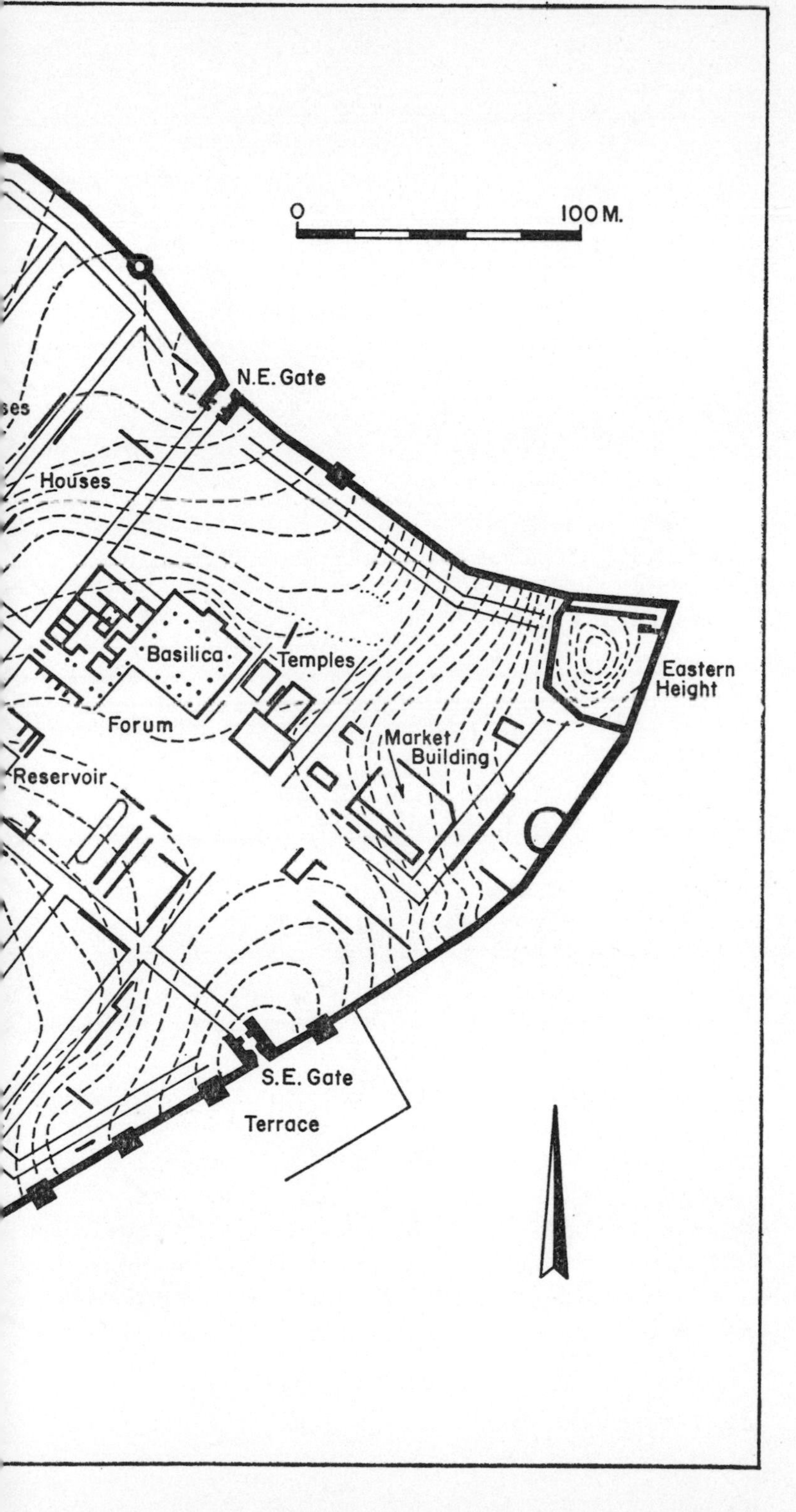
0
100 M.
N.E. Gate
ses
Houses
Basilica
Temples
Eastern
Height
Forum
Market
Building
Reservoir
S.E. Gate
Terrace

single-storey dwellings (but not of the Pompeian atrium type), made of local materials (rubblework and mortared masonry). Their number cannot be certainly estimated. Sixty per cent of 33 acres is not an extensive space, so that there could not have been a lot of them. But, as Thucydides reminds us,[46] the size of a town is not completely revealed by the amount of space that its wall encloses. Many of the *coloni* at Cosa, and the same is true of Alba Fucens, must have lived on the *territorium* outside the town proper, and even there the centuriation is no positive guide to their number, since allocation of uncenturiated land was common enough. In any case at Cosa the remaining traces of centuriation are not very extensive.[47]

The failure of the surviving ancient sources to record the original number of settlers at Cosa reduces one to conjecture. The excavators guess that Cosa may have had 2,500 or thereabouts. This would be abnormally small for that period: between 313 and 218 the recorded numbers for Latin colonies are either 4,000 or 6,000. As a matter of fact the hill at Cosa could not accommodate either 2,500 or 4,000 families. If the available area favours the smaller figure, the one thousand reinforcements Cosa got in 197 might indicate the larger: one quarter of the original complement seems more likely than two-fifths.[48] Whatever the original total of settlers, it is certain that many of them must have lived on their holdings, perhaps miles away from Cosa itself. Its *territorium* was large and could easily provide for them.

The frequent parallels that one can draw between Cosa and other colonies show that the Romans must have had a master plan or 'blue print' for a *deductio*. By the time that they applied it at Cosa they had already had much experience in using it, having established no fewer than thirteen Latin and six Citizen colonies since 338. Hence it is not surprising that they could make the town so typical and so excellent an example of colonization. It displays a neater and tidier arrangement of town wall and rectangular grid of streets than does Alba Fucens thirty years earlier. It abundantly confirms Cicero's description of a *colonia* as 'a watch-tower and bulwark'.[49] And it even confirms that a *colonia* was founded with the formalities and ceremonies traditionally believed to have been observed at the foundation of Rome itself. At any rate, the excavators think that they have found evidence of them. Immediately under the central cella of the Capitolium there is a crevasse in which were found what appear to be remains of the burnt offerings which were a prominent feature at any foundation ceremony, along with the ploughing of the ritual furrow and the removal of the *groma*.

CHAPTER II

PRISCAE LATINAE COLONIAE

COLONIZATION TO 338 BC

THE POLICY OF ATTEMPTING to strengthen a frontier or other strategic position by establishing a community of soldier-settlers on it has been adopted by many nations in both ancient times and modern, and the Romans were no strangers to it. They were following an old Italic practice. In the days before their rise to greatness *coloniae* are said to have been founded by not a few of their fellow-inhabitants of Italy: Aequi, Etrusci, Latini, Samnites, Umbri, Volsci. The Romans themselves are recorded as already knowing the practice in the days of Romulus, and even if this be an exaggeration they must have become thoroughly familiar with it during their close association with the independent Latini before 338.[50]

From the earliest days of the Roman Republic, if not from the time of the Roman Monarchy, the Romans were allied with the Latin communities, collectively and in one or two instances individually, for the defence of Latium. The Cassian Treaty of 493 definitively formalized a military understanding which had existed, with interruptions, from very early times.[51]

The tasks of the alliance were twofold: to liberate, where possible, the parts of Latium that had fallen under the rule of alien intruders and, also where possible, to push the boundaries of Latium forward to a defensible frontier. Of these two tasks the former took a great deal of time and effort to complete; the latter took even longer. (It was still going on, in a way, in the days of the Empire.)[52] These were joint tasks for the Romans and the Latin League acting together. But, while discharging them, there was nothing to prevent either of the high contracting parties from embarking on enterprises of its own: the conquest of Veii by Rome falls into this category. But it was as a result of action that Romans and the Latin League took in common that colonies were born.

When an enemy was defeated and expelled from an area, the allies habitually established a colony on it, composed of both Roman and Latin settlers. Each of the colonists received a portion of the liberated soil, to enable him to maintain himself and his family by subsistence farming, and he became a member of a new civic community organized to protect the area against any renewed enemy threat.

The surviving ancient texts that tell of this process are Roman or Roman-inspired, and not unnaturally they stress the Roman role in it. They suggest that it was invariably the Romans who decided when and where to found these settlements. Indeed the all-Roman character of the enterprise is so emphasized that Livy, for example, repeatedly calls them, quite simply, *coloniae Romanae*, conveying thus the impression that they were founded exclusively by and for Romans. This, before 338, is to exaggerate the role of the Romans. The establishment of any colony in this early period could not have been a matter for their sole decision. By themselves they could have done little more than agree to participate in a colony: the initial decision whether or not to establish it had more probably been taken by the Latin League, no doubt after consultation with the Romans. One ancient text actually implies as much. The initiative, of course, could have varied with the occasion. The Romans presumably proposed the colonies for the frontier with the Etrusci, whereas the Latini more probably suggested those for the Volscian zone. Certain it is that the Latini, no less than the Romans, always had the right to contribute settlers; and that the decision in the last analysis rested with the Latin League is indicated by the fact that each colony, on its creation, became another Latin commonwealth, independent and sovereign, and was immediately admitted to the ranks of the Latin peoples comprising the Latin League. In conformity with this, any Roman who had joined it ceased to be a Roman and became instead a citizen of the new community. A better title for these colonies, and one with ancient authority, is *Priscae Latinae Coloniae*.

The following list of *Priscae Latinae Coloniae*, fourteen in number, brought into being in this way before Rome dismantled the Latin League in 338, may not be complete, and it can hardly be fully trustworthy in other respects either. But it probably does go back to some kind of official, perhaps priestly, record, even though no authentic details of the actual foundings have survived. How numerous the colonists were, or how selected, what proportion were Romans and what not, how they reached the sites—these are matters about which practically nothing is known. The use of the word *colonia* to describe them, however, does suggest that the settlers received land-lots, but of what size, and how surveyed and assigned to them, it is impossible to say.

Fidenae (Castel Giubileo) on the hill that controls the last Tiber-crossing above Rome, Cora (Cori) on the slope that dominates the north-western route around the Volscian Mountains (Monti Lepini), and Signia (Segni) on the powerful site that overlooks the valley to the east of the same mountains, are all attributed to the semi-mythical period of the Roman Monarchy. Their strategic purpose is obvious: Fidenae was to hold the line of the Tiber against the Etrusci and Falisci, Cora and Signia the line of the Volscian Mountains against the Volsci and Aequi (*Pl. 35*).

During the next hundred years and more, other colonies were added to these three and were founded with similar military objectives. Velitrae (Velletri) (494), on the southern rim of the Alban Hills, dominated the gap between the latter and the Volscian Mountains; and Norba (Norba) (492) surveyed the Pomptine marshes from a stupendous and well-nigh inaccessible bluff: both were intended as bastions against the Volsci. Antium (Anzio), an anchorage on the coast of Latium, and itself a strong-point of the Volsci, is said, most improbably, to have been snatched from them and converted into a colony in 467. Ardea (Ardea) (442), where a branch of the Latini, the Rutuli, had had their stronghold from prehistoric times, straddled the southern approaches to Rome. Labici (418), on high ground near Labico, excluded the Aequi from the Algidus pass, which pierces the rim of the Alban Hills. Vitellia (near Valmontone) (395) was custodian, with Velitrae, of the corridor that separates the Alban Hills from the Volscian Mountains. The headland of Circeii (Monte Circeo) (393) was sentinel against Aurunci and others at the southern limit of Latium. Satricum (Conca) (385) was the keypoint between Antium and the Alban Hills. Setia (Sezze) (383 or earlier), on the southern underfalls of the Volscian Mountains, helped Circeii to keep watch on the gateway to Latium. At almost exactly the same time, *c.* 382, the speakers of Latin pushed their north-western frontier beyond Fidenae and made Sutrium (Sutri) and Nepet (Nepi) their new outposts there: these two places were 'the keys to Etruria', twin fortresses like Circeii and Setia, Sutrium controlling the route to Volsinii via the forbidding Ciminian forest and Nepet the route to Falerii and ultimately to Umbria: the Celts had shown as recently as 387 how vulnerable this region was.[53]

All these sites were skilfully chosen, and defence considerations were uppermost in their selection. All of them were militarily useful and most of them naturally strong. Almost every one was perched on a hilltop; some were flanked by ravines; streams protected others and forests camouflaged yet others. Ostensibly peopled by peasant-farmers, they were in fact powerful bastions, and their strategic contribution was notable. They formed a network of fortresses, controlling river crossings, mountain passes, roads and tracks, and they could frustrate enemy combinations. Through them the Romano-Latin alliance was successful in completing and consolidating its grip upon Latium.[54]

By strengthening their progress thus periodically with new *coloniae*, the Romans and Latini managed to liberate Latium from all control by alien Etrusci, Aequi and Volsci: even the Celtic assault of 387 was quickly repulsed and repaired. The region became for ever Latin, the nursery from which that tongue was to be carried ultimately to the far corners of the earth. This last development was no doubt more incidental than intended, but it is some measure of the role that the colonies, wittingly or unwittingly, contributed to history.

Thus, by the year 380, the speakers of Latin had made themselves reasonably secure on the Tyrrhenian side of central Italy, as far south as Circeii and as far north as Sutrium. They still needed to practice constant vigilance and there was the continuing risk of occasional, ephemeral raids by Celts. But their successful suppression of the attempts of Volsci, Aequi, Etrusci and others to occupy and hold parts of Latium absolved them from the immediate necessity of founding more colonies, for which in any case there was now but scanty space in Latium available. Sutrium, Nepet and Setia, *c.* 383/382, were the last foundations for almost half a century, until after the Latin War (340–338) in fact, by which time the political climate had become very different.

Diminished military need was not the only reason for the lull in colonization throughout the middle years of the fourth century. Another was the growing estrangement between Romans and Latini, which prevented agreement on when and where to colonize. Once Latium had been secured against external conquest, its inhabitants began to take a critical look at its internal condition, and they were disturbed by what they found.

The Latini saw that Rome had exploited her central geographic location to make herself into a colossus bestriding their homeland. Her conquest of Veii in 396 and her subsequent viritane distribution of its territory to her own citizens was merely the most spectacular in a series of actions that had contributed to her expansion. Even the sack of the city by the band of marauding Gauls in 387 had proved to be but a temporary setback. Nor was it likely that a Rome thus grown powerful would exercise restraint and refrain from imposing her will upon her neighbours. Over a century earlier, in her first treaty with Carthage (508), she had claimed the mastery of Latium: was she not bound to claim it again? These apprehensions of the Latini were not allayed when, in 354, Rome signed an alliance with the Samnites, an Oscan-speaking people of the south, who had recently shown a disquieting disposition to expand towards Latium. As the Samnites controlled a larger area and probably a larger population than any other state in contemporary Italy, the nervousness of the Latini is understandable: the Romano-Samnite treaty might not take much account of their interests and wellbeing.

On the other hand the Romans, too, were not altogether content with what they found inside Latium in the mid-fourth century. The Latini had become reluctant rather than ready allies, and a system that automatically strengthened the Latin League with every new colony no longer suited the Romans. The *coloniae* might make Latium safe against external enemies, but they would equally make it safe against Rome. Despite the Roman element in their original population, the colonies had quickly come to adopt the outlook of the other Latin communities. They were partners with the latter in the Latin League, sharers of their sentiments and interests. They would unquestionably make common cause with them; and in fact when the confrontation between Romans and Latini eventually came in 340, it was precisely the *coloniae* that supplied the leaders for the Latin cause.[55]

The Romans then, perhaps inevitably, had become wary of this communal kind of colonization. It is significant that, when they repelled the Samnite expansion into Campania *c.* 343, no colonies were founded, uncommonly useful though they would then have been. Fortunately for Rome this First Samnite War (343–341) was short and desultory, and once it was over the two sides renewed their alliance, their object evidently being to divide the central section of western Italy into two spheres of interest. The coastal region, inhabited by Latini, Western Volsci, Aurunci and Campani,[56] was marked for the Romans, while the Samnites claimed the inland region, the territory of the Eastern Volsci and Sidicini. The middle Liris, the stretch of the river between Sora and Interamna, was evidently intended to be the dividing line between the Roman sphere and the Samnite.

The resistance of the intended victims was vigorous and led to the so-called Latin War (340–338). This conflict was fiercely fought, but it went in favour of the bigger powers. The crucial battle took place somewhere near Suessa Aurunca and as a result of it the political picture in this part of Italy was drastically altered. The Sidicini and Eastern Volsci passed under Samnite domination, and the Latini, Western Volsci, Aurunci and Campani were brought completely under Roman.

The area which the Romans now claimed to control (southern Etruria, Old Latium, and northern Campania) can be conveniently

Fig. 5 Latium Adjectum

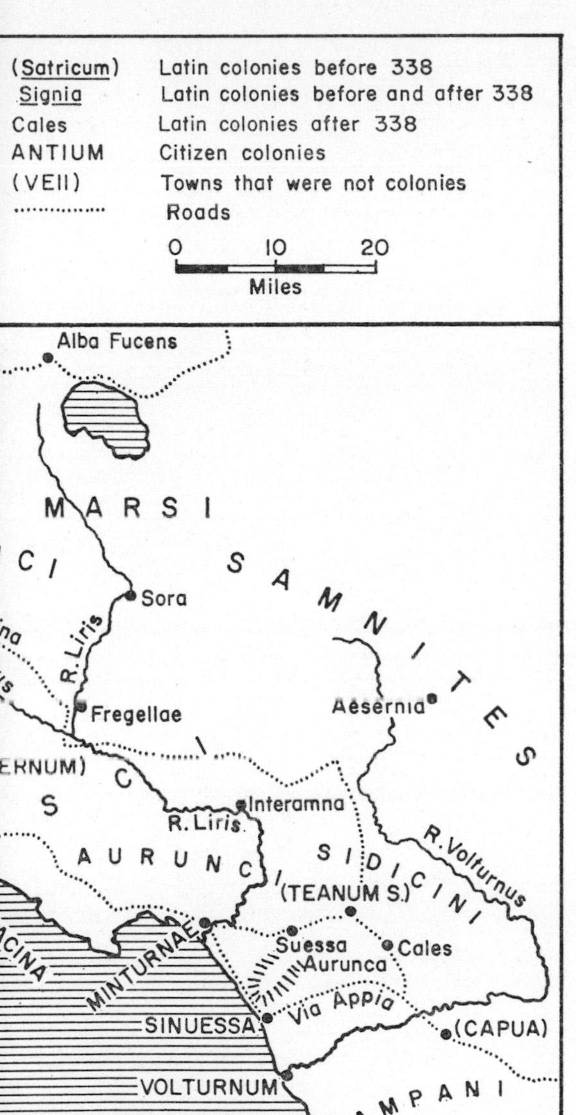

(Satricum) Latin colonies before 338
Signia Latin colonies before and after 338
Cales Latin colonies after 338
ANTIUM Citizen colonies
(VEII) Towns that were not colonies
Roads
0 10 20
Miles
Alba Fucens
MARSI
SAMNITES
Sora
R. Liris
Fregellae
Aesernia
Interamna
R. Liris
AURUNCI
SIDICINI
(TEANUM S.)
R. Volturnus
MINTURNAE
Suessa
Aurunca
Cales
Via Appia
SINUESSA
(CAPUA)
VOLTURNUM
CAMPANI

called Latium Adjectum (Enlarged Latium),[57] and as they had dismembered the Latin League they faced the necessity of establishing some kind of political order there. Their solution was to organize the whole area as a group of communities, all tightly bound to Rome, but divided into three categories: *municipia*, that is city-states that were incorporated into the Roman state, some with its full citizenship, others with only partial; *civitates foederatae*, that is city-states that were technically independent of Rome but linked to her by treaties of alliance; and *coloniae Latinae*, that is city-states that remained theoretically sovereign but were inextricably involved with Rome.

Annexation of the whole and its centralization around Rome would have solidified her control of Latium Adjectum, and her statesmen must have considered this. But even though they did annex some territory from the defeated and allot it by viritane distribution to Roman citizens, they evidently decided that stubborn problems of administration and assimilation made it impossible for them to absorb the entire region at this time. Without a civil service Rome could not govern it, at least not directly and completely; and without some sudden change of mentality she could not weld its inhabitants into one unified nation, at least not immediately. Had all of Latium Adjectum become a unitary city-state centred on Rome, distance alone would have prevented many of its inhabitants from exercising the rights of their new citizenship and so prevented them from being regarded as citizens, above all by themselves. This would have meant alienation for those of them who came from towns of consequence with long and proud traditions of independence, or from towns of speech and culture different from the Romans' own. For this reason Rome imposed her three-tiered settlement. On the whole it was not ungenerous, it was certainly very original and ingenious[58] (Fig. 5).

Municipia. Many of the communities in Latium Adjectum were incorporated into the Roman body politic. In her earliest days Rome had annexed some of her neighbours by the simple but effective process of transferring their whole populations, physically and permanently, to Rome. This crude method, however, could not be practised indefinitely. There was a limit to her own

A ninth-century AD
›nception of a land
›mmission at work:
shows nine toga-clad
›mmissioners,
›pparently discussing
nd-grants. They
ay, however, be
locating land for
ritane distribution,
nce the founding
›mmission for a
›lony normally
ımbered three, not
ne (p. 19 and
ote 17).

Manuscripts of the
oman surveyors'
ritings contain
ustrations of
›lonies. Here we
ave a Colonia
ugusta, probably
rawn as a model,
ith rivers,
ountains, town
alls etc.
›nventionally
presented in the
anner normal in
ch miniatures.

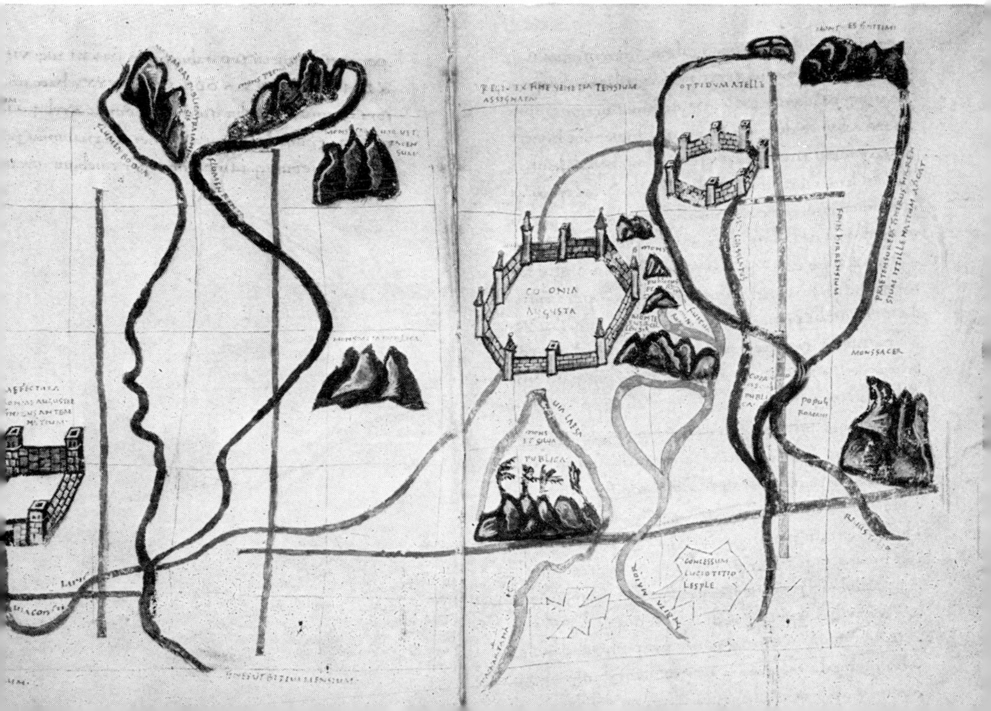

3 This drawing authentically represents Tarracina-Anxur (Note 111): the Via Appia runs past centuriated land to the town walls; a river crosses the town as in antiquity; and on the right is Pescomontano (for which see Plate 46).

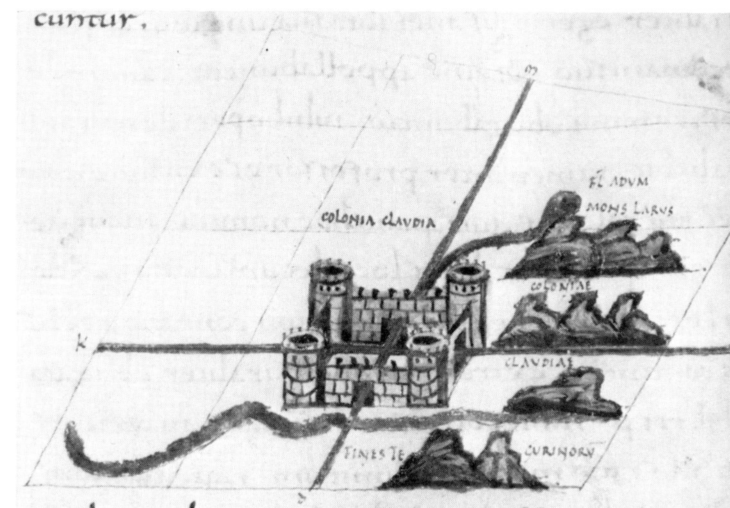

4 A miniature clearly showing the centuriation of a Colonia Claudia bordering on the Tegurini, which may mean that it purports to be Aventicum (Avenches) in Switzerland. But Vespasian, not Claudius, colonized Aventicum (Note 311). East is at the top of the plan, to conform with Roman practice.

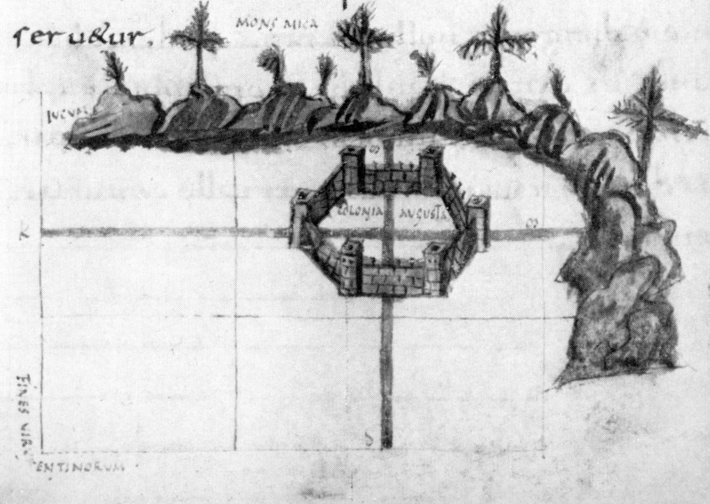

5 A picture of a Colonia Augusta, fancifully hexagonal but graphically portraying the intersection of *decumanus maximus* and *kardo maximus*: actually these roads rarely met thus at the very centre of the town (p. 22).

6 Aerial photograph of republican centuriation at Luceria (Lucera) in southern Italy, revealing rectangular rather than square subdivisions around the modern airstrip (Note 25). Arrows indicate farm houses flanking the double-ditched 'centurial' road.

7 Air view of Beneventum (Benevento) in southern Italy, disclosing the strategic nature of the site, an important road centre that also controlled several river crossings (p. 63).

8 Denurius of *c.* 23 BC from Augustus' foundation at Emerita (Merida) in Spain, showing the town's monumental entrance: contrast the gateway in Plate 26. (Roman colonies of the Empire, unlike Citizen colonies of the Republic, could issue their own coins.)

NVMINI CEREI IVSSVS ERIT IVDICATI IVRE
VS IN IECTIO ESTO ITQVE EI S F S FACERE LICE
DEX ARBITRATV IIVIRI QVI QVE I D P LOCVP
ESTO NI VINDICEM DABIT IVDICATVMQVE
ET SECVM DVCITO IVRE CIVILI VINCTVM HAB
SI QVIS IN EO VIM FACIET AST EIVS VINCITVR
PLI DAMNAS ESTO COLONISQ EIVS COLON
CCIƆ CCIƆ D D ESTO EIVSQVE PECVNIAE C
LET PETITIO IIVIR QVI QVE I D P EXACTIO IVDI
O QVE ESTO
IIVIRI QVICVMQVE ERVNT II IIVIR I IN EOS SING
LXII LICTORES BINOS ACCENSOS SING SCRIBAS
NOS VIATORES BINOS LIBRARIVM PRAECO
HARVSPICEM TIBICINEM HABERE EIVS POTE
QVE ESTO QVIQVE IN EA COLONIA AEDILER
IIS AEDIL IN EOS AEDIL SING SCRIBAS SING PV
COS CVM CINCTO LIMO IIII PRAECONEM HARV
CEM TIBICINEM HABERE IVS POTESTAS Q ESTO E
NVMERO QVI EIVS COLONIAE COLONI ERVNT H
TO IISQVE IIVIR AEDILIBVSQVE DVM EVM MA
BEBVNT TOGAS PRAETEXTAS FVNALIA CEREOS
BERE IVS POTESTAS Q ESTO QVOS QVISQVE
RVM ITA SCRIBAS LICTORES ACCENSOS VIATO
TIBICINEM HARVSPICEM PRAECONEM HABEBIT
OMNIBVS EO ANNO QVO ANNO QVISQVE EO
APPAREBIT MILITIAE VACATIO ESTO NEVE QVI
VM EO ANNO QVO MAG APPAREBIT INVITV
MILITEM FACITO NEVE FIERI IVBETO NEVE EV
COGITO NEVE IVS IVRANDVM ADIGITO NEV
DIGI IVBETO NEVE SACRAMENTO ROGATO NE
ROGARI IVBETO NISI TVMVLTVS ITALICI GALL
VE CAVSA EISQVE MERCES IN EOS SINGVL QVI
RIS APPAREBVNT TANTA ESTO IN SCRIBAS SI
HS ∞CC IN ACCENSOS SING HS DCC IN LICTO
SING HS DC IN VIATORES SING HS CCCC IN LI
RIOS SING HS CCC IN HARVSPICES SING HS D
CONI HS CCC QVI AEDILIB APPAREB IN SCRIB
SING HS DCCC IN HARVSPICES SING HS C IN

11 Bronze tablets, now in Madrid, containing extensive fragments of the charter of Julius Caesar's colony at Urso (Osuna) in Spain (see p. 135 and Note 198). The photograph shows the first nine surviving paragraphs of this unique document.

9 Coins reveal much about Roman colonies. This issue from Caesar-augusta (Saragossa) in Spain mentions the duoviri of the colony and the legions whose veterans peopled it, and also shows the *vexillum* that conducted them to it (pp. 24, 87, 145, 155).

10 The tracing of the ritual furrow the bronze plough drawn by a w steer and white heifer: p. 24) o appears on colonial coins. sestertius of *c.* AD 111 shows Emperor Trajan, appropriately c in the role of founder.

12 A land register in marble, found at Arausio (Orange) in France, somewhat resembling the bronze *forma* of a colony (p. 26). The allotments recorded in this fragment, however, are the wrong size for a *centuria* of 200 iugera.

13 Air view of Minturnae (Minturno), the early *colonia maritima* in Latium Adjectum. Minturnae and its companion colony Sinuessa (Plate 34) controlled the road round the seaward end of the Mons Massicus: for views of its monuments see Plates 48–50.

14 Air view of another *colonia maritima*, Pyrgi (Santa Severa) in Etruria. The photograph reveals the small size of the early Citizen colonies, Pyrgi being on the tiny promontory at the bottom of the page. See also Plate 45.

15 Air view of Alba Fucens (Albe) in central Italy from the south-east, looking along the Via Valeria to the civic centre (pp. 34, 84 and Plate 25). As in other early Latin colonies, the walls follow the contours of the site.

16 By contrast, Allifae (Alife) on level ground in southern Italy, colonized under the Empire, was symmetrically square. Moreover its town walls were not polygonal, but brick-faced mortar (much of the brick veneer, however, has long since vanished).

17 In imperial times a colony was likely to have its own amphitheatre. The heavily restored example pictured here is at Luceria: it was typical in being situated just outside the town itself.

18 Under the Empire colonies were commonly laid out in a grid of square city-blocks, but few showed such axial regularity as Thamugadi (Timgad), Trajan's foundation in north Africa. Its triumphal arch is also a particularly fine specimen.

absorptive capacity and also to the practicable distance. Her neighbours were soon out of range, so to speak. Now, in the fourth century, Rome developed an original type of synoecism with her masterpiece of statecraft, the *municipium*, a non-Roman town that was simultaneously Roman by incorporation. The burgesses of such a town (*municipes*) acquired Roman citizenship while retaining a city-state of their own that was separate from the Roman state: they were in effect naturalized Romans who had not lost their own original citizenship. These communities continued to have their own corporate personalities by retaining their own local organs of government and autonomously managing their own affairs.

Municipia, however, were of two types. One type, of which Tusculum in 381 seems to be the earliest specimen, was granted the full Roman citizenship. Its burgesses were enrolled in one of the Roman tribes and when in Rome enjoyed all the rights, public and private, of native Romans. They could participate in the activities of the Roman assemblies and be elected into office (although they seldom were, into the consulship at any rate); and they could marry and enter on legally binding contracts with native-born Romans of Rome.

The other type of *municipium*, of which Caere is usually cited as the typical specimen, received only partial Roman citizenship. Its burgesses were not assigned to a Roman tribe and if they went to Rome they could not participate in the assemblies or hold office. They did, however, enjoy the private rights of Roman citizens, the *ius conubii* and the *ius commercii*.

Citizens of both types of *municipia* were, of course, called upon to discharge the responsibilities of Roman citizens: *municipes* are men liable for service (*munus*, *capere*). They might under certain circumstances be subject to the jurisdiction of Roman legal officials (*praefecti iure dicundo*) appointed by the urban praetor at Rome. Above all they could be conscripted into the Roman army and be required to pay taxes (*tributum*) for the maintenance of the Roman forces in the field: a *municipium* was not allowed to have an army of its own (nor a foreign policy either). But it is only fair to add that they also possessed the much-cherished right of the

Roman citizen to appeal to the Roman People against an arbitrary sentence from a Roman magistrate: dual citizenship did not involve only responsibilities.

The evidence suggests that after the Latin War all the Latin-speaking towns of Latium Adjectum, except those that Rome planned on having as *civitates foederatae* or *coloniae Latinae*, were incorporated as *municipia* of the first type, probably because the Romans were confident that such boroughs would fairly quickly become Roman in sentiment as well as in law; and in fact towns like Aricia, Lanuvium, Lavinium, Nomentum and Tusculum did become thoroughly Roman.

On the other hand the towns of Latium Adjectum that did not speak Latin and whose assimilation would therefore be a protracted process were incorporated as boroughs of the second type (*municipia sine suffragio*). These were the towns of the Aurunci, Campani and Western Volsci, and they included Capua. It is surprising to find so important, populous and proud a city subjected to treatment that was almost certain to guarantee its permanent disaffection. In the cases of Tibur and Praeneste Rome recognized this possibility and prudently made them allies; and some scholars have argued that Oscan-speaking Capua, too, no less than the two Latin-speaking towns, must have been a *civitas foederata* rather than a *municipium sine suffragio*, but this view has not won acceptance. The Romans, anxious perhaps to keep the number of their alliances to a minimum, may have argued that Capua was bound to be disgruntled anyway and that it would be easier to keep an eye on a refractory *municipium* than on a contumacious *civitas foederata*.[59]

Civitates foederatae. Tibur and Praeneste were ancient and populous Latin towns to whom the very idea of annexation would have been anathema and would undoubtedly have kept them in a state of smouldering rebelliousness; and although they had been mulcted of some of their territory because of their participation in the Latin War, they were still so powerful that their recalcitrance could not be simply disregarded. Wisely, Rome decided to make them allies, apparently on terms comparable with those enjoyed by the Hernici. They remained fully self-governing.

Cora also obtained a treaty of alliance, more perhaps for the sake of consistency than anything else. Cora had behaved like the Hernici in the Latin War, remaining friendly to Rome, or at any rate neutral. Hence it was logical for her at the war's end to be on the same terms with Rome as they.

These allied states, although theoretically sovereign, were denied a foreign policy of their own and were required to support Rome with troops on demand.[60]

Coloniae Latinae. For ensuring their firm control of Latium Adjectum the Romans saw the advantages of the *colonia.* From now on, however, they alone would make the decisions on colonization. The capacity to safeguard Latium which the *Priscae Latinae Coloniae* had demonstrated before 338 could henceforth be put to good use in the service of Rome. Accordingly she allowed seven of the bastions, whose geographical situation seemed especially strategic, to remain intact. These seven even continued to be known as *coloniae Latinae*, even though the Latin League had now disappeared and their allegiance now belonged exclusively to Rome. So far as the ancient evidence goes, Rome did not found them anew or send additional colonists to them at this time; she simply defined their constitutional status as that of Latin colonies. Technically they were non-Roman, but at the same time they were not regarded as completely foreign.

Ardea, Circeii, Nepet, Norba, Setia, Signia and Sutrium were the select seven. Whereas the other communities of Latium, apart from allied Cora, Praeneste and Tibur, had been politically absorbed, or rather in the view of some of them politically obliterated, these seven were going to continue exercising their autonomous independence within certain limits as Latin communities. It is true that they were not allowed a foreign policy of their own and, still further to ensure that they did not combine into a new Latin league that might one day challenge Rome, they were forbidden to have economic and social relations with one another, for the time being at least; moreover only with Rome's permission would they be allowed to enlarge themselves by recruiting colonists. But they did retain their territory intact, and they could trade and intermarry with Rome. Ostensibly they were her independent partners. Unlike the *municipia* they had armed forces of their own, even though, when Rome had need, they were obliged to supply a quota of troops which served under the Roman high command. Clearly they were a privileged group of communities. In the fourth century their status must have seemed superior both to that of the Latini who had been forcibly converted into Roman citizens and to that of the Aurunci, Campani and Volsci who had in effect been reduced to the condition of Roman subjects[61] (*Pls. 36, 37*).

How they compared with allied Cora, Praeneste and Tibur in 338 it is more difficult to say. Most scholars do not differentiate the two groups of communities but regard both as having exactly the same relationship to Rome: they were all Latini. In one sense, of course, they were: they were Latin in language and in locality. As speakers of Latin, they were Latini, and as inhabitants of Latium they were also Latini. But this need not mean that the status of both groups was identical. Undoubtedly they were very similar, but no less undoubtedly ancient documents and authors distinguish them. In some way, therefore, the group of three was slightly different, in its relationship to Rome, from the group of seven. Henceforth only the latter were juristically Latin.[62]

It is quite possible that in 338 the three allies appeared better off than the seven colonies and that the Romans intended that they should at least not be worse off: Circeii and Setia, after all, had led the rebellion against Rome in the Latin War. It is to be noted, however, that, unlike Praeneste and Tibur, the seven had not been obliged to cede land to Rome. Moreover time was on their side. Inseparably bound to Rome for defence, they were also destined, and perhaps intended, to have the closest social and economic ties with her, since for a time they were not allowed to have them with one another; and their burgesses could become Roman citizens automatically by the mere act of migrating to Rome. These close links with Rome soon reconciled the Latin colonies to their lot and made them amenable to their intended role. A special relationship grew up between them and Rome, and they soon became her associates rather than her allies. Their burgesses were even allowed to vote in the Plebeian Assembly if they happened to be in Rome when it met. There is evidence to show that Rome did not view Praeneste or Tibur with anything like the same degree of favour and indulgence.

The Latin colonies with their immediately mobilizable forces were to be the means by which Rome maintained her mastery over Latium Adjectum. All of the seven, except possibly Ardea, had been originally founded on territory wrested from the Etrusci, the Falisci or the Volsci, for whose irredentist aspirations they could therefore easily become the targets. Accordingly prudence dictated that they should cling to Rome now that they no longer had the Latin League to cling to. For Rome this was a most satisfactory arrangement, since it relieved her of the necessity of permanently garrisoning strategic points and frontiers with contingents from her own citizen body. Nepet and Sutrium could keep watch on the disgruntled natives of southern Etruria, and Setia and Circeii on the incorporated and resentful Aurunci and Volsci of Latium Adjectum, while Norba and Signia contained the Volsci of the Monti Lepini. For the moment there was no Latin colony similarly to mount guard over northern Campania, but one was not going to be long in coming. Besides keeping watch over the conquered, the colonies could also help to repel any attacks from neighbouring regions.

To protect Latium against assaults from the sea, Rome used colonies of a different and entirely new kind, the so-called Citizen colonies. These were extensions of Rome herself, and a pair of them were planted at the strategic coastal points of Ostia and Antium on territory that she had annexed and added to the large and unbroken bloc of Ager Romanus surrounding the city. The demonstrated value of the *Priscae Latinae Coloniae* in early Latium may have given her the idea for these Citizen colonies, although various considerations induced her to make them considerably smaller than their old Latin prototypes.

Both Latin and Citizen colonies were obviously envisaged as pairs;[63] and later it was common practice for colonies to be founded two at a time, occasionally in widely separated regions. This seems to resemble the preference of the Romans for creating their new citizen tribes in pairs.

The incorporations of 338 provided Rome with a much larger pool of manpower for her armed forces than heretofore, in the event of an assault on Latium. But the more dissatisfied elements in her enlarged state, especially the citizens of the *municipia sine suffragio*, might not make very reliable soldiers. This enhanced the importance and the prestige of the continuing Latin colonies. As close associates, willing and perhaps eager to defend their intact and autonomous commonwealths, these Latini might be counted on to make better and more useful fighting men than reluctant Roman subjects conscripted against their will, and they would be certainly much less costly to the Roman state. Thus, even though it may be conceded that the large-scale use of the *municipium* in 338 'contributed far more than the Roman colony to the making of Rome's subsequent constitutional history', the retention of the Latin colony after the dissolution of the Latin League is also to be reckoned a masterpiece of statecraft: the Latin colonies, it has been well said, were the real instrument in the romanization of Italy.[64]

CHAPTER III

COLONIAE LATINAE

THE CONQUEST OF ITALY TO 218 BC

THE COMMUNITIES, that after the Latin War preserved their separate political identities with the status of Latin colonies of Rome, provided her not only with a welcome addition to her own armed strength, but also with a model of the institution to use in future struggles for survival or expansion; and an occasion for employing it was not long in coming.

The agreement between Romans and Samnites in 341 had specifically assigned the Oscan-speaking Sidicini of Teanum to the Samnite sphere, and in 337 this people, according to Livy, attacked the Aurunci. Presumably they were trying to sever the tenuous Roman communications with newly annexed northern Campania across Auruncan territory. A branch of the Aurunci, the Ausones of Cales, made common cause with the Sidicini and their Samnite overlords, no doubt with the hope of thereby freeing their nation from Roman domination. The Roman response was to capture Cales and establish a Latin colony there. The site neatly counterpoised Samnite-controlled Teanum, and it dominated an easy route between the Samnite positions along the middle Liris and the plain of northern Campania. It could thus also keep a watchful eye on the suspect *cives sine suffragio* of Capua.[65]

The decision to found the colony at Cales was taken in 335 and carried into effect in the following year with 2,500 settlers. Most of these must have been Roman citizens and on joining the colony they lost their Roman citizenship, obtaining burgess rights in the new Latin community instead. But they did not represent a loss of military manpower to Rome, since for the most part they were lacklands who would not have served in the Roman army anyway. In fact they meant an addition to the armed strength of Rome since, now become landholders, they were eligible for the armed forces of Cales and hence for the quota that that Latin colony supplied on demand to Rome. Furthermore non-Romans could have been included among the settlers, and these were not necessarily ethnic Latini: Aurunci, Campani, Sidicini, Volsci or even others may well have been amongst them. All the settlers, however, Romans and non-Romans alike, became Latini so far as Roman Law was concerned. Relative to Rome they enjoyed the same rights and owed the same obligations as the inhabitants of the seven communities that had remained Latin colonies after the Latin War. Henceforth men could be Latini regardless of their origin. Thus, with the colonization of Cales, there was born the juristic concept of Latin status, which came to be known later as Ius Latii or simply *Latium*[66] (*Pl. 40*).

All the colonists, Romans and non-Romans alike, received plots of land. They were not an exceptionally large group when compared with some of those sent out to colonies later, but they may have been all that were possible for the resources of Rome at that time. It is to be noted that no second colony was founded simultaneously with Cales.[67] Perhaps the Romans were not prepared to commit more than one colony with a moderate number of settlers to what was for them a new departure. In any case the 2,500 settlers were numerous enough to be able to develop their own municipal life.

The colonization of Cales in 334 certainly was a new departure, one of the great crucial events in the story of Rome. The town was far distant by the standards of those days and could be reached only by a roundabout route that followed the coast as far as Minturnae and then swung inland. By establishing settlers there Rome was announcing that she was going to found new Latin colonies wherever necessary, even if it meant challenging the strongest power in contemporary Italy. Besides this, she was establishing a pattern for future extensions of her power. The Latin colony was regularly to be the instrument of her expansion over the Italian peninsula, her 'bulwark of empire', serving sometimes as a springboard for a forward leap and always as a defence at a vulnerable gap.[68] It proved to be a tool of the greatest efficacy.

Cales was soon joined by another Latin colony. The steady advance of the Samnites towards the Liris had assumed menacing proportions. Cominium, Atina, Casinum, Arpinum and presumably Aquinum had fallen into their hands, and they had so alarmed Luca (Castro dei Volsci?) and Fabrateria (Ceccano?), Volscian communities west of the river, that in 330 they both appealed to Rome for protection. Their request did not go unheeded.

In 328 the Romans set up an obstacle to any more Samnite penetration of Volscian territory along the middle Liris by planting Fregellae on a site that controlled both the crossing of the Liris near its junction with the Melfa and the route to the Tyrrhenian Sea via the col between the Ausonian and Auruncan mountains.[69] Nor was this all. Almost simultaneously another colony had been founded, in 329, this one of the Citizen type, at Tarracina, on the coast of Latium Adjectum: the territory had been taken from the Samnites' allies, the Volsci of Privernum.[70]

For the Samnites the colonization of Fregellae was more than an affront: it was an act of war. Very probably they had legal right on their side. The Romano-Samnite treaty, signed in 354 and renewed in 341, seems to have recognized the middle Liris as the dividing line between the Roman sphere of interest and the Samnite, and Fregellae was unquestionably on the eastern, that is the Samnite, side of the river. The Samnites might choose to overlook Tarracina, small and far away from their own territory. But a Latin colony in the next year was too formidable an affair to be ignored. So the Samnites made Fregellae a *casus belli*.

The hostilities with the Samnite tribes (Caraceni, Caudini, Pentri and Hirpini) were to last, with interruptions, for over half a century, from 326 to 270, and this protracted struggle settled the fate of peninsular Italy by bringing it irrevocably under the domination of Rome. The colonies founded during the course of the long conflict were in great measure responsible. This was the golden age of the Latin colony.[71]

The first important campaign of the Second Samnite War witnessed the entrapment and forced surrender of a Roman army at the Caudine Forks in 321. Rome was obliged to lay down her arms for the time being and evacuate Fregellae and, it may be supposed, Cales as well. A quinquennium of uneasy armistice ensued, the so-called Caudine Peace. But by 316 the Romans felt strong enough to renew the struggle and their first action was significant. They sent a force eastwards across Italy to the Adriatic for the first time. On reaching the Adriatic this force turned south and seized and colonized Luceria, a Samnite-controlled bastion on the far side of Samnium. This powerful site on a hilltop, where the highlands of Samnium meet the plains of Apulia, is the key to the eastern approaches to Samnium. Through this Latin colony the Romans were able to fasten an iron grip on south-eastern Italy which was never entirely shaken loose, not even later by Hannibal or the Social War insurgents.[72]

The Latin colony at Luceria was identical in size with the one at Cales, 2,500 settlers. While not really large, this number represented a formidable undertaking in view of the distance and roundabout route involved, and it was probably all that Rome felt it prudent to establish then. A pair of colonies at so isolated and exposed a distance seemed out of the question at a time when she had heavy calls on her available manpower nearer home (*Pl. 39*).

Even as it was, the effort to colonize Luceria had temporarily weakened the Romans in western Italy, where once again they suffered defeat, at the very moment that their force was engaged in the operations at Luceria. In 315 the Samnites advanced past the dismantled fortress-colonies of Cales and Fregellae in order to split Latium Adjectum asunder, and they crushed a Roman army at the Lautulae pass, which controls the coastal communications between Latium and Campania. They then advanced into Old Latium, spreading great alarm as they went. They were not halted until they reached the Latin colony of Ardea. Its loyal resistance enabled the Romans to regroup their forces, and in the very next year (314) they won a crucial battle, probably somewhere near Tarracina. They promptly followed up this victory with two pairs of colonies, to protect the frontier against the Samnites and to safeguard communications with Campania, by sea and by land.[73]

One pair of Latin colonies was planted in 313, at Saticula, the border fortress defending the approaches to the Caudini Samnites, and at Suessa, the Auruncan stronghold controlling one of the roads to Capua. The other pair of colonies had come into being by the next year (312), respectively at the offshore island of Pontiae, to guarantee communication with Campania by sea in the event of the Samnites severing the land routes, as well as to defend the coast of Latium against sea-borne attacks, and at Interamna on the eastern, that is the Samnite, side of the Liris at its confluence with the Rapido, where there was an important river crossing. Besides these two pairs of colonies, the Romans also re-established their earlier pair, Cales and Fregellae, whether with increased strength or not we do not know.

The number of settlers needed for the four new and two refounded Latin colonies would have been huge, even if the colonies had been only of the same size as Cales in 334 or Luceria twenty years later; and in fact they seem to have been larger. Interamna, at any rate, received 4,000 *coloni*, a figure recorded for other foundations after it. No doubt a significant proportion of the colonists were obtained from elsewhere than Rome itself, and they may even have included some freedmen. Many of them, however, must have been native Romans. Investment of her man-power on this wholesale scale must mean that in Roman eyes Cales, Fregellae and Luceria had abundantly demonstrated their strategic usefulness.[74]

The three pairs of Latin colonies in the west and the isolated Latin colony in the east might fairly be described as the fetters of Samnium.[75] In an effort to pry them loose the Samnite leaders sought allies in central and northern Italy. The support they won in the Second Samnite War from the central Italian tribes (Marsi, Paeligni, Hernici, Aequi) and from the Etrusci was half-hearted and short-lived, and it had a consequence that they could not have relished. It convinced the Romans of the need for Latin colonies in central Italy; and once the Second Samnite War was over (304), they immediately proceeded to found some. In 303/302 a pair were sent to Sora and Carseoli to provide additional strength to the Liris frontier and to impede the cooperation of Samnites, Hernici, Marsi and Aequi;[76] and at about the same time, to safe-guard the Via Valeria and the Via Salaria, the principal routes across the middle of Italy, another pair were sent, to Alba Fucens (303) on Aequian territory and to a place called Nequinum on Umbrian, which they renamed Narnia (299) after the nearby river for apotropaic reasons.[77] These four colonies constituted an attempt not only to insulate the Samnites from Etrusci, Umbri and Gauls, but also to keep surveillance over the warlike tribes of the central Appennines, the Sabini, Aequi, Marsi, Paeligni and Vestini. For this task they had to be large, and they were. Sora and Carseoli received 4,000 *coloni*, the increased number adopted for the Latin colonies ten years earlier. But to Alba no fewer than 6,000 were sent, a figure that received immediate justification when the 4,000 despatched to Carseoli in 302 encountered such vigorous resistance from the natives that it took them four years to establish their colony[78] (Fig. 6; *Pls. 15, 47*).

The Romans, however, even yet had not completed an iron cordon all the way to the Adriatic coast: there was a way around it at its eastern end. And even if this had not been the case, a little time would have been needed to make it watertight; and this was not granted them. The Third Samnite War broke out in the very year that the Latin colony at Carseoli finally got settled (298), and the Samnites wasted no time. They forged an anti-Roman combination of Gauls, Etrusci and Umbri in the north, and in 296 their general Gellius Egnatius pierced Rome's 'military bulkhead across central Italy'[79] with a large army to join forces with these northern allies.

It may well have been the recently founded Latin colonies that saved Rome. Even as it was, Gellius Egnatius' grand coalition came within an ace of shattering the Roman army at Sentinum in Umbria in 295; and had it been larger, as it would have been but for the Latin colonies keeping the central Italian tribes asunder, it must have won the crucial battle. In the event Sentinum was a great victory for Rome. Two years later (293) she followed it up by heavily defeating the Samnites on their own soil at Aquilonia, and this second victory ensured her final triumph (290).

Even before the Third Samnite War had quite reached its end, she had split the Samnite tribe of the Hirpini from the related Lucani to the south of them by planting a large Latin colony at

Fig. 6 Plan of Alba Fucens

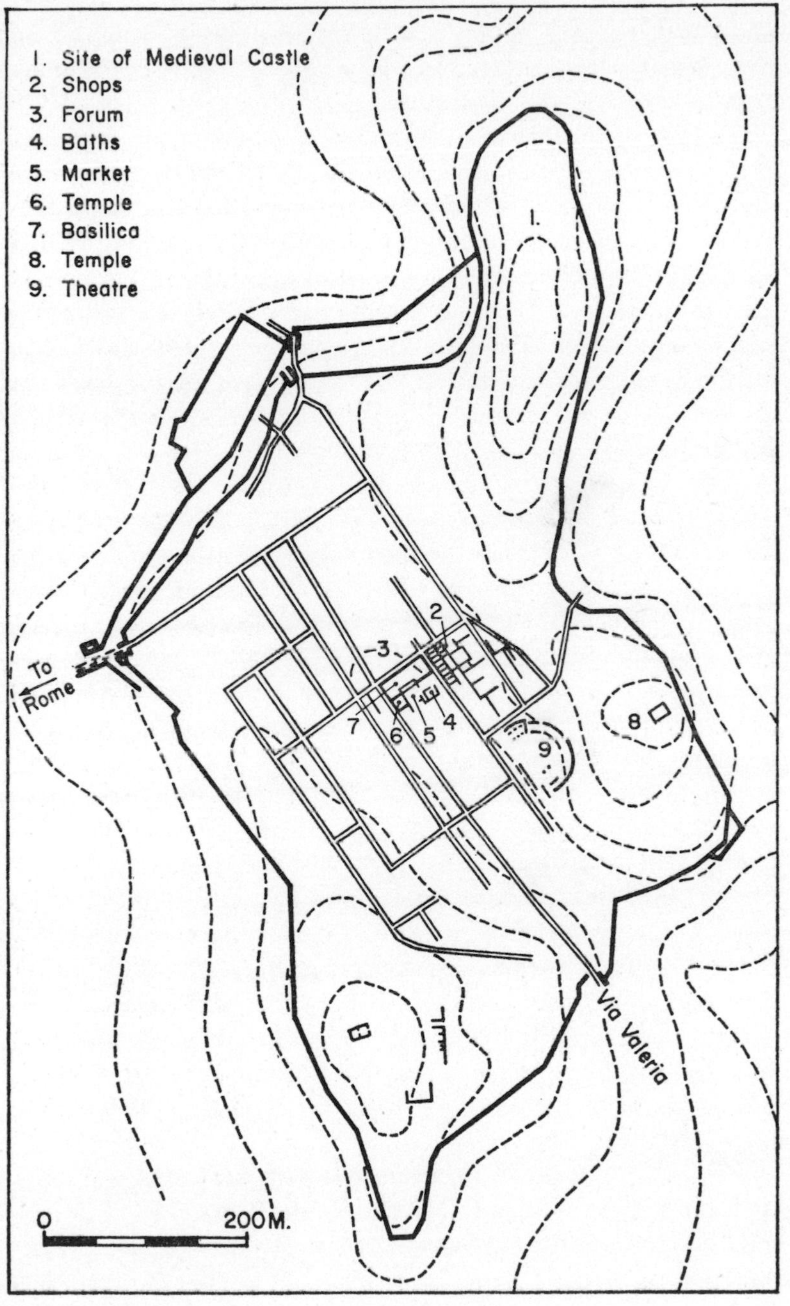
1. Site of Medieval Castle
2. Shops
3. Forum
4. Baths
5. Market
6. Temple
7. Basilica
8. Temple
9. Theatre
To Rome
Via Valeria
0
200M.

Venusia (291), on a strong and defensible ridge, surrounded on three sides by deep ravines and dominating the valley of the upper Aufidus (Ofanto), the most considerable river of southern Italy.[80]

Once the Third Samnite War was over the Romans exploited the successes that M'. Curius Dentatus had scored in central Italy during its closing stages and plugged the gap beyond the eastern end of their central Italian chain of fortresses by founding Hadria on the territory taken from the Praetuttii in southern Picenum.[81] The circuit of its walls proves that this Latin colony was not small, and from its powerful mountain site it could dominate the passage linking northern and southern Italy along the Adriatic coast. At about the same time (289–283) another colony was founded in the Adriatic region, to form a pair with it, so an Epitome of Livy implies. This was Sena Gallica, approximately 100 miles to the north, planted on territory which the Senonese Gauls had been forced to cede as the price for their participation in the Sentinum campaign. Sena was a Citizen colony, so that it and Hadria formed a mixed pair something like Fregellae and Tarracina.[82]

The hegemony of peninsular Italy which Rome was seeking to ensure with these foundations was put to a severe test a few years later in the Pyrrhic War (284–270), when she was beset by enemies on every side. In the north, south and east she sustained heavy defeats, at Arretium (*c.* 284), Heraclea (280) and Ausculum (279) respectively. In the west she was more fortunate: there Tiberius Coruncanius won a substantial victory over Etruscan Vulci (280). Even so, had these various threats been carefully coordinated to explode at the same moment, she might never have weathered the storm. She had, however, organized Italy as a network of Roman and non-Roman communities and her strategically placed Latin colonies prevented the fabric from being torn to shreds: as Cicero says, they were 'not towns of Italy but bastions of Rome's power'. Thanks to them she emerged from the struggle stronger than ever[83] (Fig. 7).

Shortly after Pyrrhus' departure and even before the hostilities engendered by him had come to an end, the Romans were already adding to the number of their Latin colonies. In 273 a pair of them were planted on the Tyrrhenian seaboard, at Cosa in the north and at Paestum in the south. These could help to guard a coastline whose vulnerability had been disquietingly emphasized, by Dionysius I's descent of old on Etruria, by Pyrrhus' recent excursion into Sicily, and by a long-standing Carthaginian disposition to intervene in Italian affairs. Cosa and Paestum also served to punish, isolate and watch recent enemies: Cosa was a port on the territory of Vulci, the powerful Etruscan city that had drawn the sword against Rome in 280; Paestum had been seized from the Lucani, the Oscan-speaking people that had so strongly supported Pyrrhus. The number of colonists is not recorded for either place, but to judge from the archaeological remains Paestum was much the larger.[84]

The Romans also took the opportunity of their victory in the Pyrrhic War to break up the confederation of the Samnite tribes. To isolate the formidable Pentri, on the one side from the Hirpini and on the other from the Caraceni, Latin colonies were used. One was founded at Beneventum in 268 and another at Aesernia five years later. Both occupied strong sites, well protected by rivers and ravines, and were important communications hubs: roads radiated from each in several directions. Beneventum, under the name Malventum ('ill met'), had been the chief town and administrative centre of the Hirpini Samnites. The change of its name into something fairer-sounding ('welcome') continued the practice, which the Romans had already employed at Narnia, of bestowing names of good import upon their colonies[85] (*Pl.* 7).

Neither of these colonies was founded singly: each coincided with a foundation in the Adriatic region against the threat of a new *tumultus Gallicus* in Italy. The Latin colony founded simultaneously with Beneventum was Ariminum (268), controlling the narrow gateway to Cisalpine Gaul between the eastern Appennines and the sea: its task was to bar the way to Gallic incursions from the north and to police the remnant of Senonese Gauls to the south.[86] It and Hadria effectively bracketed the Picentes whose subjugation immediately took place. It was in their territory that the partner for Aesernia, Firmum, was founded (264). The conquest of the Picentes (269/268) was really a sequel to that of their southern neighbours, the Praetuttii, some years earlier, and it was concluded with the forcible expulsion of large numbers of them from their homeland. They were settled much further south on the other side of Italy, near Salernum, where they formed a heteroglot wedge separating the Hirpini Samnites from their western kinsmen, the Alfaterni. On the land vacated by these Picentes Rome founded her Latin colony. The function of the suggestively named Firmum was to support Hadria, which it resembled in being a large community on a dominating mountain site some miles inland from the sea. It helped to control movements along the Adriatic coastal corridor east of the Appennines; but it also kept a wary eye on the resentful Picentes who had been left behind.[87]

Hostilities in the First Punic War broke out just as Firmum and Aesernia were being founded, and the outbreak of that great conflict very probably contributed to the decision to colonize them. In general the war was much more likely to provide occasions for maritime colonies since Carthaginian naval power made fortresses on the coast obviously advisable, especially in the closing years of the struggle when Hamilcar, the father of Hannibal, was staging sea-borne raids on Italy from his Sicilian stronghold on Mount Eryx.

Two, if not three, maritime colonies were then founded, Alsium (247), Fregenae (245), and possibly Pyrgi, and for good measure a Latin one as well. This was Brundisium, founded in 244 on territory that Rome had taken from the Sallentini over twenty years earlier. From its harbour, the best on the east coast of southern Italy, the Romans hoped to close the narrow straits of Otranto to Carthaginian or any other hostile shipping seeking to enter the Adriatic. This Latin colony was founded singly, possibly because by 244 the twenty-year struggle with Carthage had so exhausted the resources of Rome that she preferred to husband what were left for emergencies: these might include having to help Brundisium in its distant isolation. In fact the colony prospered, and as the terminus of the great south road, the Via Appia, and the jumping-off point for Greece, it became a place of real importance that greatly strengthened Roman authority in the 'heel' of Italy[88] (*Pl. 38*).

Although the hostilities in the First Punic War stayed safely distant from the Italian countryside, they nevertheless affected developments within the peninsula. Little is known about the behaviour of the Italians during the conflict; some of them, at least, were reluctant to take up arms at Rome's behest.[89] Whether to punish them or to reward ex-soldiers at the war's end, Rome apparently settled numbers of her citizens by viritane distribution on lands in central Italy that Curius Dentatus' conquests had won almost half a century earlier in 290; and to accommodate them and those who had preceded them to the area, she created two new rustic tribes, Quirina and Velina (241). At the same time she founded a Latin colony at Spoletium on a powerful mountain site in southern Umbria.[90] Simultaneously, however, the Italians became restive, and Falerii actually resorted to armed rebellion, an action that cost it dear, since it was forced to cede much of its territory and to move from its strong hilltop site of Civita Castellana to the exposed position of Santa Maria di Fálleri some miles away in the plain.[91] The exact sequence of these events is not known. It is uncertain whether the colonization of Spoletium provoked the revolt of Falerii or was a precaution against its repetition. In any event the function of its settlers, who must have included veterans from the First Punic War, was to police the neighbouring Umbri and Etrusci and also, in view of what happened next, to improve communications with Ariminum.

The suppression of the Faliscan revolt brought internal peace to peninsular Italy until Hannibal arrived to shatter it.[92] In continental Italy, however, or Cisalpine Gaul as the region between the northern Appennines and the Alps was then called, it was a very different story, even in the period before Hannibal got there late in 218. On a long view it was perhaps inevitable that Rome should seek to extend her control of Italy as far as the Alps, since these mountains must have seemed as if designed by nature herself for the true boundary of the country. But exactly when Rome decided on the subjugation of the whole Cisalpine region, a task hat took her decades to complete, is doubtful. If the actions of 237 were really the start of the systematic Roman conquest, it is indeed surprising that no colonies were planted between then and 218.

On the whole it seems likely that in the interval between the First and Second Punic Wars an advance to the Po was the most that the Romans could have been contemplating,[93] and even this was anything but easy to achieve. The Celtic tribes dwelling between the Appennines and the Alps were tough enemies. In 225 a powerful combination of them penetrated into peninsular Italy as far south as Telamon on the coast of Etruria near Cosa before meeting with defeat. Perhaps it was this exploit that led to Roman operations in Cisalpine Gaul by way of reprisal. Many Roman senators were clearly not anxious to get too heavily involved there, and they were not completely gratified when the consul Gaius Flaminius scored a triumph deep inside the territory of the Insubres in 223. In the following year M. Claudius Marcellus, the great plebeian hero, scored the first really notable victory of his fabulous military career by slaying the king of the same people to win the *spolia opima* at Clastidium.

Shortly after this in 219, probably at the urging of Flaminius, the Romans decided to establish a pair of Latin colonies right on the River Po; and to this end they recruited 12,000 settlers, half of whom were destined for Cremona on the north bank of the river and half for Placentia on the south: both places were important communications centres and river ports.

More than one ancient writer insists that the purpose of these colonies was to keep the Transpadane Gauls at bay, and this can be taken as certain. But the operation was due to become unusually complex. Early in May, 218, news arrived that Hannibal had crossed the Ebro, clearly with Italy for his destination. This news prompted the Roman authorities to order the settlers to get to the colonies, which not being on virgin sites could be swiftly made defensible, within thirty days. But the news also strengthened the determination of the Gauls to resist, and the centuriation of the colonial *territoria* encountered furious opposition. The Boii even managed to capture the three founding commissioners. Their replacements somehow completed the task, but the twin colonies had hardly been founded before Hannibal arrived to convulse all Italy (218).[94]

APPENDIX

The foundation of Placentia

According to Asconius, Placentia, whose foundation date was the last day of May, 218, was the fifty-third colony sent out by the Romans. This figure is so high that it is universally recognized to include Citizen as well as Latin colonies, in somewhat the same way that Velleius included both types in his list of colonies. That Asconius means the *deductio* in 218 and not its reinforcement in 190 is proved by the persons he names as founding commissioners for the occasion: they are the officials for the earlier occasion.

The two foundations of Placentia have been rendered famous by Frank's conjecture that they were at distinct and separate sites, at La Stradella in 218 and at Piacenza, about twenty miles to the east, in 190.[95] Frank's ingenious suggestion has found few supporters, but it is certain that colonists were sent to Placentia twice.

Mommsen drew attention over a century ago to the apparent error in Asconius' tally. According to Mommsen only thirty-four Latin and eleven Citizen colonies had been founded by 218, for a total of forty-five; and even Mommsen's figure is itself too high, since in fact there were only thirty Latin and ten Citizen colonies in 218. Moreover Mommsen did not attempt to explain Asconius' figure; he merely noted it as wrong.[96]

Actually Asconius' total will come out right if one assumes that the groups of new colonists sent to Venusia, Narnia and Placentia after the Second Punic War were officially reckoned new colonies and not just enlargements of existing ones and if one assumes further that Asconius has mistakenly given the first instead of the second *deductio* at Placentia as the fifty-third act of colonization by the Romans. It is to be noted that he calls the settlers at Placentia *novi coloni* and singles out the *equites* among them in the manner that Livy does for foundations after the Second Punic War.

Asconius clearly obtained his information from Cicero, and Cicero was very conscious of the distinction between the mere reinforcement of a colony with additional settlers and its refoundation with formal ceremonies, such as the taking of auspices and ritual ploughing of the furrow.[97] Now between 218 and 190 four Latin colonies obtained more settlers: Venusia in 200, Narnia in 199, Cosa in 197 and Placentia in 190 (it had to share its new settlers with Cremona, but Livy makes it clear that this was only one *deductio* with 6,000 *novi coloni*, the number mentioned by Asconius). We are not told explicitly whether these were refoundations or merely reinforcing operations, but it is to be noted that Livy records the appointment of three-man commissions for only three of them. Founding commissioners did not lead out new settlers under a *vexillum* to Cosa in 197. According to Livy Cosa had requested in 199 that commissioners be appointed for a new *deductio* there in order that its depleted numbers might be brought up to strength, but this request was refused. In 197, however, Cosa was permitted to enrol 1,000 additional settlers by itself, from anywhere in Italy provided that they did not include anyone who had been an enemy of Rome since 218. This, quite clearly, was no *deductio*, and Asconius therefore did not include it in his total.[98]

Besides the refoundations at Venusia, Narnia and Placentia the period from 218 to 190 witnessed the foundation of two new Latin colonies, Thurii-Copia in 193 and Vibo-Valentia in 192, and eight new Citizen ones, Volturnum, Liternum, Puteoli, Salernum, Buxentum, Tempsa, Croton and Sipontum, all in 194.[99]

Assuming then that Asconius mistook the *deductio* at Placentia in 190 for its original foundation in 218,[100] we can calculate his figures as follows (foundations before 338 not being counted of course since they were colonies of the Latin League, not of Rome):

Latin colonies, 338 to 218	30
Citizen colonies, 338 to 218	10
New Latin colonies, 218 to 190	2
New Citizen colonies, 218 to 190	8
Refounded Latin colonies, 218 to 190	3
Refounded Citizen colonies, 218 to 190	0
Total	53

So much for Asconius.

Besides him, King Philip V of Macedon also had something to say on the subject. According to the king, the policy of the Romans of granting their citizenship to manumitted slaves provided them with abundant manpower, as a result of which they had been able to found almost seventy colonies by 214 (that is, down to and including the foundation of Placentia).[101] This tally is clearly far too high. Even if to the thirty Latin and ten Citizen colonies existing in 214 we add the fourteen colonies founded by the Prisci Latini before 338, the total is still far short of the king's 'almost seventy'. Yet in 214 King Philip had good reason to inform himself as accurately as possible about the Romans and their expansion over Italy, since he was at that very moment beginning hostilities with them: hence he must have got the figure seventy from some source that he considered reliable.

The source, as Mommsen pointed out long ago, was very probably an oral one.[102] It could have garbled or exaggerated the information. King Philip or his informant may somehow have confused the despatch of Roman citizens into colonies with their division, *c.* 240, into groups of seventy for the reformed *comitia centuriata* and the simultaneous concentration of the freedmen into the urban tribes:[103] but such an explanation is more contrived than convincing. It is far more probable that the king is simply guilty of an exaggeration or, more accurately, of inexactness of language. The Roman practice of using the word *coloni* to describe settlers in viritane assignations as well as settlers in organized colonies has caused him to include both types in his total. If one could make a certain count not only of all the *coloniae*, but also of all the *praefecturae*, *fora* and *conciliabula* resulting from the viritane distributions before 214, the total would certainly approximate seventy. Whether the settlers included as large a proportion of freedmen as King Philip thought is very doubtful, but presumably there were some, just as there were some who were not Romans at all. Unquestionably the king's general inference, that the colonizing activity of the Roman state in one form or another was enormous and contributed greatly to its military might, is fully justified.

CHAPTER IV

COLONIAE MARITIMAE

CITIZEN COLONIES TO 218 BC

AT THE END of the Latin War Rome not only retained seven Latin colonies but also founded colonies of a different sort, the *coloniae civium Romanorum*, whose settlers were Roman citizens and actually the only native-born, as distinct from naturalized, Roman citizens of republican times to have two citizenships, that of Rome and that of their colony.[104] As they were communities of Roman citizens residing at a distance from Rome itself, the Citizen colonies bear an obvious resemblance to the Roman *municipia*, but they differed from them in one fundamental respect: they were Roman by origin, whereas the *municipia* were Roman by incorporation. The *coloniae*, in other words, were simply extensions of Rome, and this always affected men's view of them.[105]

During most of the Roman Republic they were held in slight regard. *Municipia* were city-states in their own right, with a tradition of independence and a history of their own, in some cases as old as, or even older than, the history of Rome herself, while the Citizen colonies were newly created and, it might be suspected, second-class appendages of the city-state of Rome. This view of the *coloniae* was clearly the official as well as the popular one. The various kinds of Roman communities are always ranked in order as *municipium*, *colonia*, *praefectura*, *forum*, *conciliabulum*, in public documents like the Lex Rubria and the Tabula Heracleensis as well as in Cicero.[106] It was only in the Roman Empire, when the Roman citizenship had acquired great value and enormous prestige and had become a highly prized possession, that the Roman *colonia* decisively asserted its superiority over the *municipium*, and this was precisely because as an extension of Rome it was then regarded as being more genuinely Roman, almost as if it were a part of Rome herself: the Roman quality of the *municipium* seemed much less authentic by comparison. The provincials, eager to parade their complete assimilation and anxious to belong to the ruling power, were largely responsible for this view of the matter.

Down to the Social War (91–87), and even later, an Italian community was not disposed to concede that its own native citizenship was less cause for pride than the Roman and consequently felt no very high esteem for a *colonia civium Romanorum*. In the fourth century particularly a small extension of Rome failed to impress. Even in 338 Rome was still only one of many states in Italy, a large and growing one admittedly, but still essentially only a local power with a citizenship much like any other.

Until the end of the Second Punic War, and even for almost a score of years thereafter, Citizen colonies were invariably founded on the sea coast, and there is ancient authority for calling them *coloniae maritimae*.[107] The first of them to be founded were the ports of Latium nearest to Rome, Ostia and Antium. A settlement was reputedly founded at Ostia, at the mouth of the Tiber, by King Ancus Martcius in the days of the Roman monarchy, but neither Livy nor Dionysius of Halicarnassus, who record the foundation, describe it as a *colonia*; nor is there any archaeological evidence for an organized settlement in the sixth century on the well explored site of Ostia.[108] Later, Ostia was unquestionably a maritime colony and its archaeological remains have been found. It was a *castrum*, the carefully constructed surviving ashlar walls of which can be confidently dated to the second half of the fourth century, in other words to the period of the settlement at the end of the Latin War. The *castrum* covers slightly more than 5 acres, an area that would have sufficed, although only just barely, as the urban centre for three hundred *coloni*; and three hundred seems to have been the standard complement for Citizen colonies before 184[109] (*Pls. 41–43*).

It is true that the figure is actually recorded before 200 of only one of them, Tarracina (329), but five of the eight Citizen colonies founded in 194 received three hundred settlers and almost certainly so did the other three. The number is to be related to the three original tribes of Rome, each of which was envisaged as supplying one hundred *coloni* for one *centuria* of land, the settlers obviously getting the traditional two *iugera* apiece. Two *iugera* per settler is actually recorded for Tarracina, and Livy clearly thought it the standard allotment in the early Citizen colonies.

A subsistence farmer and his family cannot, of course, live on so small a holding: at least three times as much is needed. Therefore the Citizen colonists must have had the use of other land, even though they did not acquire it in quiritary ownership: in fact ancient texts allude to communal land (*ager compascuus*) in Citizen colonies. The settler's personal holding was kept at the irreducible two *iugera* minimum in order to prevent any derangement of the Centuriate Assembly at Rome: Citizen colonists, like Latin, must have been obtained from the lacklands and, if given larger holdings, they might have qualified for a higher censorial class and upset timocratic control of the apparatus of the Roman state.[110]

The three hundred settlers of the earliest Citizen colonies, then, were settled on three *centuriae*. In other words, the territory of their colony was quite literally *centuriatus ager*; and that the subdivision was centuriation in this exact sense of the Latin word is confirmed by the archaeological and literary, as well as the etymological evidence. At some Citizen colony sites, and Tarracina is one, traces still survive of a survey based on *centuriae*. Moreover it is to be noted that, in conformity with this, the bigger allotments recorded by Livy for the Citizen colonies founded between 184 and 128 are almost without exception convenient fractions of a *centuria*.[111]

So small a number as three hundred settlers cries out for explanation, since a larger community would not only have made a more authentic and substantial urban commonwealth, but presumably would also have discharged its coastguard role more efficiently. Several factors were probably responsible. One was the unwillingness of the Roman state to immure thousands of its able-bodied citizens in large colonies of a type which, as we shall see, exempted them from service in the legions. A second was the

7 *Central and Southern Italy before the Social War*

impossibility of recruiting Roman citizens in large numbers for the unpopular Citizen colonies of the fourth and third centuries. A third and even bigger factor was the constitutional difficulty. In this early period the very foundation of a Citizen colony must have seemed of dubious legality, since the Roman view, if Cicero represents it correctly, was that a Roman citizen could not leave Rome and acquire a second citizenship without losing his own. The establishment of organized communities of Roman citizens in

F

remote areas did not seem consonant with the traditional concept of the city-state as an organism of reasonable size and might have proved fatal to its integrity, since a diaspora of Roman citizens scattered in pockets over the Ager Romanus would have made centralized administration virtually impossible. From motives of expediency, however, it might be acceptable for a small group of emigrating Romans to have citizenship in another community, namely their own Citizen colony; but in this early period, when the unfamiliar idea was still very radical, the same tolerance could not be extended to a large group. Even if it had been feasible, there was still the problem of administration. A really big community of Roman emigrants with full citizen rights at a distance from Rome would have been peculiarly difficult to supervise, especially in the legal and judicial fields.[112]

One way around these difficulties would have been to found Latin colonies rather than Citizen, and this was done so far as possible. The Roman state established a number of Latin colonies on the sea coast, performing essentially the same role as the Citizen colonies, and inevitably doing so more efficiently. Down to and including the period of the first two Punic Wars there were ten *coloniae maritimae*; yet there were almost as many Latin colonies on the littoral. Six were right on the coast: Ariminum, Brundisium, Circeii, Cosa, Paestum and Pontiae; and there were three more only some two or three airline miles away from it: Ardea, Firmum and Hadria. Manifestly Latin colonies with a maritime role were fully possible.[113] If Rome did not have recourse to them invariably, it was because of her reluctance, if not her positive refusal, to tolerate 'foreign' states, which is what the Latin colonies technically were, on her own *territorium*. Admittedly Latin colonies might be contiguous to Roman territory, and they were even founded on sites that had once formed part of the Roman state domain. But it was not normal for a Latin colony, at the time of its foundation, to form an enclave within the unbroken bloc of Ager Romanus centring on Rome herself. Before the year 200 it was the standard and regular practice for a colony founded at a coastal point to be Citizen if linked to Rome by a solid and continuous stretch of Ager Romanus, but Latin if separated from the Ager Romanus by an intervening stretch of non-Roman soil. Once the Ager Romanus became fragmented as the result of annexation of territory that was not physically joined to its central core, this policy had to be re-examined; but this did not occur until after the Second Punic War[114] (Fig. 7).

The Romans showed a disposition to found their Citizen colonies, like their Latin, in pairs. The partner for Ostia was Antium (Anzio), the nearest natural harbour to the city of Rome. Both colonies were planted *c.* 338: this date is recorded for Antium by Livy and is not in conflict with the archaeological evidence for Ostia. Unlike Ostia, Antium was founded on a site where an organized town already existed, and one that was old, populous and important, a former stronghold of the Volsci. As these Volsci would have to make room for the intruding colonists, relations, initially at any rate, were bound to be strained; and the admission of some, perhaps a majority of, Volsci amongst the original settlers may represent an effort by the Romans to mitigate Volscian resentment, while at the same time reflecting the very great difficulty encountered by the Roman authorities in finding settlers amongst their own citizens.[115] Whether they had trouble similarly in enrolling volunteers for Ostia we do not know. In any case the enrolment of non-Romans, as well as Romans, for the Citizen colony at Antium was in line with their practice for the Latin colonies, and it set a precedent for the Citizen colonies that was to endure for more than two hundred years: it was only in the age of the Gracchi, in the late second century, that the Romans began excluding non-Romans from their colonies (*Pl. 44*).

Nevertheless there must have remained at Antium a large number of Volsci who were not enrolled in the *colonia*, and they posed a problem with which Roman colonization was to be recurringly faced: how to order and adjust the relations of a community of *coloni* with a community of natives amongst, or alongside of, whom they had been planted. The solution found by the Romans was always pragmatic and governed by expediency. It seems that in 338 they incorporated the non-colonial Volsci of Antium into the Roman state as *cives sine suffragio*, while at the same time putting an end to the corporate existence of their civic organism. This reduced them to a disordered mass of stateless persons, the only organized community at Antium being the Citizen colony, a community of three hundred families with only the most rudimentary instruments of administration. Such a constitutional vacuum with all its possibilities for chaos could not possibly endure and some twenty years later the Roman government responded to appeals from the Antiates and authorized *patroni* from the colony to seek a solution. The result apparently was that henceforth the natives were organized in a *municipium sine suffragio* under the protection of the colony. It is impossible to say how much time elapsed before the two communities, Roman colonists and native Antiates, coalesced into one.[116]

The importance that the Romans attached to coastal defence is indicated by the fact that the only towns which Rome had specifically named in her first treaty with Carthage (508) as within her sphere of interest (Ardea, Antium, Laurentum, Circeii, Tarracina)[117] were all on, or virtually on, the coast. Clearly her purpose in making Ostia and Antium Citizen colonies *c.* 338, was to safeguard this same stretch of shore, the coast-line of the Ager Romanus, and to spare her the necessity of maintaining a fleet for doing so.

Ostia and Antium were soon followed by others: by Tarracina (Terracina) in 329 and the Minturnae–Sinuessa pair in 295. All these were obviously designed to protect Latium from sea-borne assault and thus ensure the communications between Rome and her newly-won dependencies in northern Campania. The inland route from Rome to Campania, which the Via Latina followed, went by way of the Trerus and Liris valleys and was uncomfortably close to potential enemy territory; it was tenuous, vulnerable and exposed to a quick thrust from unsubjugated Samnium. On the other hand, the coastal route, which was soon to become the Via Appia, while very much safer from land-based attack, stood in need of protection on the side of the sea. The Citizen colonies provided it. A navy would hardly have served equally well, since ancient warships could operate only in certain seasons of the year, and at no period of the year could they remain at sea for more than a few days at a time; and night-time operations were all but impossible for them. Constant vigilance by watchers on shore would be much more effective than patrolling warships for denying the coastline to enemy fleets; and to make sure that it would be always forthcoming the Romans set up what were to all intents and purposes coastguard stations. These could also serve as customs control posts, but their primary purpose was defence. They were manned with permanent garrisons of Roman settlers who were forbidden to absent themselves from their colonies for more than thirty days, even to join the regular Roman army. In fact a *sacrosancta vacatio militiae* guaranteed them exemption from service in the legions. They had to stay where they were, on the alert at all times, to resist raiders from the sea and prevent them from establishing beachheads. Their obligation to remain uninterruptedly at their coastal stations meant that they were, quite literally, *coloni maritimi*, and this is what Livy calls them in the two passages where he identifies them for his readers. Not that they were expected to go down to the sea in ships and fight. If obliged to take up arms, they fought on the beaches or in the nearby countryside. Their duty was to deny passage to enemies: normally these would be enemies landing from the sea, but they might also be enemies thrusting by land[118] (*Pl. 46*).

The function of Tarracina, for instance, was not only to defend the coast, but also to hold the Lautulae pass that ran between the Ausonian mountains and the sea. Similarly Minturnae (Minturno) and Sinuessa (Mondragone) were hastily authorized in 296, during the Third Samnite War, in order to prevent the Samnites from repeating a plundering raid which in that year had carried them around the western end of the Mons Massicus and deep into Latium Adjectum. The twin colonies blocked either end of the narrow passage between the Mons Massicus and the Tyrrhenian in very much the same way that Tarracina blocked the pass of Lautulae. Their establishment in 295 came just in the nick of time, for the Samnites did attempt to repeat their manœuvre of the previous year. But besides denying the coastal road to attackers, Minturnae and Sinuessa might also foil any attempts of sea-borne enemies to leapfrog along the littoral in search of a beachhead (*Pl. 34*).

The five Citizen colonies, that protected the coast of Latium

Adjectum while simultaneously guaranteeing communications with Campania, were the *coloniae maritimae* par excellence: they are the only ones to appear on both of the lists of *coloni maritimi* given by Livy. There were, however, in addition to them five others on either the one or the other of his two lists, and these were not confined to Latium or even to the Tyrrhenian coast of Italy.

In 290 at the close of the Third Samnite War the Romans annexed from the Sabini, Praetuttii and Senonese Gauls a wide strip of territory stretching right across Italy from the Tyrrhenian to the Adriatic. The Roman object was to push a wedge between their northern and their southern enemies and end forever the possibility of their joining hands: there was to be no repetition of the Sentinum campaign of 295. To protect the newly annexed territory at its Adriatic end they founded, at some time between 289 and 283, a Latin colony at Hadria on Praetuttian soil and a Citizen one at Sena on Senonese. Sena may not have been 'at the edge of the plains about the Po', as Polybius says it was, but it was undoubtedly a long way from Rome, and in the days before the Via Flaminia the route to it was far from easy: there was the barrier of the Appennines to cross and a detour around the territory of independent Camerinum to make. The Roman Senate would no doubt have preferred a large Latin foundation, but perhaps not enough settlers were available after provision had been made for the simultaneous Latin colony at Hadria and for the extensive viritane distribution of the newly acquired Sabine lands. Accordingly a standard Citizen colony, a small *colonia maritima*, was established at the open roadstead of Sena Gallica (Senigallia). Its purpose was to fend off Illyrian pirates as well as raiders from Cisalpine Gaul.[119]

Some twenty years after Sena events were developing that made reinforcement of the western shores of Italy seem advisable. The five original Citizen colonies there guarded only the coast immediately south of Rome, and as the section of coast immediately north of the Tiber-mouth was just as close to the city it was manifestly equally important to protect it. The Romans had long ago, in the fourth century and later, taken the precaution of annexing large parts of this sensitive section of Etruria as Roman *ager publicus*. But it was not until the menace of Carthage began to threaten that they decided that permanent coastguard stations were needed there.

The Carthaginians had been interested in the coast of the southern half of Etruria for very many years. It was there that they had found Etruscan allies against the Greeks, and it was there that the first Carthaginian inscription ever unearthed in Italy came to light a few years ago. As the Pyrrhic War was drawing to its close, Carthaginian naval power appeared to become menacing, and it was then (273) that the Romans established the Latin colonies at Paestum and, significantly, at Cosa. Now, less than ten years later, the First Punic War broke out and the Romans immediately founded a *colonia maritima* at Castrum Novum (Santa Marinella) in 264.

They also planted one at Pyrgi (Santa Severa), the port for Caere, but exactly when is nowhere recorded. They may have made it a partner for Castrum Novum and thus adhered to the custom of establishing colonies in pairs. On the other hand Pyrgi may belong to the closing years of the First Punic War, when Hamilcar's raids on the western shores of Italy convinced the Romans that it was necessary to strengthen the coast of Etruria still further: a pair of Citizen colonies were certainly founded there at that time, at Alsium (Ladispoli) in 247 and at Fregenae (Fregene) in 245[120] (*Pls. 14, 45*).

The ten places that have been listed were the *coloniae maritimae* recorded by Livy. All ten of them were very much alike. The town walls of Minturnae and of Pyrgi can be traced, or quite confidently inferred, in their entirety, and they enclose spaces almost identical with that of the *castrum* at Ostia, presupposing thus communities of three hundred families. Such small settlements with their minuscule holdings, as noted above, were anything but highly regarded, and the tradition that they were undesirable places in which to settle persisted down to Cicero's day. It is not surprising therefore that Rome had great difficulty in finding even three hundred settlers for them. Romans were just as reluctant to enrol for Minturnae and Sinuessa in 296/295 as for Antium in 338. On other occasions, perhaps all other occasions, the founding commissioners probably obtained their complement by opening the lists of intending settlers to non-Romans. We know that this was done in the case of Antium, when the Romans first began founding Citizen colonies, and in the case of Citizen colonies which they planted shortly after the Second Punic War and which undoubtedly continued many of the practices observed in the earlier *coloniae maritimae*[121] (*Pls. 45, 48–50*).

The reluctance of Roman citizens is not hard to fathom. The *coloniae maritimae* held out few prospects of worthwhile civic activity. The round of local affairs in them could not have been very exciting. They had the minimal measure of self-government, far less than the *municipia* or the Latin colonies. Their only officials were a pair of duoviri, whose competence was limited for the most part to organizing defences and military activity whenever that became necessary. The duoviri did not have judicial authority, the Citizen colonists being under the direct jurisdiction of urban officials or in some matters of *praefecti iure dicundo* appointed by the praetor in Rome.[122] Apparently only the duoviri were eligible for the senate of the colony, so that the average Citizen colonist had no real participation in public affairs. No doubt he would have been equally unlikely to have reached political office, had he stayed in Rome, belonging as he normally did to the class that could never expect to win it. But at Rome there was at least all the excitement of the popular assemblies.

Enrolment in a *colonia maritima* was in fact tantamount to disfranchisement, since attendance at meetings of the *comitia* and support from the plebeian tribunes, while theoretically possible, were very unlikely for settlers who were forbidden to be absent from their colony for more than a month at a time. Presumably the ban on absenteeism did not last for ever, since it is inconceivable that a man who joined a Citizen colony was condemning himself and all his male descendants to everlasting exile; and, whatever the situation elsewhere, descendants of the settlers in the *coloniae maritimae* near Rome contrived to profit from their proximity, to judge from the careers of the unscrupulous Postumius and others from Pyrgi. But this does not alter the fact that the original *coloni* were effectively exiled for the active portion of their adult lives.[123]

19, 20 Under the Empire provincial towns often received Latin status as a first step towards becoming Roman colonies: to advertise their 'latinity' they sometimes erected a statue of the symbolical sow and piglets (p. 126 and Note 239). To proclaim itself an extension of Rome a Roman colony, such as Aventicum, might display a sculptured representation of the wolf and twins.

21,22 The same types of buildings are found in all Roman settlements (p. 27). Saepinum (Altilia) in southern Italy, founded by the future Emperor Tiberius *c.* AD 2, is typical. It had a theatre (*above*) with an arched corridor round it at ground level; it also had a basilica (*below*) which presented its long side to the forum, as usual; the rectangular shape of its forum was also normal.

23 Under the Empire *coloniae*, as the highest type of Roman cities, were regularly embellished with monumental structures. Trajan adorned Beneventum with a magnificent triumphal arch, known today as the Porta Aurea. Besides recording the achievements of his reign, it marked the starting point of the Via Traiana, the shorter road to Brundisium which Trajan built *c.* AD 109. (Road-building was regularly associated with colonization: p. 84.)

26 Stout walls of polygonal limestone blocks protected early Latin colonies. At Signia (Segni) in Latium they still stand with their corbelled gateway, forerunner of later monumental entrances (*cf.* Plate 8). ▷

24 Signia, like many Latin colonies, had a Roman-type Capitolium: its central cella is now the nave of a church.

25 The polygonal walls normally had their outer face carefully smoothed to make scaling difficult, as here, at Alba Fucens.

27 At Norba in Latium the gateway was skilfully devised to oblige attackers to expose their unshielded side to the defenders in the beautifully constructed round tower on the right (p. 33). ▷

28 At Cosa (Ansedonia) in Etruria one entered the forum by a monumental triple arch, the earliest dateable specimen in Italy (second century BC) (p. 34). The arch has long since collapsed, but its original appearance can be easily envisaged.

29 A colony was usually linked to Rome by a military road. At Alba Fucens the Via Valeria made a right-angled turn to become the town's *decumanus maximus*: the milestone reveals that Alba was sixty-eight miles from Rome.

30 Remains of the basilica at Cosa: as usual, its long side faced the forum. In imperial times the building was transformed into a theatre, remains of the reconstruction being clearly discernible. ▷

31 Air view of Cosa looking southeast towards the port: in the foreground, a housing area, and, beyond it, the forum. The latter resembled contemporary fora in other colonies and at Rome in being a rectangle close to, even if not exactly at, the centre of the town, and in having an adjoining basilica, comitium and curia (p. 34). ▷

32, 33 At Cosa, as in other Latin colonies, public structures imitated their Roman counterparts: the comitium (*above*), meeting place for the assembly of burgesses, was round and stepped (p. 34: ignore the later crosswall). The Capitolium at Cosa (*below*) crowned the citadel and was approached by a processional way: note the three well-preserved cellae and the large cistern under the pronaos (p. 35). The smaller temple in the lower left-hand corner was built before the Capitolium.

The truth is that the *colonus maritimus* faced the bleak prospect of spending the best years of his life in the dreary round of a small outpost community where political activities and social amenities were conspicuous by their absence. Some of these communities, such as Antium or Sena Gallica, were living in juxtaposition with a hostile and bitterly resentful native population, which made dwelling in them more than a little dangerous. Others of them, like Castrum Novum, to judge from its name, were established on virgin sites and eked out a rough and primitive kind of frontier existence, which made dwelling in them uncomfortable.

The one advantage that the Citizen settler in a *colonia maritima* enjoyed was his exemption from legionary service,[124] but it is a moot point whether it was not more than counterbalanced by his obligation to stay in his colony. For that matter, he ultimately lost even this poor advantage. During the crisis brought on by the arrival of Hasdrubal to support his brother Hannibal in the Second Punic War, the *sacrosancta vacatio* was suspended for all *coloni maritimi*, except those at Ostia and Antium, and they were called upon to serve in the legions. During the panic caused by the war with Antiochus in 191, an even greater indignity befell them: they were made liable for service in the fleet.[125]

The unpopularity of the *coloniae maritimae* explains both why they were so small and why they were so few. In all, there were only ten of them, all founded in the course of a single century between 338 and 241. After the First Punic War (264–241) no authentic new *colonia maritima* seems ever to have been founded. The eight Citizen colonies that were planted shortly after the Second Punic War resembled their ten predecessors in a number of ways: they were small, they were on the sea coast and their settlers probably received very small allotments. But they differed from the earlier *coloniae maritimae* in one very essential particular: their *coloni* could not, or at any rate did not, claim exemption from legionary service. In other words they were not tied to their coastal stations in the manner of the true *coloni maritimi*.

CHAPTER V

TIME OF TESTING

THE COLONIES IN THE SECOND PUNIC WAR

WHEN HANNIBAL ARRIVED in Italy there were, so Livy implies,[126] exactly thirty Latin colonies and ten Citizen, no more and no less. The roundness of these numbers evokes both surprise and suspicion. It may of course be nothing but coincidence, especially in the case of the Citizen colonies, there being no compelling reason for the Roman authorities to 'freeze' their total at exactly ten. A total of thirty, however, for the Latin colonies cannot be so airily dismissed, owing to the universal tradition that in the days before Rome acquired control of Latium there were precisely thirty Latin communities there, all of Alba Longan origin and all joined together in the Latin League: they were symbolized in the well-known legend of the sow and her thirty piglets.[127] Not surprisingly a connection has been sought between the two sets of thirty.

That the thirty Latin colonies of Hannibal's day had been deliberately brought to that total, and no further, by the Roman authorities as 'a symbolic gesture' towards the old tradition of thirty Latin peoples in prehistoric Latium can hardly be the full explanation.[128] Latin colonies were founded when and where needed, and the Roman authorities could not, and indeed dared not, assume that exactly thirty of them, never more than that even though at first there might be fewer, were bound to be the ideal number.

It must have been a lucky chance that there were exactly thirty Latin colonies in 218. By then some of them had, of course, outlived the immediate purpose of their founding: Rome's frontiers had been pushed far beyond them. But they did not cease being Latin colonies merely because the logic of military events had left them in the rear. The same logic of military events could equally be expected to go on making additions to their number necessary. No doubt, however, the existence of the thirty Latin colonies in 218 helped to establish the unchallenged priority of the tradition that listed precisely thirty Latin peoples in pre-Roman Latium. Other traditions were undoubtedly in circulation. Dionysius of Halicarnassus in one passage records forty-seven peoples; the Elder Pliny mentions fifty-three or more; and long before either of them Cato seems to have been aware of a Latium that contained far fewer than thirty communities.[129] If the version of thirty came to prevail, then the existence of precisely that number of Latin states during the Second Punic War, the very period when Roman historiography was being born, probably had something to do with its acquiring the sanctity of a firm belief.[130]

How well informed Hannibal was about these thirty Latin colonies and for that matter about the Roman organization of Italy in general will never be certainly known. He was certainly well aware that the peninsula was not all Roman; and presumably he also knew something about its threefold character, Roman, Latin and Italian. As far as Rome was concerned, the Latin third was of the greatest military usefulness. Polybius reveals that shortly before Hannibal's arrival the collective strength of the Latini, although inferior to that of Rome herself, was a very significant component in the armed might of the peninsula.[131] And, besides their fighting manpower, the walls around their urban centres and the military highways leading to them aided the Latin colonies to discharge their strategic function very effectively. The great roads, that all led to Rome, and that formed a network embracing peninsular Italy, had not been thoroughly engineered or completely paved by Hannibal's day, but they were in good enough shape to make troop movements along them comparatively easy.

Roads or tracks must have existed from time immemorial between Rome and the sites of the earliest colonies. Practicable routes had pre-existed to Signia, Norba, Ardea, Circeii and Setia along the valley of the Trerus (Sacco) or across the rolling Campagna, and to Sutrium and Nepet by way of the defiles of southern Etruria. To get to Cales at the time of its foundation in 334 a roundabout approach was necessary via the lower Liris and the route of the later Sinuessa–Suessa–Cales cross-road through Auruncan territory.

With the coming of the colonies these earlier and perhaps primitive communications had begun to be replaced and supplemented by the great Roman highways, paved and straight-thrusting. In fact colony founding and road building were intimately connected operations, the planting of the colony usually preceding the construction of the road. The Via Latina, because of its name, is thought to be the earliest of the great Roman roads: it served Signia, Fregellae, Interamna and Cales. The Via Appia, leading to or past Citizen colonies (Tarracina, Minturnae, Sinuessa) as well as Latin (Ardea, Norba, Setia, Circeii, Suessa), was begun as early as 312 and by the time of Hannibal probably stretched all the way to Brundisium, going through or by Saticula, Beneventum and Venusia. The Via Valeria, from Rome to Carseoli, Alba Fucens and beyond, dated from 303, so Livy implies.[132] The Via Aurelia may belong to 241, and if this was the case Cosa and the other colonies on the coast of Etruria had a direct link with Rome.[133] So probably did the centre of Etruria, since it is very possible that either the Via Clodia or the Via Cassia dates from 225: if not the Via Cassia itself, then certainly its predecessor ran to Sutrium and the heart of Etruria by the last quarter of the third century. The Via Flaminia, completed just before Hannibal reached Italy, went through Narnia and past Spoletium to reach Ariminum. It is true that the great road linking Cremona and Placentia with Rome came after Hannibal's day; but there were Roman roads to the northern Appennines, and non-Roman roads, so Livy says,[134] ran over these mountains. Thus even these distant colonies were by no means completely without communications (*Pls. 7, 15, 47, 48, 51, 52*).

By 218 military forces could move to and from all the colonies quite expeditiously. This, of course, means Hannibal's forces as well as Rome's, but the advantage lay with her: for, even if

Hannibal reached the colonies, as he frequently did, their massive walls were impregnable to the means at his disposal. He had no siege train and was therefore obliged to pin his hopes to the possibility that they might be induced to become disloyal to Rome.

Here, however, he was doomed to disappointment. The Latin communities in general were loyal to Rome. Admittedly their 'independence' was not complete, but in compensation they enjoyed considerable intimacy with her. Their settlers could acquire Roman citizenship by the simple act of migrating to Roman territory and taking up residence there; and if, instead of emigrating to, they merely visited Rome, they could vote in the Plebeian Assembly there.[135] Furthermore they enjoyed the legal right of intermarriage with, and of conducting contractual business transactions, including valid land sales and purchases, on equal terms with, Roman citizens. Yet these close relations with Rome, which made the Latini in practice less than foreign even though still something less than citizen, did not by any means cut them off from the Italians. On the contrary they could also intermarry and trade with the latter. Above all, a Latin colony enjoyed the cherished right to order its own affairs according to its own laws, and it could amend, repeal, replace or enlarge these laws as it saw fit. Naturally it administered justice in its own courts. Its territory was its own, and its burgesses paid no tax on it to Rome. Even if the Latin colony did have to supply a quota of troops to Rome on demand and pay for their upkeep, it supervised and controlled its own military forces. The colony was so much its own mistress that normally Roman officials could not exercise authority in it or even set foot in it in their official capacity: it was run by its own magistrates. As if to emphasize its right to sovereign autonomy with unmistakable clarity, a Latin colony could issue its own coins, and not a few of them did so, usually in bronze, although five of them, all founded before 268,[136] coined also in silver. In fact the issues of the Latin colonies are a prominent feature of the numismatic history of Italy in the days of the Roman Republic.

As self-governing city-states the Latin colonies must have been free to choose any constitution they liked, but they preferred to order themselves according to the forms of Roman political organization, and because of this readiness, if not positive eagerness, to imitate Rome they present a fairly uniform picture. A Latin colony resembled Rome in having a popular assembly, a senate and two chief officials. These latter, like those of the early Roman Republic, were called by the old Latin title of praetor; and in addition to them the Latin colonies had officials of lesser consequence.[137] For these, however, the picture is less standardized although they are all alike in having Roman titles. The college of quaestors might number seven (as at Beneventum), or five (as at Paestum, Firmum and, later, Aquileia), or perhaps three (as at Venusia). Similarly instead of two aediles there were sometimes three tresviri (as at Ariminum, Spoletium and, later, Bononia). Praefecti were neither universal nor of identical function: at Luceria they seem to have been a special commission for superintending construction of the town wall. So far as is known, only Venusia had plebeian tribunes.

The magistrates were elected annually by the assembly of the colony: an interrex, named by the local senate, conducted the elections when no magistrates were available. There is no need to believe that Rome regularly engineered the choice of her own nominees despite the common assertion that she always made sure that effective control in the states within her sphere of interest should be safely in the hands of the well-to-do. In ancient society it was normal for the wealthy to exercise political power, since only they could afford the expense attached to office-holding; and this must have been the case in the Latin colonies, regardless of any action by Rome. Once elected, their praetors performed the functions to be expected of chief state executives, including the administration of justice. The duties of the lower officials seem to have been roughly the same as those of their Roman equivalents.[138] All of the officials must have been quite busy. There were public works, ceremonies, games and finances to superintend, and order had to be maintained: for this last they possessed certain powers of coercion.

Obviously the Latin colonies enjoyed almost complete administrative autonomy, a fact that helps to explain the strength of their support for Rome. Other factors promoting it were the origin of a very large proportion of their settlers from Rome and their military dependence upon her. Initially planted, as often as not, as buffer states between Roman territory and hostile populations bitterly resentful of their presence, the colonies needed the armed support of Rome for their very survival. Moreover a modification in their relationship to Rome *c.* 268 may have had the effect of attaching them still more closely to her. The change in status affected Ariminum and probably all the Latin colonies subsequently founded.[139]

The Citizen colonies were even stronger in their allegiance to Rome, naturally so since they formed an actual part of the Roman state. This latter fact affected their local government. The earliest of them may have been administered directly from Rome for some years after their establishment *c.* 338. But the need for leaders in times of trouble, and on other occasions too, must have become obvious very quickly, and from a very early date, if not from the actual beginning, every Citizen colony must have had its local administration. Its chief officials, as in the Latin colonies, were two in number; and it has even been suggested that these were originally called praetors, just like their Latin counterparts.[140] There is, however, no reliable evidence of this and in itself it seems very unlikely in the case of officials who did not possess jurisdictional powers. The epigraphic evidence suggests that the highest officials in the Citizen colonies were always called duoviri except for a very short period at the end of the second and the beginning of the first century.[141] Presumably, like the praetors of a Latin colony, they were annual officers elected by the assembly of the colony, but with duties that were almost exclusively military. The Citizen colony also undoubtedly had its own senate, of thirty members apparently in pre-Hannibalic days, a self-perpetuating body of co-opted ex-duoviri.[142] But it had very little else in the way of communal organization. There is no evidence that in the period before the Second Punic War it had any officials other than its duoviri, and small communities founded with three hundred settlers would not really need more than two magistrates. Later, when large Citizen colonies began to be founded, starting in 184, two officers could scarcely have been enough and consequently larger local senates and more officials must then have been created[143] (*Pls. 57, 59*).

The degree of independence and sovereignty possessed by the colonies and the extent of their intimacy with and dependence upon Rome made them proof against any offers or temptations with which Hannibal sought to allure them. This was also generally true of the *municipia* apart from the Oscan-speaking ones with partial Roman citizenship in the south. After Cannae (216) Capua went over to Hannibal.[144] Her dependencies, Atella and Calatia, also joined Hannibal, as did a number of the Oscan and Greek allies of Rome in southern Italy, although in some cases through *force majeure* rather than through conviction.

For the most part Hannibal failed in his attempt to win the Latini and Italians away from Rome. He could not induce any colony to side with him; nor was he able to carry any of the heavily fortified strongholds by assault. Expected to support and, if need be, to afford havens to the forces of Rome and her allies, the colonies discharged the role magnificently, down to 209 at any rate. Their military usefulness was incomparably greater than that of the areas of viritane distribution, which proved to be very poor recruiting grounds.[145] Placentia proved an asylum for the refugees from the battle of the Trebia (218), Venusia for those from Cannae (216). Venusia again was repeatedly a base for the southern operations of 'the sword of Rome', the great M. Claudius Marcellus.[146] Other colonies had an incalculable effect on the strategy with which the war was waged, by their mere existence forcing the Carthaginian into decisions that went sorely against his grain. Thus, the fortress of Ariminum, even though it could not by itself have prevented Hannibal from going round the Appennines in 217, any more than it prevented Hasdrubal from doing so ten years later, nevertheless had more than a little to do with Hannibal's decision to take the costly route over the mountains to get to the south; and it also retarded the flow of Gallic recruits to him once he got there. The troops at Ariminum were certainly instrumental in slowing down Hasdrubal's advance along the Adriatic coast in 207, thus allowing time for one Roman army to come across from Narnia and another to come up from Luceria and join together to wipe him out at the battle of the Metaurus. Furthermore it had been the necessity to watch the bastion of Venusia that had prevented Hannibal from marching north to join his brother immediately upon the latter's arrival in Italy.

On one occasion (216) the cluster of colonies near the middle and lower Liris and Volturnus almost enabled 'the shield of Rome', Fabius Maximus Cunctator, to trap Hannibal: the Carthaginian escaped only by bluffing the Romans with his ruse of burning faggots on the horns of oxen. In 211 this same group of colonies accounted both for the confidence of Rome when threatened by Hannibal's march and for the recapture of Capua despite his efforts at relief.

The Citizen colonies were no less steadfast. They saw to it that neither reinforcements nor supplies reached Hannibal by sea, and at the same time they kept the communications open for Rome.

For the colonies, however, the price came high. Placentia and Cremona, distant and isolated, were under such ceaseless assault from the Gauls that finally, despite prodigies of valour by Catiline's ancestor, M. Sergius Silus,[147] the morale of some of their colonists cracked, and they fled. Hadria, Firmum, Luceria, Beneventum, Venusia, Sinuessa and Minturnae all had their fields devastated, some of them repeatedly, by the passage of Hannibal's army. An even sterner trial came after the Roman disaster at Cannae in 216. Defection of *municipia* or allies in the south, or their subjugation by Hannibal, inevitably increased the calls on the Latin colonies for soldiers.[148] The colonies evidently responded well, but for some the effort became intolerable.

In 209 twelve of the Latin colonies announced that they could fight no longer: they had been bled white and could not send any more troops or find the pay for any. The recusant twelve were: Ardea, Nepet, Sutrium, Alba, Carseoli, Sora, Suessa, Circeii, Setia, Cales, Narnia, Interamna. The other eighteen, led by Fregellae, assured Rome she could still count on them to supply their quotas and, if need be, even more than their quotas of troops.

In the sequel it emerged that the twelve had not been quite so completely drained of their manpower as they alleged, even though they were undoubtedly finding it very difficult to field the troops demanded of them.[149] Most of the twelve were near to Rome and all were Latin colonies of long standing, five of them indeed belonging to the original group of seven of 338. They had probably lost many of their native sons by emigration to Rome and were short of soldiers in consequence: it is to be noted that after the war two of them, Narnia and Cales, had to be reinforced with new groups of colonists. Some of them may have preferred to keep their soldiers at home to defend their own farms and fields, which, it is fairly clear, was precisely what the more distant colonies, such as Placentia, Cremona and Venusia, were doing. All of them must have noted that the Romans had allowed themselves some relaxation of their own war effort, reducing the number of legions from twenty-three or more, probably twenty-five in 212, to twenty-one in 210,[150] so that it was perhaps time for the Latini, too, to get some relief. In any case, the war was going better and there was not the same sense of urgency: Syracuse, Capua and Tarentum had all been recovered, and in 209 it could not be foreseen that within a year Hasdrubal would bring another Carthaginian army to Italy to provoke the most serious crisis since Cannae.

For the time being Rome could do nothing. The troops that the twelve colonies were supposed to supply she found elsewhere as best she could: in her need of men she even abrogated the solemnly guaranteed exemption from legionary service of the maritime colonists. It was not until 204 that Rome found herself able to punish the recalcitrant twelve. Each of them was then required to produce from the ranks of its wealthiest burgesses for service outside Italy twice as many infantry as had ever been fielded by it in any one year since 218 and in addition to supply 120 cavalrymen (or three extra infantrymen for every trooper short of the 120). As the twelve colonies were not charged with secession or with giving aid and comfort to Hannibal, it is evident that the Romans recognized at least the partial justice of their claim to have had their strength overtaxed.

On the whole, the punishment meted out by Rome may not appear exceptionally severe to us. To the Latini, however, it must have seemed far otherwise, especially as it was accompanied by the stipulation that henceforth all twelve colonies were to follow the census procedures of Rome, send solemnly attested copies of their census returns on a prescribed form to Rome, and levy an annual tax from their burgesses on the same scale as Rome did from hers.[151] Hitherto the Romans had merely stated how many troops a Latin colony should supply: they had not interfered directly in the colony to dictate the manner of counting and raising the men. Henceforth they were going to scrutinize each of the twelve carefully and, in effect, administer its military forces. Clearly this was an infringement of the autonomy of the twelve as well as a deprivation of one of their most highly regarded privileges. It was also an indication that the Second Punic War had made Rome much stronger relative to her Latin associates and Italian allies than she had been before the war began.

Italy had emerged from the war still organized along the lines that Roman statecraft had devised. But Rome was now far more powerful than before: it was she, not her partners, who acquired provinces and large-scale reparations out of the defeat of Carthage. This state of affairs was to affect colonization along with much else.

APPENDIX

'Ius Duodecim Coloniarum' sive 'Ius Arimini'

In a celebrated passage Cicero mentions a group of twelve colonies in such a manner as to suggest that they differed from other colonies; exactly how, he does not say, merely remarking that their burgesses could receive bequests from Roman citizens (and that apparently was something that all Latini could do anyway). Cicero names Ariminum as typical of the twelve, perhaps because it was the first to enjoy the status that characterized them all. Hence it has become customary to refer to the grade of dignity of these communities as either the Ius Arimini or the Ius Duodecim Coloniarum. Cicero makes it clear that he is not referring to Citizen colonies: hence his twelve are to be sought amongst the Latin colonies, but their identity has never been firmly established.[152]

There are two well-known groups of twelve Latin colonies. First, there are the refractory twelve of 209. But as Ariminum was not one of these, Cicero cannot be referring to them, unless his text is faulty. The latter possibility has, of course, been suggested: it has been proposed to amend his text to make it refer either to Ardea or Interamna (instead of Ariminum) or to eighteen colonies (instead of twelve).[153] But this kind of palaeographic legerdemain fails to carry conviction.

The other well-known group of twelve Latin colonies are the last twelve to be founded, which began precisely with Ariminum in 268. Mommsen suggested long ago that these must be Cicero's twelve, and he defined Ius Arimini as an inferior kind of Latin status.[154] This theory has been widely accepted and various attempts have been made to show how the latinity of the twelve was inferior: they could not coin in silver, their burgesses could not intermarry with Roman citizens, their burgesses could not migrate freely to Rome. Here, however, is the flaw in the theory: no evidence can be found to prove beyond doubt that colonies founded in 268 or later did have reduced rights. The alleged ban on their silver issues is an *argumentum e silentio*, and even if such a ban existed it did not apply only to them; disapproval of marriage between Latini and Romans cannot be demonstrated until imperial times when Latin colonies were no more; the restriction on Latin emigration to Rome began in 187, not in 268. Not only is it impossible to prove that Latin rights were reduced in 268, but it actually seems more probable that they were improved then.[155] As Bernardi points out, there is no very obvious reason why Rome should have become more imperious towards her Latin associates in that year. On the contrary, their proved loyalty in the Samnite and Pyrrhic Wars gave her good reason to be more considerate towards them, and in fact the Latin colonies founded from 268 on seem to have been even more intimately involved with Rome than their predecessors: it is significant that not one of them was to be found among the colonies withholding further aid in 209. Finally, Cicero's text, so far from suggesting that the *duodecim coloniae* were worse off than the others, seems rather to imply the reverse.

Some years ago the present writer, who at that time accepted the guess that colonies founded in 268 or later were worse off, suggested a third group of twelve as the ones that Cicero had in mind: namely, those of the eighteen loyal and dependable Latin colonies of 209 that were founded in 268 or earlier: there were precisely twelve of them, Ariminum being the last. But although this hypothesis takes account of Cicero's implication that Ius Arimini was a favoured rather than an inferior status, it founders upon the exploded theory of a reduction in Latin rights in 268.[156]

Perhaps the identity of Cicero's twelve will never be certainly known; but it does seem certain that the last twelve Latin colonies to be founded began with Ariminum and that Cicero's twelve enjoyed exactly the same rights as communities of Roman citizens in the matter of making wills and inheriting legacies. Elsewhere Cicero points out that all Latin colonies could acquire whatever they pleased of these Roman testamentary rights simply by passing legislation of their own parallel to the Roman laws.[157] This may mean that settlers at Ariminum and the other eleven places obtained full testamentary equality with Roman citizens automatically and without the necessity of their colony going through this formality of passing an enabling act. Possibly it was this that differentiated the twelve from the other Latin colonies.

On the whole, then, it looks as if Cicero's twelve were the last twelve Latin colonies to be founded, beginning with Ariminum and ending with Aquileia. If they were rather more favoured than the earlier colonies, it may have been because Rome was already experiencing difficulty in finding settlers for her Latin colonies and therefore sought to entice them with an improvement of status; or possibly she modified the Latin status, assimilating it more to the Roman citizenship, in order that it might serve as a suitable substitute for the *civitas sine suffragio*, which she seems never to have granted again from 268 on.[158]

CHAPTER VI

TIME OF TRANSITION

THE AFTERMATH OF THE SECOND PUNIC WAR

COLONIZATION HAD BEEN HALTED for the duration of the Second Punic War, but with that struggle now over reasons were soon found for new foundations. Some parts of Italy, including some colonies that had suffered severely in the war, were, if not derelict, in at least serious need of settlers. Colonies might provide careful surveillance of areas lately rebellious, and they might confer the further benefit of caring for veterans of the war. Above all colonies would prevent certain regions from becoming strategic liabilities in a period when Rome was going to be faced with a new or continuing round of conflicts. Annexation of the Iberian peninsula would entail unending campaigns of pacification in Spain; Philip V of Macedon had to be punished for his support of Hannibal, and this meant Rome getting involved inextricably in the tortuous world of the Hellenistic monarchies; and, much nearer home, accounts had to be settled with the Celts in the north, who had helped Hannibal and remained in arms after his defeat. All of this seemed to make colonies necessary.

Peninsular Italy had to be safeguarded against attack by Hellenistic monarchs who controlled, or were thought to control, large fleets; and if the menace of another Celtic attack or of a renewed assault from Spain was to be permanently removed, continental Italy had to be subjugated. Clearly colonization would continue to be dictated by military necessity. The foundations might be incidentally useful for accommodating urban lacklands or soldiers home from the war (although the colonies that were founded, for the most part, came too late for the Hannibalic veterans).[159] But such an economic and social purpose would be equally well served by viritane distribution of land, and in fact provision was made for veterans in this way in southern Italy at the expense of communities that had sided with the Carthaginians. The colonies were intended to support a military programme, not to make provision for the needy.

Appreciation of the necessity for colonies was one thing; their actual establishment was something else. The Second Punic War had changed many things and not least the outlook and attitude of the ordinary Roman citizen. He was no longer burning with the zeal of the peasant-soldier, ready at a moment's notice to exchange his ploughshare for a sword. After 200 the reluctance of the Romans to face the rigours and the risks of life in a *colonia* became increasingly more marked; and no matter how obvious the strategic desirability for any given colony, the Roman authorities were not going to find it easy to recruit settlers for it.

One part of Italy, the south, had suffered severely in the Second Punic War and therefore seemed particularly vulnerable and exposed in 200. It was here, accordingly, that the Roman authorities first sought to repair the damage that Hannibal had done. Venusia, isolated from the Latin-speaking world ever since its foundation in 291, had been not only cut off periodically but also threatened continuously with sudden assault during the long years that Hannibal had roamed the south enjoying the support of its Oscan-speaking peoples. Yet, even when encircled, Venusia had never faltered in its duty to Rome, much less surrendered to the enemy: its sufferings and its losses must have been acute. In 200, as soon as possible after the war, the Romans, as an essential first step for the restoration of their authority in the region, reinforced Venusia with a fresh group of settlers. Yet soon after this Venusia was showing signs of oscanization, so that one wonders how many of the new settlers in 200 were Romans born and bred.[160]

The strengthening of the shore line received attention next. As the operations against Philip V of Macedon would require Roman naval strength to be concentrated in the Adriatic, there was concern lest the Tyrrhenian coast might be left insufficiently protected. Hence it was decided to plant Citizen colonies there, especially on its southern portion, since a number of foundations already studded the shores of Etruria and Latium. Planning of colonies in Campania had in fact begun very soon after the war, four of the Citizen type being projected. Like the maritime colonies of old, they were to have the general coastguard function of repelling any sea-borne assault; but since an assault by a Hellenistic monarch on the west coast of Italy was somewhat improbable, they would be free to fulfil other functions too. One pair at Puteoli and Salernum could serve as customs stations, a role envisaged for them as early as 199. They could also keep guard over areas of disaffection. Salernum was on soil taken from the disloyal Picentini, and Puteoli was close to Hamae, the shrine and rallying-point of the rebellious Campani. The other pair at Volturnum and Liternum, both planned in 197, were on territory that had been taken from Capua for her support of Hannibal; evidently they, too, were intended *inter alia* to keep an eye on dissident Campani[161] (*Pl. 53*).

The decision to plant these colonies was taken in the Roman senate, dominated at the time by Scipio Africanus and his faction, and it may be that this colonization programme was a favourite project of his. It is to be noted that, when he later fell out of favour, he retired to one of these colonies, and not a particularly attractive or salubrious one, Liternum, to spend the closing years of his life there.[162] Be that as it may, the actual founding of the colonies did not take place until 194, conclusive evidence that there was difficulty in finding settlers for them. Indeed, by the time that the recruits had finally been mustered, the programme had been enlarged, because of the menace that Antiochus the Great's fleet was expected to pose, especially should Hannibal get the command of it. Accordingly in 194, besides the colonies planned in 199–197, two more pairs of Citizen colonies were founded, all of them on the coast and on the territory of ex-rebels: Sipontum and Buxentum were planted on the soil of Arpi and of the Lucani respectively, while Croton and Tempsa were on land that had once belonged to the Bruttii.[163]

The four pairs of colonies founded in 194 were all small. They obtained three hundred settlers apiece. This figure is actually recorded for five of them (Puteoli, Salernum; Volturnum, Liternum; Buxentum) and it was possibly only Livy's desire to avoid repetition and be succinct that prevented him from recording it for the other three as well. Thus all eight Citizen colonies together amounted to a mere 2,400 settlers, fewer than Rome had planted in her first Latin colony in 334. Almost certainly the allotments were correspondingly small, even though their size is not given by Livy. They were probably no larger than the traditional two *iugera* each, since even in later Citizen colonies, where bigger holdings had become the rule, they sometimes amounted to no more than five or six.

Clearly the eight Citizen colonies of 194 resembled in some ways the ten maritime colonies of earlier days: as Livy says, they were sent *in oram maritimam*.[164] But they were not identical in every respect. The *coloni* of 194 were not really *maritimi*, since they were not tied to the coast. They might be called upon for service in the legions, or even in the navy, and hence they were not visualized as permanently at their stations on the littoral. As if to emphasize this aspect of their duties, the Roman authorities ruled that henceforth no Citizen colonists, not even those in the old *coloniae maritimae*, should any longer be exempt from service in the regular armed forces.

These colonies of 194 also differed from the earlier Citizen colonies in another respect. At least three of them were founded on what might be described as detached fragments of the Ager Romanus and were thus cut off from the main body of Roman territory. Croton, Tempsa and Sipontum could be reached from Rome only by crossing non-Roman territory. Two more of them, Buxentum and Salernum, if not actually separated from the main bloc of Roman territory, were attached to it only by a tenuous and tortuous strip of land. In an earlier day all five of these places would have been not Citizen, but Latin colonies; but to find settlers for this number of Latin colonies would have been quite impossible in 194.

The eight Citizen colonies were far from enticing, and this made it difficult for Rome to find settlers willing to go to them. To get them the founding commissioners had to go beyond the ranks of Roman citizens, and the evidence suggests that the non-Roman volunteers were more interested in acquiring Roman citizenship than in actually taking up residence in the colonies.[165] It is true that one of the colonies, Puteoli (Pozzuoli), soon became the busy and prosperous port for Rome. Salernum (Salerno) was also to become a place of great importance. But in general the sites were unattractive. The great days of Croton (Crotone) were long since behind it. Tempsa (near Santa Eufemia) and Volturnum (Castel Volturno) have remained poor hamlets to this day. Liternum (near the Lago di Patria) was an unhealthy swamp;[166] and Sipontum (near Manfredonia) and Buxentum (Policastro) were so dreary that their settlers soon ran away from them.[167] The renegade *coloni* may have argued that their liability for legionary service meant that they were not really expected to stay indefinitely at their coastal stations. The fact that the Roman authorities discovered only by accident that they had absconded indicates how forlorn and forgotten these outposts were; and it also suggests that the panic fear of Antiochus' naval power which had brought them into being had not lasted for very long. Had apprehensions remained lively, it is inconceivable that the authorities at Rome would not have kept in close touch with the colonies. Steps were taken to rehabilitate Sipontum and Buxentum, but the ineluctable conclusion was also drawn: the day of the small Citizen colony was clearly over.

Nor would it be possible to substitute Latin colonies for small Citizen ones. The Roman government learned this at once, when it sought, precisely at this time, to establish a pair of coastal colonies of the Latin type in the 'toe' of Italy, namely Copia (193) at Castrum Frentinum on the territory of lately revolted Thurii, and Valentia (192) at Vibo (*Greek* Hipponium) on soil taken from the Bruttii.[168] The optimistic names given to both places indicate the Roman intention to have them become places of real consequence; and, in both places, land allotments were reasonably generous, twenty *iugera* at Copia and fifteen at Valentia, with even more than this for cavalrymen, in an effort possibly to create local aristocracies which would serve as the administrative class.[169] Yet it proved very arduous to find settlers. Somehow 3,300 were raised for Copia and 4,000 for Valentia, and they probably included many non-Romans. Livy reports that at Copia the number was disappointingly small and that in both places land was set aside for additional colonists who, it was hoped, might nevertheless appear.

The truth is that, after the Second Punic War at a time when many Romans had obtained land by viritane distribution at the expense of disloyal Italian states, Rome did not have sufficient manpower left both to reinforce old Latin colonies that had been ravaged by war and at the same time to found new Latin colonies, even though these latter were planned on a somewhat smaller scale than those of the third century.[170] Moreover, even if she had had an unlimited supply of manpower for all these purposes, she may not have been willing to lose it to Latin colonies. It was better to keep it under her own control than be denied the use of it by Latin colonies claiming to be overburdened and exhausted. Above all, however, it seems certain that Roman peasants, even if available in large numbers, would not have been as amenable to the idea of joining a Latin colony now as they had been in the fourth and third centuries. By now Roman citizenship had become valuable as a result of the overwhelming predominance with which Rome had emerged from the long struggle with Hannibal, and Romans, even land-hungry Romans, were not disposed to relinquish it in exchange for the citizenship of a Latin colony. Apart altogether from this there were many Romans who were not prepared under any circumstances to leave urban amenities for distant farm life in possibly hostile surroundings. For these various reasons recruits were simply not to be found in any numbers for Latin colonies at this time.

This can be seen in the north even more clearly than in the south. Scipio's victory at Zama had not brought peace in Cisalpine Gaul. There, urged on by Hannibal's agent, Hamilcar, the Gauls continued fighting; and the Ligures, too, were in arms. In 200 the Celtic Boii even managed to do what the great Carthaginian captains had been unable to accomplish: they captured the Latin colony of Placentia together with some 2,000 of its settlers. Half of its inhabitants, it is true, managed to escape, nor were the Boii able to repeat their feat at Cremona. But they had made it very clear that there were difficult days ahead for the Romans in the north.[171]

The first step taken by the Romans was to strengthen their communications with the area. The Latin colonies at Narnia, a key point on the Via Flaminia, and at Cosa, the port halfway up the coast of Etruria, both needed reinforcements and the Roman government authorized 1,000 new settlers for each, in 199 and 197 respectively. The Roman authorities, however, refused to take the responsibility of finding the settlers for Cosa and that colony got them by itself as best it could from anywhere in Italy. It is clear that the 1,000 at Narnia also included many Italians.[172] Evidently recruits were in very short supply, and it is therefore not surprising that almost a decade elapsed before there was any more colonization north of Rome. Finally, in 190, the Romans succeeded in mustering 6,000 recruits for the reinforcement of Placentia and Cremona. Simultaneously they decided to found near these places a pair of new Latin colonies on land ceded by the Boii; but in this they were being very over-optimistic. By offering very large allotments of fifty *iugera* each they attracted 3,000 colonists for one new foundation on the site of the Etruscan settlement of Felsina at the northern end of the principal pass over the Appennines. They planted the colony in 189, giving it the optimistic name of Bononia (Bologna). But not even the prospect of fifty *iugera* of free land could allure sufficient settlers for the second Latin colony, and it accordingly was never founded.[173]

It may be suspected that many, and perhaps even a majority, of the recruits which the Romans did manage to enlist for their colonies in these years were non-Romans: the reinforcements at Cosa certainly were. But finding even them presented the Romans with a very difficult dilemma. Emigration was depopulating the non-Roman states of Italy to the point where they were finding it almost impossible to supply their quotas of troops for the incessant wars throughout the Mediterranean basin, and as they made up two-thirds of the armed forces, and on the more difficult battlegrounds such as Spain apparently an even higher proportion, the Roman authorities, with memories of 209 in mind, could not let them lose still more population. In 188 they stopped extending the Roman citizenship to Italians, and in 187 the Senate responded to Latin protests against the number of Latini that were being permitted to settle in Rome by restricting the Latin right to migrate freely to the city: they expelled 12,000 Latini who had moved there recently and henceforth permitted no Latin to emigrate to Roman territory, unless he left an adult son behind him in his own Latin community.[174]

This regulation, however, could be very simply, if somewhat ingeniously, evaded: an emigrating Latin merely arranged to have his son become the nominal slave of a co-operative Roman, who would 'liberate' him and thereby make him a Roman citizen by manumission: thereupon he was free to join his father. So the Latin communities continued to lose population. One sign of it was the need to bring the Latin colony at Cales back to strength shortly before 184: Claudius Pulcher somehow succeeded in raising a group of settlers and added them to it.[175]

In 177 the Latin communities found it necessary to renew their protest, their spokesman on this occasion being perhaps the eloquent Lucius Papirius of Fregellae.[176] The Senate now ruled that it was illegal for a Roman citizen to liberate a slave without first solemnly swearing that it was not a case of pre-arranged manumission to effect a change of citizenship, and it expelled all the Latini who had immigrated since the previous Latin protest. These measures may have had some effect on the influx of Latini into Rome, but it may well be doubted whether they caused the Romans to stop enrolling Latini in their colonies.[177]

Such expulsion of enfranchised immigrants, instigated by the non-Romans themselves though it was, must have strengthened the Romans' innate conviction of their own superiority; and it no doubt helped to breed that xenophobic exclusiveness which became so notable a feature of their behaviour later in the century. But in the early part of the century it is good evidence of a shortage of recruits for Rome's colonies.

By 190/189, when Placentia and Cremona were reinforced and Bononia founded, all of the Cisalpine Gauls except those in sub-Alpine areas had been conquered, and colonies were now needed to consolidate the Roman grip on the Gallic lands. The three just named were not enough to provide fully adequate protection to the improved and very much shortened communications which had been constructed to Cisalpine Gaul in 187, the Via Aemilia from Placentia to Ariminum and a second Via Flaminia over the Appennines from Arretium to Bononia.[178] In an earlier age colonies of the Latin variety would have been founded, but Latin colonies were now clearly out of the question. Accordingly the Romans decided to use Citizen colonies instead; for them Roman citizens could be conscripted perhaps in the last resort, but it would probably be possible to find volunteers for colonies that enjoyed the Roman citizenship.[179] This marked a big turning-point in the history of Roman colonization. Before the Second Punic War Latin colonies were the rule and Citizen colonies the exception; the exact reverse now obtains.

Sipontum and Buxentum had familiarized the Romans with the idea of Citizen colonies on parcels of Roman territory that were isolated and separated from the main bloc. But now, *c.* 185, the Romans had to go further and make up their minds to an idea that was even more novel, namely the possibility that Citizen colonies might have to be large and far away from the sea, if not sent outside Italy altogether. By conceding this, the Romans completely changed the character of their Citizen colonies, making them into settlements of the greatest consequence. The golden age of the Citizen colony was still to come, but the way to it was opened now, in the first quarter of the second century.

One of the first steps was a reform of voting procedures in the Roman Tribal Assembly which may have made it possible for Citizen colonists to participate more easily in the activities of that body. This, however, was by no means the only political repercussion of the radical change in colonization. Hitherto the Senate had controlled it. It was chiefly on the initiative of the Senate, and even on its orders, that colonies had been founded. *De iure*, perhaps, only the Plebeian Assembly could decide when and where to found a colony; *de facto* the Senate had acted for the People and made the decision. Undoubtedly the preference of the Senate had been for Latin colonies; and since the Second Punic War, it had been responsible for all foundations of new Latin colonies or reinforcements of old ones. But large Citizen colonies were not going to be left indefinitely to the discretion of the Senate. The man responsible for a foundation became its patron and the settlers in it became his clients,[180] and a large Citizen colony could provide a more influential retinue than a *colonia maritima* or a large Latin colony might be expected to do. Not surprisingly, therefore, aspiring statesmen were soon no longer content to let the Senate monopolize colonial policy. Individuals began to pursue vigorous and independent colonizing programmes of their own and this was bound to affect the purpose, the siting and the composition of colonies. For the moment, it is true, the Citizen colony continued to be in the main a strategic instrument, but it is significant that rivalry for the role of founding commissioner had already become very keen.[181]

In 184 Potentia (S. Maria di Potenza) and Pisaurum (Pesaro) were founded on the Adriatic coast, in Picenum and the Ager Gallicus respectively. They were Citizen colonies and probably the earliest large ones, although that distinction is usually thought to belong to Mutina and Parma in the following year. That Potentia and Pisaurum were large is suggested by the size of their allotments: six *iugera* per colonist are evidence of agrarian settlements, not coastguard stations. They were, it is true, on the coast and seaboard Citizen colonies were traditionally small affairs. But Luna, just seven years later, received 2,000 coloni, and it was a Citizen colony on the littoral. For that matter it is not unlikely that the first large Citizen colonies should have been located where hitherto all Citizen colonies had been. Another indication that Potentia and Pisaurum were more than villages is the action of a Roman censor in 174 in objecting to his colleague's construction of public works in these towns, presumably on the ground that they were big enough for their own local officials to undertake such tasks. In small Citizen colonies activity by the Roman censors would have excited no comment. Finally it is worth noting that the only colonies actually named in the Epitomes of Livy for the period after the Second Punic War are precisely these two and four others, all of them large (Bononia, Parma, Mutina, Aquileia).

Velleius, too, actually names Potentia and Pisaurum, while ignoring no fewer than eight of the other Citizen colonies planted between 200 and 177. Evidently these two towns were reckoned important.[182]

Like the pair of Citizen colonies planted just one year later, Potentia and Pisaurum may have had 2,000 settlers apiece. This might be the figure which the Roman authorities had been used to obtaining for Latin colonies from the Roman citizen body since the end of the Second Punic War. It certainly seems unlikely that they could have mustered more than this in 184. Whatever the figure, they had to go beyond citizen ranks for their colonists and enrol non-Romans, who became Roman citizens when they joined their colony. The poet Ennius, a Messapian from Rudiae, was one of their number.[183]

Potentia and Pisaurum were not only on the coast but also on the Via Flaminia, so that they must have been intended to secure the communications with Cisalpine Gaul along the Adriatic side of Italy. The next year (183) similar measures were planned for the other side of the peninsula. A pair of Citizen colonies were projected on territory in Etruria that Rome had annexed long before. The foundation of one, the important road centre of Saturnia (Saturnia), was completed in 183, and of the other, Graviscae (Porto Clementino), two years later. As with the previous pair, the number of settlers is not recorded, but it was probably 2,000 in each. This is clearly indicated for Saturnia by Livy, who couples its foundation with that of Mutina and of Parma, each of which obtained this number; and its still-traceable town walls would be suitable for a community of this size. About Graviscae only *a priori* conjecture is possible, but it seems unlikely that it would have differed in size from the other Citizen colonies founded at this time: its 5-*iugera* allotments were certainly comparable, being identical in size with those at Mutina.[184]

Mutina (Modena) and Parma (Parma) were founded simultaneously with Saturnia, each of them getting 2,000 settlers. Like Saturnia they were situated well away from the sea coast, and they resembled Latin colonies unmistakably. In fact they were fulfilling the purpose of a Latin colony that had been projected, but never founded, as the partner for Bononia in 189, for they were to help the latter to control the northern exits of the passes over the Appennines.[185]

Mutina and Parma were not only large and far from the sea, but even beyond the political boundaries of Italy. The absence of comment on this novel aspect is presumably due to their being well within its geographical boundaries, far to the south of the Alpine barrier. Certainly their settlers were regarded as being on Italian soil for purposes of title to their land, and presumably for other purposes as well.[186] In 179 the Roman tribal lists were drawn up on a local basis: the details are unknown, but one effect of it may have been to enable settlers in Citizen colonies, including Parma and Mutina no doubt, to participate more easily in Roman public life.[187]

The three pairs of Citizen colonies between 184 and 181 tightened the Roman grip on the gateways to continental Italy, setting the stage for the exploitation of Cisalpine Gaul and the final subjugation of the Ligures at its western extremity. M. Aemilius Lepidus, the consul of 187, who was not only the head of the founding commission for Mutina and Parma but also the builder of the great highway from Placentia to Ariminum, was clearly a strong advocate of these developments; and his action has immortalized his name: the Cispadane district of Italy is still called Emilia. His hand was undoubtedly strengthened by the action of 12,000 Transalpine Gauls who crossed into Cisalpine Gaul from the east in 186 with the peaceful but firm intention of settling there together with their wives and children: they emphasized the need for Roman defenders in the north (Fig. 8).

These Gauls were expelled and, as an obstacle to any renewal of their attempt, it was decided to found a colony at Aquileia, at the head of the Adriatic, astride the roads leading to the passes over the Julian Alps. Livy tells us that the Roman Senate debated at great length in 183 whether this colony, too, ought not to be a Citizen one.[188] He does not record the arguments for and against, but the factor at issue must have been its distance from Rome: it was some 450 miles away, almost at the limits of geographical Italy. Up until now no organized community of Roman citizens

8 Cisalpine Gaul

had been settled at this distance from the mother state, and Roman opinion, or at any rate senatorial opinion, could not easily contemplate so unparalleled an action. The notion of a Latin community far away, on the other hand, was much less strange, presumably because the Nomen Latinum was not visualized as possessing territorial unity: it inhabited scattered pieces of territory, no single one of which had primacy. Latin status by now was firmly established as a juristic rather than an ethnic concept that was not attached to a given geographical area, but could flourish anywhere. Years before Aquileia, Latin colonies had been planted beyond the Italian frontiers of their day—at Placentia, Cremona and Bononia; and ten years after Aquileia the Romans gave the status of a Latin colony even to a place in far-off Spain.[189]

The Senate therefore decided that the colony at Aquileia should be Latin, and there at once ensued the inevitable difficulty of finding the settlers for it, a difficulty doubtless compounded by all the large Citizen colonies that had so recently drained off all the surplus manpower. Even allotments on the generous Bononian scale and the presence of gold deposits near by failed to entice more than 3,000 recruits plus some centurions and cavalrymen, and it took a long time to round up even these: at any rate, they did not reach Aquileia until 181. This number was in fact too small for so remote and exposed a site, and in 179 it proved incapable of preventing a repetition of the Gallic penetration of seven years earlier. Thereupon the Romans renewed their search for settlers and decided also to link up Aquileia with the highway network of peninsular Italy. The road materialized first, an extension of the Via Aemilia in 175. It took longer to find the 1,500 additional settlers: they arrived at Aquileia only in 169.[190] These measures, however, started Aquileia on its way to greatness. By 148, when Rome had linked it further, with Cremona, Placentia and ultimately Genua, by means of the Via Postumia, it was firmly established. Its later development into one of the most important cities of the Roman Empire was an appropriate destiny for the last of those establishments that had played so notable a role in the expansion of Rome: after Aquileia no Latin colony was ever again actually founded.[191]

Meanwhile Roman subjugation of the Ligures had been going steadily on. Cicero's sneer about easy triumphs won at the expense of this people conveys a false impression. They were far from negligible foes and, according to Livy, kept the Romans very much on their mettle during the interludes between the really great wars. In 194 they penetrated right to the walls of Placentia and they actually overran the Citizen colony of Mutina six years after its foundation. Even after eighty years of warfare the Romans managed to force a way through them around the gulf of Genoa only with the utmost difficulty. Etruscan Pisae (Pisa), immediately to the south of them, could bear witness to their prowess, since they had succeeded in wresting the Tyrrhenian coast immediately above it, north of the River Macra, from Etruscan hands.[192]

As a barrier to any further progress by this redoubtable people Pisae offered territory to Rome in 180 with the specific request that a Latin colony be founded on it. The Etruscans' motive was no doubt to win favour with the mistress of Italy as well as to provide for their own protection; and Aquileia probably encouraged them to hope that the colony could be a Latin one, which is what they preferred as being more likely to guarantee their own continued independence. The Romans sent a three-man commission, headed by Q. Fabius Buteo, of a clan that had long had interests in Etruria, to investigate the Pisan offer, and three years later a colony of 2,000 settlers with $6\frac{1}{2}$ *iugera* of land apiece was established at Luna on the bay of Spezia to deprive the Ligures of a prime port for their age-long piracy and to block their road southward down the Tyrrhenian coast. But it was not a Latin colony: it was a Citizen one of the new large type. The resentment of the Pisans was undisguised but fruitless; and Luna, aided by a forced mass transfer of Ligures to southern Italy, discharged its task successfully.[193] Henceforth peninsular Italy felt few qualms about threats from continental Italy until the close of the second century. Thus the early phase of Roman colonization reached its end. For the time being no more colonies were needed.

List of Latin colonies

Priscae Latinae Coloniae, founded by the Latin League in concert with the Romans

Fidenae	Romulus	Labici	418
Cora	501	Vitellia	395
Signia	495	Circeii	393
Velitrae	494	Satricum	385
Norba	492	Setia	*c.* 383
Antium	467	Sutrium	*c.* 382
Ardea	442	Nepet	*c.* 382

Coloniae Latinae, founded by the Romans alone

Signia		remained Latin colonies after the Latin War
Norba		
Ardea*		
Circeii*		
Setia*		
Sutrium*		
Nepet*		
Cales*	334	
Fregellae	328	
Luceria	314	
Saticula	313	
Suessa Aurunca*	313	
Pontiae	313	
Interamna*	312	
Sora*	303	
Alba Fucens*	303	
Narnia*	299	
Carseoli*	298	
Venusia	291	
Hadria	289–283	
Cosa	273	

* The twelve colonies which withheld aid to Rome in 209 are marked with an asterisk.

Coloniae Latinae (continued)

Colony	Date	
Paestum	273	
Ariminum	268	the Duodecim Coloniae of Cicero?
Beneventum	268	
Firmum	264	
Aesernia	263	
Brundisium	244	
Spoletium	241	
Placentia	218	
Cremona	218	
Thurii Copia	193	
Vibo Valentia	192	
Bononia	189	
Aquileia	181	

CHAPTER VII

SOCIAL AND ECONOMIC OUTLETS

THE COLONIES OF THE GRACCHAN AGE

WHEN COLONIZATION WAS RESUMED with the despatch of a group of settlers to Auximum (Osimo) in Picenum, an event usually assigned to 157 but much more probably belonging to 128,[194] its scope and aim had markedly changed. After the lapse of half a century this is not entirely surprising.

Various reasons had been responsible for the cessation of colonization. In the first place, there was no military need between 177 and 128. In peninsular Italy there had been servile uprisings but no armed resistance by Italians to the supremacy of Rome since the attempted revolt of Falerii in 241. In continental Italy the Ligures and most of the Gallic tribes had been defeated and, despite some trouble with the Salassi in 143, Roman authority had been established well to the north of the Po. Beyond the Alps there was no contiguous power that could pose a really dangerous threat at this time.[195] Hence there was no very urgent reason for colonies.

Secondly, as the state domain was not needed for strategic colonies, the oligarchy that 'managed affairs, both civilian and military'[196] preferred to exploit it either for their own profit or for that of the state, instead of giving it away to settlers in the form of allotments.

Thirdly, private jealousies and mutual quarrels reinforced the nobles' view that it was better for the Roman public domain to provide rents for the state than farms for colonists. Colonial foundations were only too likely to engender attempts by the great noble Roman houses to monopolize the office of founding

34 Sinuessa (Mondragone), a *colonia maritima* on the coast of Latium Adjectum, blocked the passage round the seaward end of the Mons Massicus (p. 77): the mountain appears at the top of the photograph.

35 Fidenae (Castel Giubileo), allegedly colonized by Romulus and regarded by Dionysius of Halicarnassus as the model for later Roman colonies (pp. 40, 42, 149). It controlled the last Tiber-crossing above Rome.

36 This air view reveals how Setia (Sezze Romano), from its lofty site on the southern slopes of the Volscian Mountains, dominated the southernmost part of the Pomptine Marshes, which can be seen in the lower left-hand corner of the photograph. Setia was one of a pair of Latin colonies that stood as sentinels guarding the access routes on the borders of Old Latium, Circeii being the other (p. 43).

37 Air view of Nepet, clearly showing the ravines that give the site its exceptional strength. It and Sutrium formed a pair of Latin colonies in the same manner as Setia and Circeii. Their purpose was to control the approaches to Rome from the northwest, and for that reason Livy calls them *claustra Etruriae* (p. 43). In particular, Nepet dominated the road to Falerii and the Falisci, allies of the Etrusci.

39 Air view of the site of Lucera (*cf.* Plate 6), clearly revealing the military possibilities of the hill on which this early Latin colony stood. Situated where the Appennines meet the Apulian plain, Luceria controls the routes between central and southeastern Italy. Although distant and isolated when founded (p. 58), it soon became the great stronghold of Roman interests in that part of Italy.

38 Remains of the two columns erected by Trajan to mark the terminus of the Via Appia at Brundisium (Brindisi). The road originally ran to Capua, but was extended to the Adriatic, probably when Brundisium became a Latin colony (Note 88).

◁

40 Latin colonies, being theoretically sovereign states, issued their own coins, mostly of bronze. Five, however, also minted in silver, including Cales (Calvi) in Latium Adjectum. This didrachm, showing Victoria in a *biga*, probably belongs to the second century BC.

43 Roughly squared tufa blocks, part of the east wall of the five-acre castrum at Ostia, the original *colonia maritima* (*c.* mid-fourth century BC). ▷

41,42 Although its usefulness as a port at the Tiber-mouth promoted its rapid growth, Ostia remained an open roadstead until the Empire. This sestertius of Nero, *c.* AD 66 (*above*), celebrates the first harbour to be constructed there, that of Claudius. By imperial times Ostia was a large and flourishing town. This relief of *c.* AD 200 (*below*), now in the Museo Torlonia, shows its harbour and various protective divinities. The two freighters are probably wine ships: a welcoming party (left) approaches the larger vessel whose sail is decorated with the wolf and twins and the letters V L (Votum Libero?); dockers (right) unload the smaller craft.

44 Antium (Anzio): remains of the harbour. Unlike Ostia, its sister colony on the coast of Latium, Antium became a fashionable resort, much frequented by the Caesars.

45 The town walls of Pyrgi (for which see also Plate 14). No ancient writer records the date of this *colonia maritima*, but it probably belongs to the third century BC (Note 120). Its walls, which here form the substructure for a Renaissance building, can be traced in their entirety. They enclose a space of about five acres, almost identical with the castrum at Ostia (p. 71 and Plate 43), and their fine polygonal masonry confirms the date suggested for the colony.

commissioner. Already at Luna in 177 rivalry of this kind had perhaps provoked some kind of a struggle.[197] Certainly henceforth no great noble house, if it could help it, was going to allow any rival house to receive a backing of thousands of client supporters at one stroke by becoming patrons of a colony. The easiest way to prevent imbalance from developing was to make sure that no colonies at all were founded.

When colonization began anew exactly fifty years later at Auximum, its explosive possibilities were immediately appreciated. The territory on which Auximum stood had belonged to Rome for many years and one wonders why a colony should have been thought necessary there at this particular time. Military considerations are not to be completely excluded, since the essential characteristic of colonies as strategic bastions was at no time entirely forgotten;[198] and if the 128 date is correct this strong hill-site, twelve miles inland from Ancona, was colonized at the precise moment when the Gracchan land-law had made Italians, and even Latini, very restive. One task for it may have been to maintain surveillance over Picenum, where the Italian city of Asculum was potentially dangerous, exactly how dangerous was to be balefully revealed in 91. Nevertheless, in 128, there was no immediate or overt military threat,[199] so that there must have been more than just a strategic motive for what appears to have been a foundation of some size[200] (*Pl. 55*).

Auximum may well represent an attempt by Tiberius Sempronius Gracchus' opponents to outstrip the influence which his faction had gained from his contentious agrarian law. By now a Citizen colony was a very different affair from the poor hamlets of yesteryear with their minuscule holdings. It was a medium-sized community peopled by settlers with moderate-sized plots of land and capable of providing some social amenities for them. Because of its increased size it also had some political life of its own, with a more sophisticated communal organization, of which the use of the title 'praetor' for the chief officials at Auximum is symptomatic. Furthermore by now, as has already been noted, the Citizen colonist could probably exercise his citizen rights at Rome with more facility than formerly. All of which made the Citizen colony seem much more attractive to the urban proletariat. Accordingly, if Tiberius Gracchus' faction had won accretions of strength, piecemeal and gradually, by viritane distribution of inalienable lots, his opponents might hope to counter this effectively at one stroke with a colonization that gave allotments to thousands. Colonization ceased thus to be mainly military in its aim and became political and economic.

Auximum may represent a fresh departure in another way as well, namely in its composition. In the Gracchan age a spirit of Roman exclusiveness was abroad, insisting that free land was for Romans only. Apparently only Roman citizens could be recipients of Tiberius Gracchus' allotments,[201] and just five years after Auximum Gaius Gracchus encountered bitter opposition when he sought to enrol non-Romans for a colony in Africa. The conclusion would appear to be ineluctable: whereas non-Romans had regularly been eligible for Citizen colonies in an earlier day, Auximum in 128 was restricted to Roman citizens; and there seems to have been no difficulty in finding the colonists. Indeed there may have been enough for another colony at the same time.

This was Heba (S. Maria in Borraccia, near Magliano) in Etruria, a place virtually unknown until rendered famous in 1948 by the discovery of a bronze tablet there throwing much light on electoral procedures under Augustus. Its remaining ruins suggest that Heba, although hardly ever mentioned in ancient literature, was at one time a place of consequence. With Saturnia, it controlled the valley of the River Albinia (Albegna), the communications artery leading from the Tyrrhenian coast to the great religious shrine of Fanum Voltumnae in central Etruria; and near by there were mineral deposits to exploit, on Mount Amiata, as well as agricultural land. Heba had certainly been an inhabited site since early Etruscan times, and it was no less certainly a colony in Roman. Nothing, however, is known about its colonization. An inscription proves that it was a *colonia* in the early Empire when it bore a title of the type fashionable before 100: in other words, it looks like a Citizen colony and one that was earlier than the Social War, since had it been Latin it would have become a *municipium* after that conflict. Also it was probably later than 167, since it is not mentioned in the surviving text of Livy. It could belong to 128.[202]

When the Romans in that year resumed colonization on land that had long been theirs, they may have decided to found colonies in pairs as in earlier days, and then proceeded to plant Auximum some miles inland from the Adriatic and Heba not far from the Tyrrhenian. Perhaps Tiberius Gracchus' opponents were trying to discredit his programme by colonizing a region which he had loudly proclaimed to be derelict and which his land commission had conspicuously left to languish. This would mean that for Heba, no less than for Auximum, the motive was political and economic rather than military.

In any case, by 128 careerist politicians at Rome were well aware of the political value of sponsoring a colony. This can be inferred, interestingly enough, from the description of colonizations of a much earlier age in the pages of Livy and Dionysius of Halicarnassus. According to these authors, the proposal to found a colony sometimes led in the fifth and fourth centuries to faction-strife between well-to-do aristocrats and the champions of the down-trodden plebeians, a picture of the early Republic that must have been inspired by developments in a later age; for assuredly no contemporary record was kept of the debates that accompanied a colonization in those far-off days.[203] It is true that the actual foundations were almost certainly reported by the pontiffs on their *tabulae*;[204] but these priestly records were too scanty to have included detailed accounts of the arguments and disputes that flared whenever a foundation was mooted. The tales in Livy and Dionysius of plebeians agitating for colonies in the face of aristocratic reluctance contradict the assertion, also found in Livy, that sometimes colonists could be obtained only with the utmost difficulty. They must be figments of some annalist's imagination modelled on events in the Gracchan age. It was in the late second century, not in the fifth, fourth or third, that provision for the urban poor and unemployed became the primary motive for a *colonia*, with plebeian tribunes playing a major role in its foundation. Already in the first third of the second century, these officers of the plebs had sometimes made the official proposal for a colonization, but evidently in collaboration with the Senate.[205] By the last third of the century they were doing so unabashedly for political reasons of their own. This may explain why it now became the rule for only Roman citizens to benefit from colonization.

In fact the Romans had assumed a very high-handed attitude towards the Latini and the Italians since the Second Punic War, and the dissatisfaction of the non-Roman inhabitants of the peninsula was growing intense.[206] They resented the discriminatory practices that had become all too common now that Rome had developed into the strongest Mediterranean power. Rome was the only state in Italy that had profited territorially from the wars that all of them had fought in common. Only Roman officers could aspire to the highest commands with all their opportunities for influence, power and swift enrichment. Roman soldiers were likely to get the bigger share of the plunder and non-Roman the bigger share of the hardships and the fighting. Increasingly, non-Roman towns were being exposed to Roman arrogance while being excluded from Roman citizenship.[207] Despite their alleged independence, Latini and Italians were finding themselves subject, without redress or even appeal, to the *fasces*, those symbols of Roman authority. These things were resented, and resented bitterly, and they would have exploded into violence long before this had it not been for the material advantages that the local aristocracies derived from the Roman connection. The ruling group in a Latin colony or in an Italian allied town were not disposed to organize an anti-Roman movement, for the simple reason that Rome ensured their political pre-eminence in their own communities and permitted their participation in the profitable exploitation of the Roman provinces and of the Roman state domain. Tiberius Gracchus, however, had disregarded these privileges of the Latin and Italian gentry,[208] and this was probably one of the causes that led first to complaints and finally to conspiracies: the Social War (91–87) was the ultimate, inevitable outcome.

The resentment by the Latin colonies of Roman behaviour was in general much less pronounced than that of the Italian allied communities, probably because of the more favoured treatment which their greater intimacy with Rome won them.[209] Even so, the status of the Latini had become less desirable. Good evidence of it is the difficulty the Roman authorities had after the Second Punic War in finding Latin colonists: Romans were no longer prepared to exchange their precious Roman citizenship for the inferior Latin variety. Nevertheless the Romans had at least been mindful of Latin interests when striking a treaty with a trans-Adriatic people and they were prepared sometimes to give Latini a share, even if an unfair share, in viritane distributions of public land, while omitting to do the same for Italians.[210]

The Romans always showed an instinct to grade individuals, or even whole communities, at varying levels, and this instinct manifested itself now, not only between Latini and Italians but even between Latini and Latini. Some Latin colonies had preserved their 'Latin' character undefiled and were regarded by the Romans with particular indulgence. Others had come strongly under alien influence and were much less highly regarded. Two such Latin colonies were Fregellae, which had been largely oscanized by a mass immigration of Samnites and kindred Paeligni, and Venusia, which was heavily affected by its all-enveloping, Oscan-speaking environment.[211]

The Roman attitude was revealed in 125 at the very time when the non-Roman inhabitants of Italy first began to clamour for the Roman citizenship. The consul M. Fulvius Flaccus, a Gracchan supporter, endorsed the Italians' claim and proposed further that any of them who preferred it should obtain the Roman right of appeal rather than the Roman citizenship. But his proposals were brusquely rejected, and Fregellae is alleged thereupon to have taken up arms. The Roman answer was to send an army to the town and wipe it off the face of the earth. It was replaced in 124 with a new and presumably all-Roman colony at nearby Fabrateria Nova (La Civita, near Falvaterra).[212] The Romans did not go to these drastic lengths with Venusia, although according to a contemporary witness, Gaius Gracchus, they had no compunction about brutally murdering one of its inhabitants, presumably a speaker of Oscan, on the most trivial of pretexts. It would appear, however, that simultaneously the Romans sought to bind the governing class in the Latin colonies still more firmly to themselves by passing a law which conferred Roman citizenship henceforth automatically on office-holders in Latin colonies, while permitting them apparently to remain members of their Latin communities.[213] This unprecedented action was shrewd and far-sighted and was well calculated to guarantee the continuing loyalty of Latin communities, since these office-holders became automatically decurions in their local senates.

Such was the situation when Gaius Sempronius Gracchus, most celebrated of all the plebeian tribunes, entered on his office on 10 December 124. There can hardly be any doubt that he already appreciated how extremely useful colonization could be in promoting that popularity without which neither he nor any other plebeian tribune could hope to get his programme endorsed and ratified by the Plebeian Assembly. Whether or not one accepts the conjecture mooted above that Tiberius Gracchus' opponents had improved on his agrarian legislation and made it seem inadequate by comparison with their own colonization of Auximum and Heba, Tiberius' brother was fully aware that by now colonies were much more likely to make an instantaneous mass appeal than viritane distributions. Any illusions he may have had about this would have been surely dissipated at the very beginning of his tribunate.

He became plebeian tribune at the end of the year in which the Citizen colony was established at Fabrateria Nova, and although so far as is known he had nothing to do with that colonization, he could not have failed to appreciate its significance: it curried favour with the urban proletariat by taking land away from disgraced Latini and giving it to needy Romans.

Clearly an agrarian law of the type Gaius' brother had sponsored with its viritane grants of land was not enough: colonization would be much more effective and speedy in gaining Gaius the support that he foresaw he would need. Therefore he planned a number of Citizen colonies. He himself did not need to make the actual proposal for any of them: one of his political supporters could do that. But that the policy was his there cannot be the slightest doubt. Ancient writers explicitly say so, and the Gromatici Veteres do not hesitate to label the colonies they list for this period as Sempronian.[214]

The Romans had long ago adopted the habit of improving the names of the places where they founded their colonies. They had substituted Narnia for Nequinum, Beneventum for ill-sounding Malventum, Copia for Thurii, and Valentia for Vibo. Gaius Gracchus followed this practice, all the more eagerly probably since his father had done it before him. In 183 the latter had been one of the founding commissioners who had given the name Saturnia to a Citizen colony in Etruria at a place called Aurinia or something similar. Gaius, no doubt with propaganda in mind, adopted such nomenclature from divinities for his own colonies. Three of them, all on the sea coast, are known, two apparently belonging to 122 (Neptunia at Tarentum [Taranto] under the 'heel' of Italy, and Minervia at Scolacium [Squillace] on the 'sole') and one apparently authorized in 123 (Junonia at the site of Carthage in Africa). The proposal for the last-named colony was not made by Gaius himself but by a certain Rubrius, plebeian tribune in either 124/123 or 123/122, about whom virtually nothing is known, but who must have been Gaius' close associate. Gaius himself was one of the founding commissioners for Junonia, but was fated not to complete his task.

Junonia would obviously have to be a transmarine colonization, and this aspect of it at once encountered violent criticism. Gaius' political enemies alleged that it was denying poor Romans their birthright, dragging them off into exile. Furthermore Junonia might grow and some day outstrip its metropolis: Carthage had done this once before; so had Massilia and some other places. In any case a community of Roman citizens should not be established in a place so far away from Rome that it weakened the cohesiveness of the Roman citizen body, least of all on provincial soil where it presented the additional problem of taxation, since such soil could not be held in quiritary ownership. It is not surprising that, before long, rumours were circulating that divine opposition was being manifested in the form of omens at the site.[215]

As colonial commissioner Gaius had been seeking some of the 6,000 settlers projected for Carthago-Junonia from non-Roman

Italy. His motive may have been not merely to revert to the practice of an earlier day, but also to quieten the clamour about Roman citizens being uprooted from their native land. Whatever his aim, instead of allaying criticism, he exacerbated it. He had now exposed himself to the further charge of attempting to promote by furtive means his unpalatable policy of enfranchising Italians. In the end his opponents triumphed, and his plan for a *colonia* on the site of Carthage had to be abandoned: Rubrius' law for the colony was repealed.[216]

There is, however, one feature of Gaius' colonies that has long been recognized. He sought to enhance their political usefulness to himself by consolidating the support not only of the urban poor but also of the business class, that section of the Roman population that he had favoured with his judiciary law and that was soon organized into the equestrian order. Some of Rome's paupers undoubtedly became landholders in the colonies at Tarentum and Scolacium. But even in these places the *coloni* also included men who were not paupers but who were interested in commerce, for which indeed both sites were well suited. Carthago-Junonia was even more obviously making provision for the well-to-do, since there the agrarian settlers were in many instances men of substance: allotments of two hundred *iugera*, a whole *centuria*, could hardly be worked except by a man with some capital. Plutarch is certainly exaggerating when he says that Gaius obtained almost all his colonists from the rich,[217] but there were evidently enough of the latter included to rob his colonies of their popular aspect; and this fact, along with their other objectionable features, made colonization a much less effective political tool for him than he had hoped.

In any case it was a tool that could be turned against him with relative ease, and it soon was. In 122 his fellow tribune and political opponent, M. Livius Drusus, undermined Gaius' whole position by the simple expedient of outbidding him. Drusus proposed to found no fewer than twelve colonies, each with 3,000 settlers taken from the poorest of the poor. Although little is known about Drusus' dozen, certain pronouncements can quite confidently be hazarded about them. First, they must have been intended to be Citizen colonies; the suggestion, sometimes put forward, that they were to be Latin, fails to take account of the prevailing political climate. Secondly, they must have been restricted to Roman citizens: after the furore aroused by Gaius Gracchus' attempt to recruit non-Romans for Carthago-Junonia, it is inconceivable that Livius Drusus would have failed to stress the all-Roman character of his own foundations. Thirdly, they represented something new in Roman colonization: not even Gaius had proposed to provide for the dregs of the city in so blatant a fashion.[218]

Commissions for founding one or more of these twelve colonies were actually appointed, with Drusus himself very virtuously, if somewhat ostentatiously, declining to accept a post on them: he was not going to be another Gaius Gracchus. Nevertheless it is doubtful whether any of his colonies were in fact ever founded, although one or two of the colonies labelled 'Sempronian' in the Gromatici Veteres may possibly have been his.[219] After Gaius Gracchus' downfall there was, of course, no longer any need for Drusus to persevere with his scheme. His proposed colonies had served their purpose and could now be safely allowed to die, along with Gaius; but later politicians did not hesitate to follow his example and provide colonies for the urban unemployed.

During what was left of the second century, colonization continued to be exploited as an instrument for the making of political fortunes. Even settlements that undoubtedly served a strategic purpose were now likely to be proclaimed as aiming primarily at something else, such as the economic benefit of the masses at Rome; and within a comparatively short space of time colonization could be described as a device for getting rid of the dregs of the population and the politically undesirable and for re-peopling the empty spaces of Italy.[220] Thus, Narbo Martius (Narbonne) *c.* 114, Dertona (Tortona) in 109 and Eporedia (Ivrea) in 100, if these last two were in fact colonies, occupied highly strategic sites. Narbo in southern Gaul safeguarded, as it was intended to do, the road from Italy to Spain against any Volcae who might prove hostile; Dertona in Cisalpine Gaul controlled the passage between the Ligurian Alps and the Po basin and confined the Ligures to their native mountains; and Eporedia, at the entrance to the Val D'Aosta in Piedmont, was the key to the two Saint Bernard passes and, so Strabo expressly informs us, was a check upon the Salassi. Yet for all three of these places political and economic motives were mixed up with the military and may have predominated.[221]

Narbo Martius met with strong opposition in the Roman Senate, doubtless on the ground that it was too distant to be a suitable site for a community of Roman citizens. That it was nevertheless founded suggests that Gaius Gracchus' missionary work had not gone entirely for naught. The founder of Narbo, L. Licinius Crassus, obviously imitated Gaius, promoting his colony as a 'popular' measure, naming it after a divinity and seeking some of his settlers among the financial and commerical class. His programme evidently satisfied the Plebeian Assembly, and to make it more palatable to the Senate he could point out that, even though Narbo was beyond the Alps, it was not, like Junonia, beyond the sea; and it could be reached without undue difficulty by land. He also made some concession to conservative, senatorial opinion: his colonists apparently did not get their land in quiritary ownership, as colonists in Italy did, but as a perpetual, hereditary possession.[222]

The ulterior and probably principal purpose of the colony at Dertona, if there was one, was to reinforce the political strength of the Aemilii in Cisalpine Gaul. It was an important communications centre on territory won from the Ligures by the consul M. Aemilius Scaurus in 115. It undoubtedly contributed to the perpetuation of Emilia as the name for the Cispadane region.[223]

Eporedia, on territory that Rome seems to have acquired in 140, was a town founded, so the Elder Pliny says, as the result of a Sibylline injunction. Perhaps, therefore, it was an attempt on the part of Saturninus' senatorial opponents to counter and outdo his agrarian legislation. If a colony was planted at this place, it may also have been because the nearby gold deposits of Victumulae could be counted on to make it economically attractive.[224]

Clearly, strategic considerations were even now by no means overlooked when colonies were being proposed, but no less clearly the emphasis had shifted. In the last third of the second century, the foundations were more particularly intended to serve other functions, such as the relief of urban unemployment or the promotion of trade and commerce.[225]

Roman road construction—and this always went hand in hand with colonization—indicates the same thing. Before the Gracchan age ten great roads had been built, the Via Latina or possibly the Via Appia (312) being the earliest. They were all primarily for military purposes and all of them were an integral part of the strategic system for which the colonies were the linchpins. But between 133 and 109 no fewer than eight new roads were built, all largely for economic purposes: one of their main functions was to provide communications with the regions where the beneficiaries of the Gracchan agrarian legislation were settled.[226]

It can be confidently assumed that only Roman citizens participated in Narbo, and in Dertona and Eporedia too, if they were colonies, but there is no way of knowing to what extent this exclusion of non-Romans contributed to the outbreak of the Social War in 91. Evidently there was some protest, since Saturninus in 100 felt it necessary to stipulate that each of the colonies, which he wanted Marius to found (but which never materialized), should contain three non-Romans.[227] In general, however, colonies must have been regarded as deterrents to Italian unrest. In the Citizen colonies the outlook and behaviour were bound to be Roman, and in the Latin colonies policy was controlled by the local senates which, infiltrated during the past third of a century by ex-office-holders with Roman citizenship, were virtually all-Roman by 91. It is no wonder that thirty-two of the thirty-three Latin colonies remained firmly loyal to Rome when the Social War broke out in that year.[228] The only one to join the Italians in the great rebellion was Venusia, and there ethnic considerations were an important factor.

Accounts of the Social War (91–87) have to be painstakingly pieced together from sporadic and fragmentary scraps of information, but one thing emerges clearly: for Rome it was touch and go, and it was the colonies that saved her. Had the Latin colonies in particular joined the insurgents, or even remained neutral, she must inevitably have gone down to defeat. No doubt the Citizen colonies did what was required of them in the near-run struggle. Above all they ensured uninterrupted passage of sea-borne supplies and of provincial fighting men to Rome, while denying all such aid and comfort to the embattled Italians; and this was an important service. But it cannot compare with that rendered by the Latin colonies. They were in the very thick of what ancient testimony regards as the most ferocious struggle that had ever been waged in Italy.[229] Carseoli was apparently sacked, Alba Fucens violently assaulted, Beneventum, Firmum and Luceria intermittently cut off, and Aesernia finally captured. Had it not been for the breathing-spell which the stubborn resistance of Alba and Aesernia gave to Rome late in 91, in the opening weeks of the hostilities, she might well have suffered irreparable disaster.

In 90 and 89 the enfranchising acts were passed, which conferred Roman citizenship on all of Italy south of the Po and converted it into a vast congeries of *municipia* and *coloniae*.[230] This did not affect the status of the Citizen colonies, although presumably it put an end to any still-existing 'double communities' of which they formed part. Any Italian community that had been living alongside of, but with inferior status to, a Citizen colony, now on acquiring Roman citizenship became indistinguishable from it and was bound to fuse with it. But by this time there could not have been many such double communities left in Italy. Gracchan Neptunia and Tarentum may have formed one: if so, they now merged, and the surviving fragment of the Lex Tarenti may be part of the law that was passed to regularize their union.[231]

Meanwhile the internal development of the large Citizen colonies had naturally made great headway. The simple and rudimentary constitutions of the old maritime colonies were a thing of the past.[232] The colonies had become increasingly complex, and by now had come to resemble the organisms that they were to be later in the Roman Empire.

In the late second and early first centuries there was some wavering between praetor and duovir as the title for their chief officials, and some colonies actually used the double designation praetor duovir, but ultimately the traditional duoviri remained as their principal public officials.[233] Their authority was, however, much greater than it had been before 184. By the first century the independence of the Citizen colony in the management of its religious, financial, judicial and even military affairs was well developed and it was reflected in its constitution. Some conception of what public administration was like in a Citizen colony *c.* 63 can be obtained not only from what Cicero implies about Puteoli, but also from the proposals made in that year for the projected colony at Capua: quaestors, aediles and censors were envisaged, with wide judicial powers included among their functions.[234] The Social War, however, was hardly responsible for this kind of development; it had become inevitable from the moment that large Citizen colonies began to be founded.

The Latin colonies, on the other hand, were immediately and very materially affected by the Social War. As a matter of fact it brought about their disappearance. All of them became Roman *municipia* overnight[235] and either through choice or through persuasion replaced their praetors with quattuorviri, and the quattuorviral constitution now became the standard one for Roman *municipia* everywhere.[236] Once the Latin colonies were thus assimilated, what one might call their active and dynamic history came to an end.

Not that the expression *colonia Latina* ceased entirely to be used. For a time it was bestowed on towns whose inhabitants, because of their good services and their degree of romanization, seemed worthy to receive the Latin status. These towns, however, had never been actually colonized; that is, settlers had not been marched out to them, allotted parcels of land, and organized into self-governing, closed communities. Such towns, and after 89 they were all in the provinces, were said to possess Ius Latii, or more simply *Latium*: that is, their relationship to Rome was similar to that of the Latin colonies before 89. In this latter year the towns in the Transpadane region of Cisalpine Gaul were made Latin colonies of this honorary type by Pompeius Strabo, who was thus the father of the titular colony as well as of Pompey the Great.[237] But their title of *colonia Latina* was not only purely nominal, it was also very short-lived: the Emperor Augustus seems to have put an end to it.

APPENDIX

The later history of the Latin status

Some indication of the transitory character of the so-called titular Latin colonies can be obtained from the fact that the earliest of them, those created by Pompeius Strabo in 89, had already obtained the Roman citizenship by 49. After that date there were some titular Latin colonies in Narbonese Gaul, the creations of Julius Caesar: Vienna, the administrative centre of the Allobroges, was the most celebrated of them.[238] But soon Augustus, eager to enhance the status of the true *colonia*, frowned on the use of the title for a community that had never been formally colonized, even though its inhabitants had been pronounced Latini by the formal grant of the Ius Latii. Instead of *colonia* such a community might call itself *municipium* or *res publica*: if it had any other title, we do not know with certainty what it was.[239]

Latini who were burgesses of such a regularly organized urban community were known as Latini *coloniarii*, both in continuation of the old tradition and in an effort to distinguish them from Latini *Juniani*: these latter were not members of a 'Latin' community, but were individual Latini, ex-slaves who, because irregularly manumitted, were not allowed to acquire Roman citizenship like other freedmen, but were granted Latinity instead.

Under the Empire, as under the Republic, the 'coloniary' Latini were closer to the Romans than any other 'foreigners', and the imperial jurists, like Livy, regard the world as divided into Romani and Latini on the one side and aliens on the other. In fact, Ius Latii became for the Empire what *civitas sine suffragio* had been for the middle Republic, a destiny adumbrated for it perhaps as early as 268, when the granting of *civitas sine suffragio* may have been discontinued and the Ius Duodecim Coloniarum instituted.

It was a halfway house to the Roman citizenship. A *res publica*, whose burgesses had been declared Latini, was well on the way to obtaining the rank of a Roman *municipium* and ultimately even of a Roman *colonia:* Lambaesis in Africa is a good example.[240]

Ius Latii itself underwent some refinement. In the reign of Hadrian (AD 117–138) mention is made of *Latium Minus* and *Latium Maius*. The former was simply the old republican right which conferred Roman citizenship on the magistrates of a Latin town. *Latium Maius*, on the other hand, conferred Roman citizenship, not only on all the local magistrates of a Latin town, but on all the local senators (decurions) as well: it was found, principally if not exclusively, in Africa,[241] and its purpose presumably was to induce the local well-to-do to join the curial class.

After AD 212, when the Emperor Caracalla promulgated his Constitutio Antoniniana and thereby made all free inhabitants of the Empire, except a very few, Roman citizens, Ius Latii no longer had any significant meaning.

CHAPTER VIII

COLONIAE MILITARES

COLONIES IN THE AGE OF REVOLUTION

ACCORDING TO VELLEIUS, *coloniae* after Eporedia were *militares*, that is, settled with demobilized soldiers.[242] The expression may be poorly chosen, since the vast majority of the colonies so far founded could not unreasonably be described by the same adjective; but it has some justification, since the expression Citizen colonies is now irrelevant, all authentic colonies being henceforth *coloniae civium Romanorum*, and it is convenient to have a generic description to distinguish those of them that were settled with veteran soldiers. Even so, like so much else about colonies in Velleius, the statement that foundations from now on were *coloniae militares* is not strictly accurate. A number of the colonies founded between 100 BC and AD 30, the year in which Velleius was writing, were intended for non-military settlers; and, under Augustus, even the expression *colonia civica* occurs. Conversely some of the colonies founded before 100 may have been used to absorb ex-soldiers, those planted in 194 for instance.[243] It is only fair to add, however, that it was not until 100 and later that provision for veterans became the principal, as distinct from an incidental, aim of colonization.

Therewith a new element was introduced into the whole process. Hitherto colonies had regularly been established on territory acquired by conquest. But there was now no longer much of this left unused in Italy.[244] Consequently veteran colonies were likely to be founded on land that had been purchased or possibly confiscated, and ever more increasingly they were likely to be founded outside Italy altogether. The pattern had been indicated by Carthago-Junonia and set by Narbo-Martius.

The impetus for this new kind of colonization had been initially given by Marius' army reform. Finding himself obliged to care for the paupers whom, contrary to the earlier Roman tradition, he had enrolled for a set period in his army and had then discharged, he sought to assuage their land hunger with the help of his temporary political ally, L. Appuleius Saturninus. But Saturninus' agrarian legislation in 103 concerned itself chiefly with viritane distribution.[245] Moreover Marius himself seems to have been responsible for practically no formal colonization. Only one colony is attributed to him. This was Mariana, a Citizen one, founded in the tradition of Gaius Gracchus overseas, on the island of Corsica, although it is unknown whether, like Junonia, it aroused a storm of opposition.[246] But Marius' action in providing for his veterans had much greater influence than the dearth of foundations by him might have led one to expect. Land distributions to his veterans, whether in viritane or in colonial style, built up a formidable retinue of clients for him both in Italy and in Africa,[247] and even if Marius himself did not realize the full implications of this, his rival Sulla was quick to appreciate its import. At the first opportunity he improved on Marius with characteristic thoroughness, to reward his soldiers, to punish his opponents, and to ensure the continuation of his own system of government.

After winning the mastery of Italy at the Colline Gate on 1 November 82, Sulla proceeded to found many colonies, one of them on the island of Corsica, to offset the Colonia Mariana no doubt.[248] The motive of these foundations was not strategic in the old sense, since there were no longer any foreign enemies to cause the Romans much concern in peninsular Italy. In fact, as a result of the Social War, all Italy now enjoyed Roman citizenship, and the *territorium* of Rome now extended to the limits of the peninsula. This meant that there was no obtaining land for colonization through conquest in Italy, and there was little existing state domain there still available: the largest single bloc of it still remaining was so productive of revenue that there was little disposition to carve it up for colonies. In the provinces, it is true, there undoubtedly was state domain and to spare, but the two foundations on Corsica did not fully reconcile Roman public opinion to the idea of colonization abroad. Sulla therefore decided on colonies in Italy, and he would get the land for them by expropriation. It probably never occurred to him that he might purchase it.[249] At any rate, he did not pay cash for it: he simply seized it as he saw fit. Sulla's colonies thus helped him to make good his boast that he never forgot either a friend or a foe. They were established at various points throughout the Italian countryside or in already existing cities, and they were peopled with his soldiers. At one and the same time he was able to compensate his supporters and chastise his enemies. He confiscated land from the communities that had opposed him in the Civil War (83–80), centuriated it and gave it in allotments to his trusty veterans, who with their military tribunes and centurions were organized on it into closed, self-governing communities alongside the despoiled victims. The Italian cities were exposed to the rigours of what Cicero calls 'the anguish of the Sullan period'.[250] Some of them not only had to cede land, but were also reduced in status with impaired citizen rights. 'Double communities' returned with a vengeance (*Pls.* 54, 56).

One result was that the title *colonia* came to be prized, and prestige began to accumulate about the name, at first grimly, but gradually with increasing respect, until ultimately, under the Empire, the *colonia*, a community of non-independent origin, displaced the *municipium*, with its tradition of ancient sovereignty, as the foremost type of Roman city.

In the Sullan period too, as Velleius notes,[251] the custom began of adding descriptive adjectives to the name of a colony as an honorific gesture to its founder. Sulla's own foundations are likely to include the word Veneria in their official title, since he claimed to be the protégé of Aphrodite. Yet, despite this aid to identification, it is by no means possible to name all his colonies or even to know how many they were. *A fortiori*, there is no record of the number of *coloni* assigned to each nor any very easy way of conjecturing it, partly because the ancient texts give varying estimates of the number of legions Sulla demobilized and partly because he used viritane assignation as well as colonization.[252]

One region that suffered severely was Etruria, a Marian stronghold. Not all of the places that were mulcted of land there, and then saw colonies planted on it, are known, but they certainly included Arretium and Faesulae. The effect of Sulla's activity was to promote the romanization of Etruria. Its numerous bilingual tombstones belonging to the last century BC indicate a rapid spread of Latin, and Sulla's colonies must have been greatly responsible.

Nearer Rome, Praeneste, a hotbed of anti-Sullan sentiment, became a *colonia* and bitterly resented it.[253] Southern Italy, where the Samnites had resisted Sulla to the very end, also did not escape. Viritane distribution there seems to have been on a vast scale, but some colonies were founded as well, at Abella (?), Abellinum, Ausculum (?), Nola, Pompeii and elsewhere. In the resulting 'double communities' relations were tense: Cicero specifically says so in the case of Pompeii.[254] In this part of Italy, too, Sulla's ruthlessness contributed powerfully to the disappearance of non-Latin Italy: after him the vernacular Oscan swiftly declined (*Pl. 56*).

Sulla's colonization is notable not only because of the manner in which it promoted romanization, but also because of the precedent that it set for future masters of the Roman state. Sulla did not seek authorization from either Senate or People for his colonies. He merely assumed that the Lex Valeria of 82, which conferred dictatorial powers upon him, allowed him to do just as he pleased,[255] and this precedent was followed by his successors. Julius Caesar availed himself of the powers granted him in 49 and 48; the Triumvirs invoked the Lex Titia that appointed them. Before Sulla the foundation of a colony had resulted from an act of legislation by the Roman People, usually on the motion of a plebeian tribune, and as this law of the People was regularly preceded by a senatorial decree in early times, it is not too wide of the mark to say that down to Luna (177) the Senate and thereafter the Plebeian Assembly had controlled colonization policy. Henceforth this was to be no longer the case. From now on, the powerful men who succeeded in making themselves masters of the Roman state decided when and where to found colonies. Future colonies were going to depend upon the will of an individual, and he would be the one to obtain all the credit from the foundations and, much more important, all the following of clients that went along with them. Sulla, and those who came after him, were not going to let founding commissioners win prestige and power for their own houses: the ruling dynast would have appointees of his own to supervise the actual establishment of a colony, perhaps members of his own family.[256] The newfangled nomenclature reflects the changed state of affairs clearly: the adjectives added to the title of the colony are likely to include the name of the dynast in adjectival form.

In what remained of the Roman Republic there were repeated occasions when demobilized soldiers expectantly awaited settlement. Until the dictatorship of Julius Caesar viritane distributions normally accommodated them, but there may also have been a few colonies, including some perhaps beyond the bounds of Italy. About these, however, only vague information survives. Pompey and his sons, for instance, seem to have been active in Spain, but it is not possible to say whether their settlements, or those of Junius Brutus and Claudius Marcellus at places like Corduba and Valentia, ought properly to be styled *coloniae*.[257]

Undoubtedly the next person after Sulla to found colonies on a large scale was Julius Caesar. Like the earlier dictator, he made extensive use of them, but, unlike Sulla, his motive was not merely to settle ex-soldiers. Admittedly his earliest distributions of allotments, in Campania in 59, when he was consul, did provide for the troops that Pompey had brought back with him from the east, but perhaps only incidentally. Rullus' proposed agrarian law of 63 suggests that Caesar had long nursed plans for settling the impoverished unemployed of Rome, whether freeborn or freedmen, on land allotments, and the Campanian distribution of 59, accommodating 20,000 recipients, represents his first effort of the kind.

Even later, after Caesar became dictator, this motive still existed, perhaps inevitably, since he had to do something for the thousands whom he had deprived of the grain-dole. Accordingly, as soon as he had secured supreme power, he began founding colonies. Most of these were outside Italy, but he must have been responsible for some colonies inside the country since it is very improbable that all the *coloniae Juliae* epigraphically attested there belong exclusively to Octavian. A refoundation of Castrum Novum in Etruria, for example, may have been a colony of Caesar's.[258] The veterans, without whose aid Octavian could hardly have challenged Antony, unquestionably obtained land in Italy, and not all of them by viritane assignation.

In general, however, Caesar preferred to conserve his reputation among the Romans for *clementia* by founding his colonies on provincial soil rather than on land confiscated in Italy.[259] The conqueror of Gaul did so with all the more alacrity since he must have been aware of the useful role played by the colonies when it had been a matter of consolidation, expansion and assimilation inside Italy itself. In his view there was no reason to halt the process at the frontiers of Italy, even though those frontiers had by now reached the Alps: he was even prepared to plant settlements in the Greek-speaking east. He seems, however, to have been quite Roman in his view of provincial soil: it was to be kept distinct from Italian, and even colonies planted on it, extensions of Rome herself though they theoretically were, were not to escape the land-tax, and their settlers would not hold their land in quiritary ownership, even if they were not subject to the direct authority of the governor of their province.[260]

In colonizing abroad Caesar was the authentic successor of Gaius Gracchus. He was not contemplating a series of colonies like Narbo-Martius, linked to Italy by direct highway, but settlements which could be reached only by crossing the sea. In fact, he was the first to plant colonies overseas on a really large scale. If the policy did not involve him in the same difficulties as it had Gaius Gracchus, it may have been due to the broadening of Roman horizons since Gracchus' day, but even more to Caesar's dictatorial mastery of the state: this enabled him to do things which Gaius, dependent on the fickle and uncertain goodwill of the popular assembly, could not achieve. Not that Caesar went uncriticized. There was grumbling, and one result of his overseas colonization was the wide circulation of the baseless rumour that he was planning to shift the capital of the Roman world to some faraway site such as Alexandria or Troy.[261]

It may have been the transmarine nature of Caesar's colonization that caused Velleius to ignore it. Regarding Gaius Gracchus' attempt to found colonies outside Italy as his most pernicious legislation,[262] Velleius could not bring himself to record Caesar's similar but much more prolific and successful venture, careful though he usually was to emphasize the importance of Roman colonization. Fortunately Velleius' omission does not leave us completely uninformed. The deficiency is to a great extent repaired by the Gromatici Veteres and by epigraphic evidence. Many inscriptions survive with the telltale words Colonia Julia. As these usually formed part of the titulature of a Caesarian foundation, some estimate of Caesar's colonization becomes possible. Unfortunately a colony planted by Octavian before 27, when he became Augustus, was also normally styled Colonia Julia and cannot always be distinguished from one of Caesar's foundations.[263]

One thing is clear: the colonies founded by Caesar were very numerous. According to Suetonius, he settled no fewer than 80,000 *coloni* in the provinces, and he and Augustus between them seem to have founded almost as many colonies as all other Roman emperors put together.[264] Theirs was the golden age for the Citizen colony just as the Samnite Wars had been for the Latin.

The expression 'Citizen colony', however, will henceforth not be used; 'Roman colony' will be substituted for it, Caesar's colonies, like those of all his successors, being peopled by Roman citizens. He himself did not live long enough to found all that he intended, and it was left to one or other of the triumvirs to carry out his plans.

Like the Latin colonies of former years, Caesar's were often linked up by a network of roads, and they usually had large dependent territories. In certain other respects, however, as will be seen, many of them resembled the earliest Citizen colonies. Many of his colonies were intended for the defence of Roman territory, but there were also undoubtedly some that, like the colonies of the Gracchan age, were designed to help Roman indigents or to promote Roman commerce. Yet others of them were *coloniae militares*, like Sulla's, and provided for ex-soldiers.

Norba, Metellinum and Praesidium Julium in Lusitania, in the most distant part of the Iberian peninsula, all probably Caesarian, were clearly fortresses serving strategic ends: they were keeping an eye on the tribes north of the River Tagus. The Caesarian colonies in Illyricum must have had a similar purpose; but here it is particularly difficult to decide which colonies were really his. In Africa, besides refounding Carthage, he seems to have planted a number of other colonies (Carpis, Clupea, Curubis, Hadrumetum, Hippo Diarrhytus, Neapolis, Thapsus), all of them on or very near the coast and some of them perhaps not much larger than the original *coloniae maritimae*. Although they may have been settled, in part at least, with *proletarii*, it is reasonable to suppose that their principal purpose was to deny Africa as a base to anyone for anti-Caesarian operations.

That Caesar used colonies as places of settlement for the urban poor is shown by the surviving charter of one of his foundations, Urso in the Spanish province of Baetica.[265] The document, engraved on bronze tablets, is now housed in the National Museum at Madrid, and, although this extant copy dates from Flavian times, it preserves Julius Caesar's original regulations. (He himself had not lived to see them carried out and Marc Antony had supervised the actual foundation of the colony.) Officially the settlement was Colonia Julia Genetiva Urbanorum, the *urbani* obviously being city-dwellers. They included even freedmen who were expressly pronounced eligible for the local senate, just as freedmen were in some of Caesar's colonies in Africa[266] (*Pl. 11*).

Another Caesarian colony founded for economic or social reasons was the most celebrated of them all, Corinth, it too brought into civic existence after the dictator himself was dead. Its *coloni* were freedmen for the most part,[267] many of them presumably Greek-speaking; and this, taken in conjunction with its siting, shows that the colony could not have been agrarian. It was manifestly intended to revive the mercantile glories of the city that Mummius had destroyed in 146 (*Pl. 57*).

A similar motive existed in the case of another city that Rome had obliterated in 146. The colony at Carthage, like the one at Corinth, was brought into being after the Ides of March, and

Caesar's role in the revival of Gaius Gracchus' scheme is further obscured by Octavian's action in recolonizing it with some 3,000 settlers about fifteen years later.[268] But there appears to be no doubt that Caesar did plan it, and with a commercial purpose in mind. Its settlers seem to have come from the urban proletariat in the main, although they included some veterans.

Buthrotum in Achaea was another Caesarian colony that found its settlers among the urban poor,[269] and the same may be true of Dyme and of the colonies that Caesar established in Asia Minor (Apamea, Heraclea Pontica, Lampsacus and Sinope). Besides Urso, other colonies of his in the Spanish province of Baetica may have had a predominantly economic motive, even when, as at Hispalis (Seville), their *coloni* included veterans: the latter were there, no doubt, to guard against any revival of Pompeian sentiment.[270]

Naturally Caesar did not overlook his former soldiers. Members of his famous tenth legion were enrolled in the addition which he made to the colony at Narbo, while Arelate (Arles) got soldiers of the sixth.[271] Thapsus, in Africa, is also generally regarded as a colony of veterans; and there were undoubtedly others.

Caesar may also have been the first person to create a titular Roman colony. As honorary Latin colonies had been a familiar notion ever since Pompeius Strabo created the first of them during the Social War, analogous Citizen colonies were bound to make an appearance sooner or later. These were communities of Roman citizens officially called *coloniae* without ever having undergone the colonization process: they were no more genuine *deductiones* than the so-called titular Latin colonies were. Their title was a purely honorary one, but one that soon came to be eagerly sought after. For a *colonia*, as a community that traditionally originated from Rome, could be regarded as an extension of Rome herself, and the greatness and unrivalled prestige of Rome and her Empire made cities, especially provincial cities, very eager to be styled *coloniae* since they could then exuberantly claim to form part of the grandeur and majesty of Rome. Later it was common practice for the emperors to bestow the title of *colonia* as a mark of imperial favour upon cities that had never been formally colonized and the recipients proudly displayed it. The heyday of colonies of this type was clearly long after Caesar. In fact it is usually said that there were none of them until the reign of Claudius (AD 41–54), and it is the case that it was then rather than in Caesar's day that the title of *colonia* had acquired the great prestige that so impressed provincial cities. Nevertheless Caesar may have anticipated Claudius, since his colony at Tarraco in Spain looks like a titular one, and so possibly does Nova Carthago.[272]

Apart altogether from any titular colonies that Caesar may or may not have created, he unquestionably incorporated many cities as Roman *municipia*, and these could not have differed much from titular Roman colonies except in name.

He also granted Latin rights to a number of cities, above all, as might have been expected, in Gaul. By the middle of Augustus' reign the Gallic province of Narbonensis had thirty Latin communities which were sometimes referred to as Latin colonies, meaning titular colonies of course, and Caesar must have been responsible for most of them. As we have seen, however, Augustus himself disapproved of this use of the title *colonia Latina* and it was soon discontinued as a consequence. On the other hand Augustus gave Roman status to some of Caesar's Latin communities: it was he, rather than Caesar, who was responsible for the group of Roman *municipia* in Spain that were soon to supply senators of distinction to Rome.[273]

Caesar's colonization was obviously extensive, and its pattern, displaying every kind and species of colony, suggests a carefully pondered plan to exploit the institution of the *colonia* to the utmost.

In the period of civil war and confusion after his murder colonization took on the aspect of pragmatic improvisation and vindictiveness that it had worn under Sulla: as in the latter's day, there is no mention of comitial legislation. The 'liberators', the Triumvirs, everyone with a role to play, such as Dolabella or Munatius Plancus, acted out of sheer expediency, giving little thought to the real needs, strategic, economic and cultural, of the Roman world. To strengthen their position,[274] the Triumvirs enriched their supporters, took vengeance on their enemies, and victimized the innocent. They were completely ruthless in their methods of procuring the land they needed for their ventures, callously seizing it wherever it seemed suitable and sometimes alleging that they were simply carrying out a project of Caesar's. Some land they allotted on a viritane basis; but they also organized and planted well over a score of colonies inside Italy, as well as many abroad: some of the latter were due to the necessity for settling evicted Italians.[275] Precisely who was responsible for a foundation it is often difficult to determine. After Philippi (42) the Triumvirs agreed that Octavian should superintend the settlement in Italy of the veterans of all them,[276] and this fact, together with his ultimate triumph, has obscured the colonizing activity of his fellow warlords, since he appropriated as his own and sometimes refounded colonies of theirs that seemed worth claiming. Presumably he was also just as unscrupulous as his triumviral colleagues in obtaining land for colonies. The *Eclogues* of Vergil make it clear that he did not hesitate to confiscate it, and the later insistence of his official autobiography that he was the first to buy land for distribution to settlers,[277] a claim that has reference in the main to the period after Actium, suggests that, as Augustus, he had considerable difficulty in living down the misdeeds he had perpetrated as Octavian. Live them down he did, however, and went on to become a great founder of colonies, perhaps the greatest that Rome ever knew.

After Actium (2 September 31) he demobilized over 120,000 men. Many of these were settled in Italy in colonies whose names are known from the list in the third book of Pliny's *Natural History* or from the presence of the words Colonia (Julia) Augusta in many an inscription. In all, Augustus claimed to have founded twenty-eight colonies in Italy,[278] but they cannot be certainly identified. Some of them were at places that had been colonies, of either the Latin or the Citizen type, before Gracchan times (Aquileia?, Ariminum, Beneventum, Bononia, Hadria?, Minturnae, Parma, Placentia?, Puteoli?); others were at places that either had never been colonized previously or had been so only under Sulla or in the triumviral period (Abellinum, Asculum Picenum, Ateste, Brixellum, Brixia, Capua, Falerio, Florentia, Nola, Nuceria Alfaterna?, Rusellae, Teanum Sidicinum, Vena-

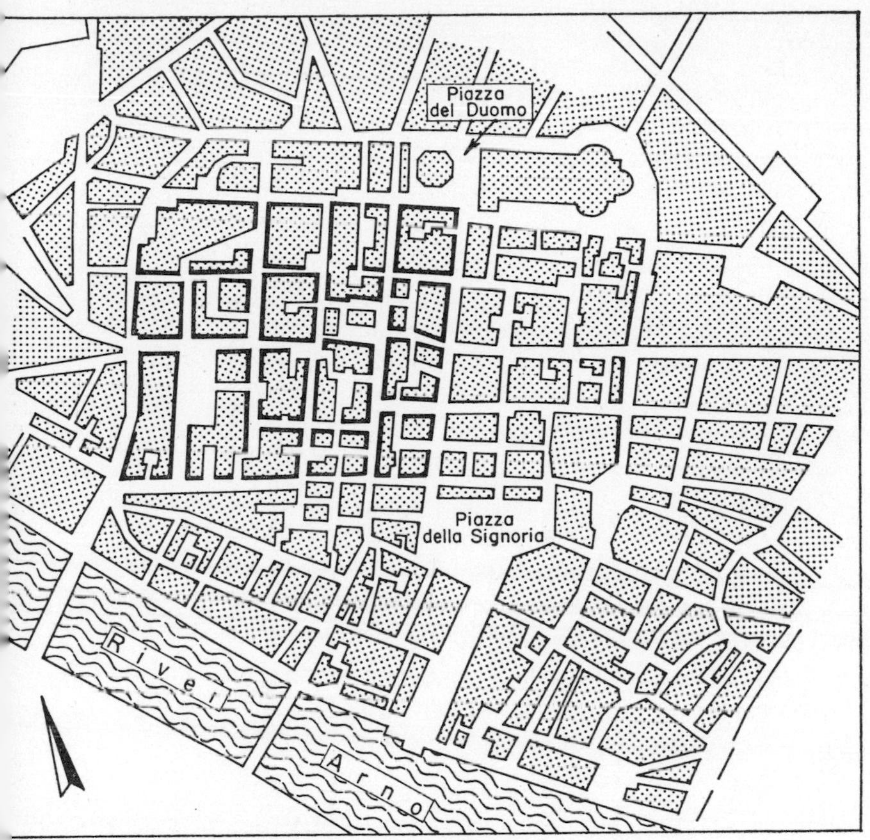

[Fi]g. 9 Plan of Florence

frum). In one or two instances his colonies were settled with civilians rather than veterans: Brixia, for example, was a *colonia civica Augusta.*[279] Augustus' assertion that he bought the land for his establishments in Italy at a cost of six hundred million sesterces is probably true, although Dio does hint that some dispossession of his opponents in Italy occurred[280] (Fig. 9).

Even more extensive was Augustus' colonization in the provinces and there, too, he claims to have bought land for the purpose at a cost of two hundred and sixty million sesterces. But he probably did not do so invariably, for a great deal of land was

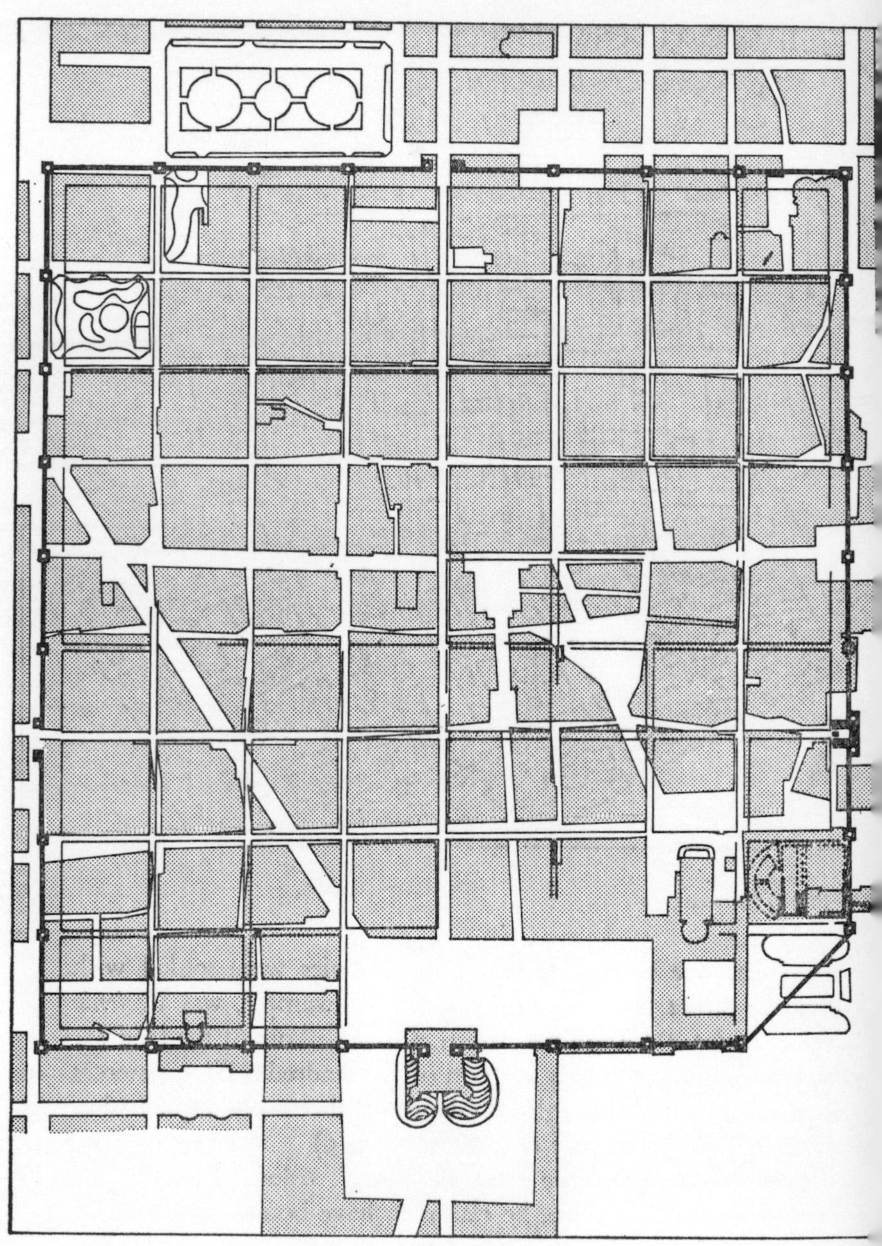

Fig. 10 Plan of Turin

involved: Augusta Emerita in Spain, for instance, had a *territorium* that was enormous. Many of his establishments were in fulfilment of Caesar's projects (Alexandria Troas and Parium are instances) and, like Caesar, he showed a preference for colonies on the coast. But his dependence on Caesar's plans has quite possibly been exaggerated: it is easy enough to attribute the guiding initiative to Caesar when a colony bears the label Julia. From the moment that Octavian learned of his adoption by Caesar's will, he sought to exploit to the full the magic in the dictator's name, which he was now legally entitled to parade as his own; and consequently, as noted earlier, any foundation of his before 27, when he acquired a name with a charisma of its own, is usually styled Colonia Julia. After 27 the titulature is more likely to contain the words Colonia Julia Augusta or Colonia Augusta, enabling the foundation to be attributed to him with greater assurance.

Besides carrying out some of Caesar's plans, Octavian-Augustus had a colonization policy of his own in the provinces. Eager to promote the glory and greatness of Rome, he sought to increase the prestige of her extension, the *colonia*. To procure respect for the title he disapproved of its being bestowed on towns that were only nominally Latin. Simultaneously he advertised his own preference by granting his colonists in Italy the right to vote for the Roman magistrates without coming to Rome and by making many of his colonies in the provinces the equivalents of *coloniae* in Italy through the grant of Ius Italicum:[281] this carried with it the right to land-tenure *ex iure Quiritium* and consequent exemption from the provincial land tax. Augustus was not prepared to treat provincial *municipia* in the same way, and as a result the *colonia* replaced the *municipium* as the most highly regarded type of Roman community.[282]

Augustus' colonies were largely in the tradition of much earlier days, making very little provision for the urban proletariat, but being rather instruments for Roman expansion. They were peopled in the main by veterans,[283] but a remark in Tacitus implies that he was not unduly concerned about their economic well-being.[284] No doubt some of his settlements had a flourishing

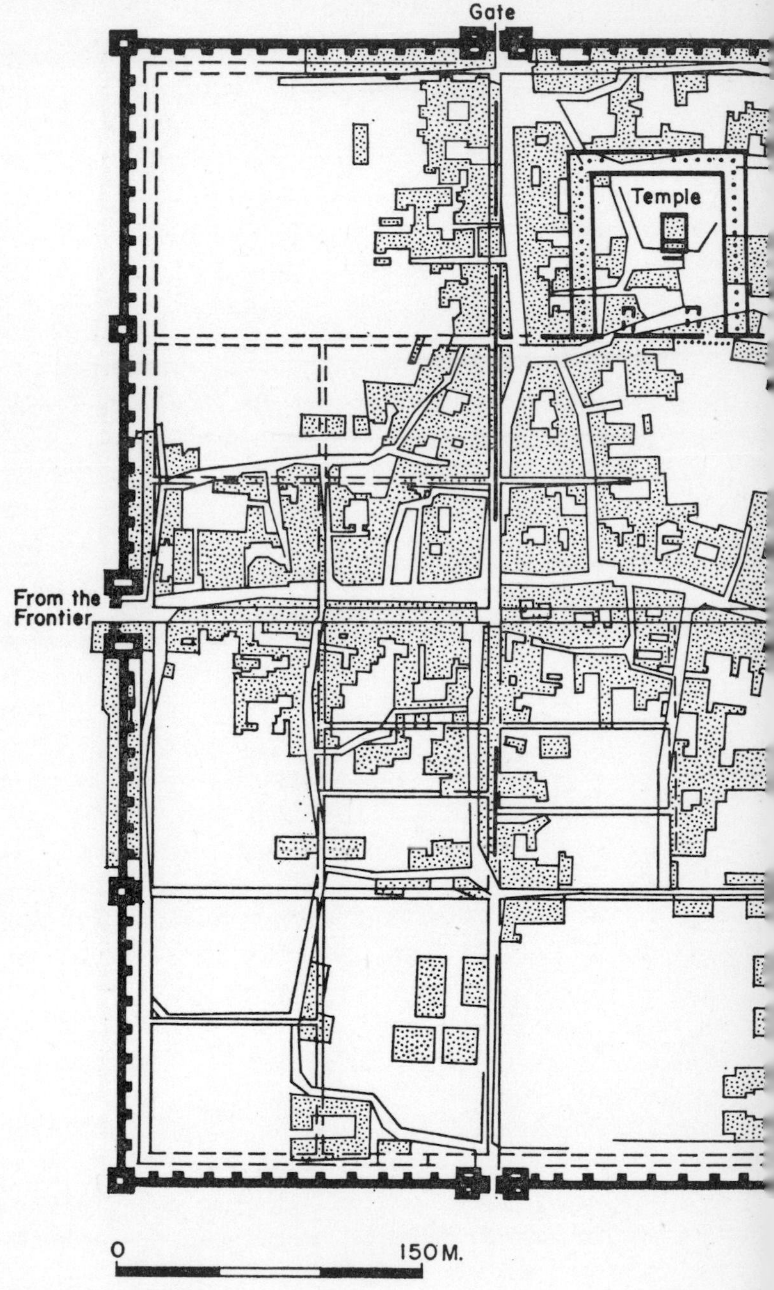

Fig. 11 Plan of Aosta

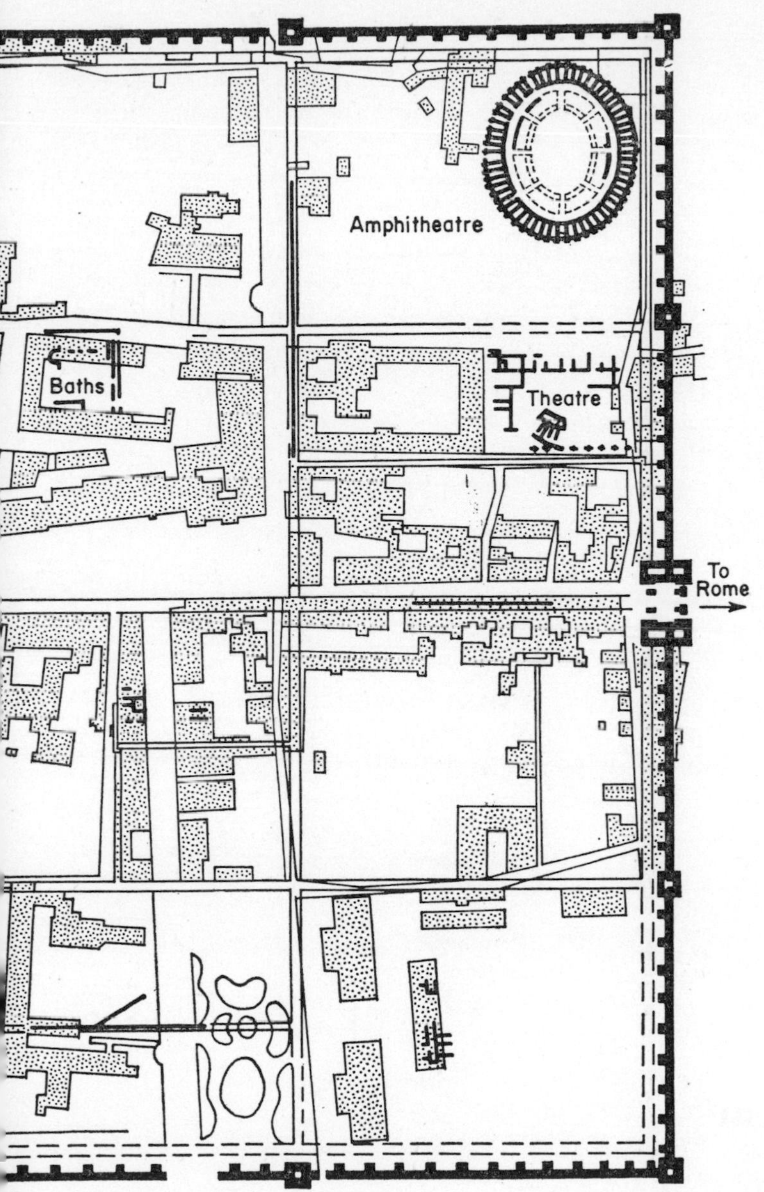
Amphitheatre
Baths
Theatre
To
Rome

trade and fostered agriculture; but more than anything else they were bulwarks of empire, built with strong walls on defensible sites and linked together by military roads. This was true even of two of the colonies which he founded in Italy, Augusta Taurinorum (Turin) (*c.* 27) and Augusta Praetoria (Aosta) (25), the latter peopled with praetorians, as its name shows. These two colonies were planted on land accruing from successful conquest and were strategically placed to control the passes through the western Alps; and they helped Eporedia to keep the recently subjugated tribes of Piedmont in check (Figs. 10, 11).

In his autobiography Augustus claims to have founded colonies of veterans in the following provinces, and it is in fact possible to identify colonies of his in all of them: Africa, Sicily, both Spains, Achaea, Asia, Syria, Gallia Narbonensis and Pisidia.[285] This is a lengthy list and it does not tell the whole story, since Augustus also planted about a dozen colonies of veterans in Mauretania, many of them on the coast, and this was not even Roman territory in his day. Presumably he colonized there with the cooperation of its client-king.[286]

Augustus was no doubt content if his colonies helped to romanize as well as defend the regions in which they were placed. But he hardly needed *coloniae* to spread Roman customs. For that purpose Roman *municipia* or even towns with Latin rights would have served almost as well; and of these he created a great many, usually to reward fidelity to Rome or to her institutions. Suetonius' assertion that he was sparing in his extension of the Roman citizenship should be viewed with caution.[287] No matter how chary Augustus was about giving the Roman citizenship to foreign individuals, he seems to have been just as ready as Julius Caesar to enfranchise, or give Latin rights to, whole communities, provided that they were sufficiently latinized.

Conscious romanization may not have been his deliberate, much less his principal aim;[288] but romanization was his undoubted achievement. It is no exaggeration to say that by his creation of *coloniae* and *municipia*, and by his grants of Ius Latii, Augustus was more responsible for the diffusion of the Latin language and of Roman practices generally than anyone else in history.

46 At Tarracina a headland (Pescomontano) fell sheer into the Tyrrhenian, barring the way along the sea-front (see Plate 3) and forcing the Via Appia to go over the hill past the temple of Jupiter Anxur. Trajan cut away the seaward side of the headland, enabling the Via Appia to go round it. At every ten feet from the top Trajan's engineers carved the height (in feet) into the surface of the rock-cutting.

47 Remains of Augustus' bridge across the River Nera at Narnia (Narni) in Umbria. The bridge carried the Via Flaminia, the great north road that linked Narnia with Rome.

48 The Via Appia at Minturnae. It formed the *decumanus maximus* of the town (p. 34), and is here shown passing the so-called east fountain. Like other Roman colonies, Minturnae had its own theatre, visible in the background.

49, 50 Two views of Minturnae (Plate 13). Here the original Citizen colony was a small settlement added to the existing Auruncan town: only a wall separated the two communities. Ultimately they fused and Minturnae became a place of some consequence. Under the Empire its aspect was that of a typical *colonia*. *Above*, the Via Appia passing a public building with arched portico; *below*, the calidarium of the public baths with remains of the hypocaustic heating system.

51, 52 The Ponte degli Aurunci near Suessa Aurunca (Sessa), a Latin colony in Latium Adjectum. Colonies often antedated their roads. To reach Cales, the earliest Latin colony indisputably their own, the Romans in 334 BC must have used, not the Via Latina whose route was not then open to them, but the coastal route to Minturnae and thence a road inland (p. 84). The bridge shown here carried the inland road in imperial times over the stream now called the Travata.

53 Early Citizen colonies were small and unattractive settlements on the coast of Italy (p. 81). But Puteoli (Pozzuoli) in Campania was one that, like Ostia, developed into a place of great importance (p. 99). A third–fourth century AD engraved glass flask, now in Prague, illustrates the town in its heyday, showing the harbour with its shipping and nearby monuments, such as a stadium, an amphitheatre and a pedimented temple standing on a lofty platform.

54 Remains of the Temple of Fortuna at Praeneste (Palestrina) in Latium. Sulla planted a much-resented colony at Praeneste, but may also have embellished the town by beginning a monumental reconstruction of its famous temple, which rises in a series of terraces up the hillside.

55 The Citizen colony at Auximum (Osimo) in Picenum probably belongs to Gracchan times (pp. 112*f.*), a date supported by its town walls, carefully constructed in ashlar masonry.

56 The forum at Pompeii in Campania, where Sulla superimposed a *colonia* of his supporters on the existing town, converting it into a double community (p. 131). The photograph shows the forum surrounded by a colonnade which goes back to a reconstruction of the second century BC (*cf.* p. 27). On the left it is flanked by a basilica. At the far end is the Capitolium: it dates from the time of Sulla.

57 Names of the duoviri at the Roman colony of Corinth are known from its bronze coins. This issue reveals that, *c.* 23 BC, in the reign of Augustus, C. Mussidius Priscus and C. Heius Pollio were in office, the latter not for the first time.

58 Roman colonies fostered the imperial cult in the provinces (p. 148). At Camulodunum (Colchester) in Britain the temple of Claudius occupied the dominating site where the Norman castle now stands. Extensive remains of its substructure permit accurate reconstruction of the entire monument: larger than most colonial temples, it had an octastyle façade and eleven columns on either side.

59–61 Coins sometimes reveal more than literature about a colony. *Left*, an issue from Bilbilis (near Calatayud) in Spain shows that the town was styled Augusta, had duoviri and may therefore have become a colony (see p. 158). *Centre*, Marsyas on a colony's coins with a wineskin over his shoulder (for example, on this issue from Alexandria Troas in Asia Minor near the Dardanelles) indicates that it enjoyed Ius Italicum (p. 156). *Right*, a favourite colonial coin-type appears on the issues of Cremna (Girme) in Lycia: the Genius of the *colonia* holding a cornucopiae and patera (p. 148).

CHAPTER IX

CONCLUSION

COLONIES IN THE ROMAN EMPIRE

THE COLONIES FOUNDED under the Roman Empire were overwhelmingly of the type that Velleius called *militares*. Many of them have been identified from inscriptions and are revealed to have had a rather elaborate titulature: besides including the word *colonia* and the name of the town, it usually contains one or more adjectives to advertise the name of the emperor who founded it and the quality of the foundation. Thus Gloucester in Britain (Colonia Nervia Glevensis) is seen to be Glevum and a colony of Nerva's (AD 96–98), and Orange, in the Gallic province of Narbonensis (Colonia Firma Julia Secundanorum Arausio), is Arausio, one of Octavian's colonies and, it is hoped, a stalwart one, peopled with veterans of Legion II. The latter example shows that this kind of nomenclature dates from the earliest beginnings of the imperial period.[289] Most emperors imitated Augustus, the professed model of practically all of them, in founding or claiming to found a lot of colonies which they hoped would develop, like his, into flourishing cities, and they did not hesitate to publicize their activity in this regard[290] (Fig. 12).

The avowed aim of these imperial colonies was to provide discharged legionaries with farms and thereby integrate them into the civilian life of the Empire. To this end their land grants were generous, especially when compared with the meagre 2-*iugera* holdings in the maritime colonies founded hundreds of years earlier. The secular trend for allotments in colonies to get larger, already clearly evident under the Republic, led to a standard grant of at least fifty *iugera* under the Empire: indeed one third of a

Fig. 12 *Colonies in the Roman Empire mentioned in the text*

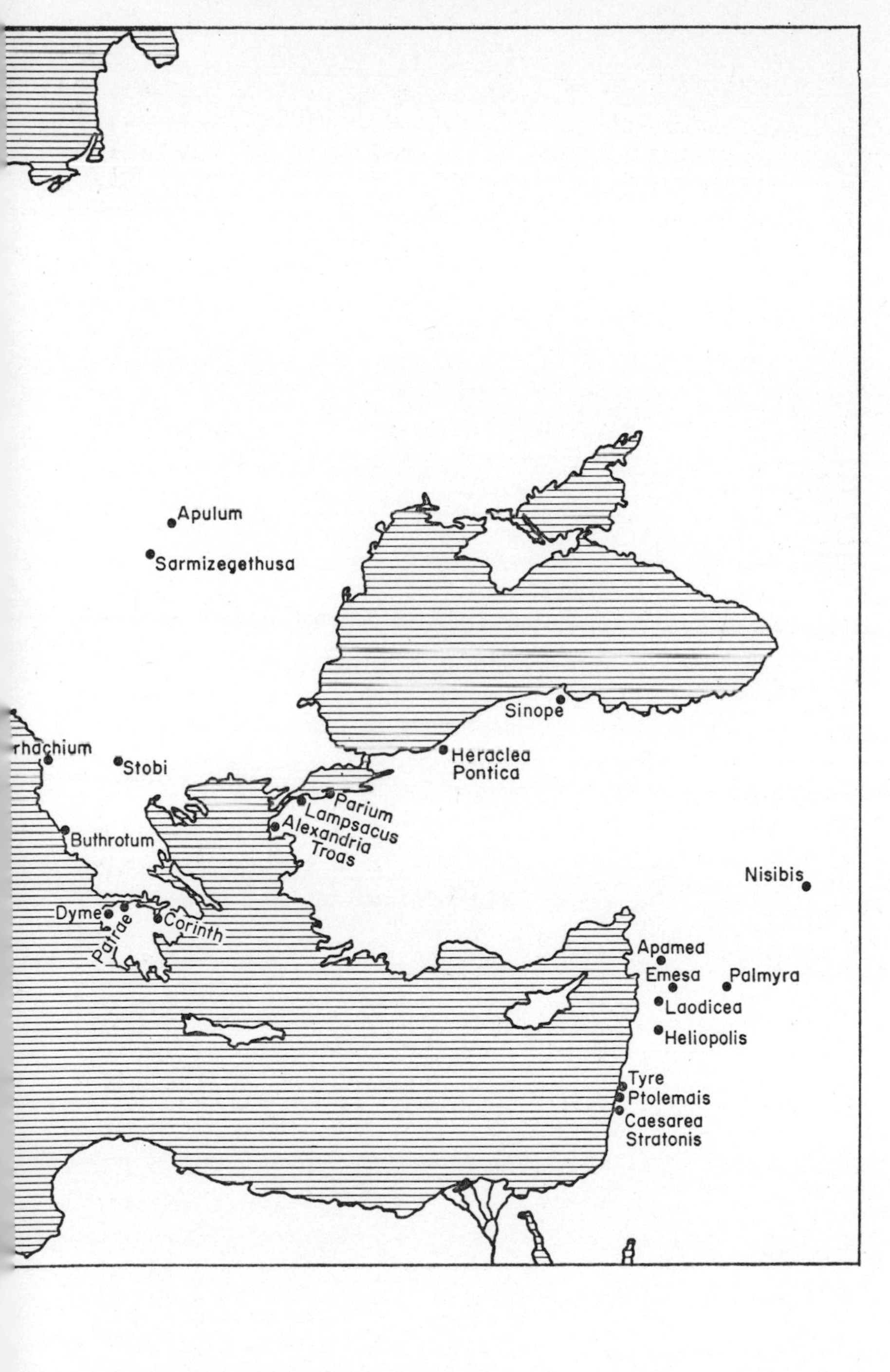
Apulum
Sarmizegethusa
Sinope
rhachium
Stobi
Heraclea
Pontica
Parium
Lampsacus
Alexandria
Troas
Buthrotum
Nisibis
Dyme
Patrae
Corinth
Apamea
Emesa
Palmyra
Laodicea
Heliopolis
Tyre
Ptolemais
Caesarea
Stratonis

centuria (=66⅔ *iugera*) appears to have been not uncommon.[291] There does not seem to have been undue difficulty in finding the necessary land. For the most part, the emperors avoided the confiscatory methods of Sulla and the Triumvirs and were careful not to seize the private property of Roman citizens. Provincial soil could serve their purpose, and it was regarded as land won by conquest and therefore readily available: but sometimes the emperors followed Augustus' example and paid cash even for it. The size of the colonies varied greatly, depending on the number of veterans being discharged: some colonies had only a few hundred settlers, yet Claudius' colony at Cologne in Germany (Colonia Claudia Augusta Ara Agrippinensium) had 4,106.[292]

Other purposes were served besides the establishment of closed civic communities of ex-soldiers. The *coloniae* were centres of Roman influence from which the Latin language spread into the surrounding sea of alien tongues; they helped to promote the imperial cult; and they familiarized the natives with Roman institutions. Their coins alone must have been a potent means for propagating Roman ideas. For the Roman colony of the Empire, unlike the Citizen colony of the Republic, could issue coins bearing its own name, and many colonies, especially those established in towns that had had mints in their pre-Roman days, did so.[293] The coins were for local use, but their legends were in Latin, and their types were Roman, sometimes with local peculiarities. Favourite motifs were the Genius and the Fortuna of the colony, usually on the reverse of the coin. In the days when coins were practically the only means of mass propaganda, colonial issues made daily impact on the consciousness of the non-Roman natives who used them (*Pl. 61*).

The question whether the emperors founded their colonies specifically with such romanization in mind has been much debated. It is certainly not difficult to name foundations where strategic or economic considerations were uppermost; and it is also possible to name colonies, which so far from romanizing their neighbours were themselves to some extent assimilated by them. Yet it is no less certainly true that the *coloniae* and the *municipia* were the vehicles through which Roman citizenship was extended throughout the Empire; and it is obvious that, whether deliberately intended to do so or not, the colonies did affect the surrounding native areas and induce them to adopt Roman ways.[294] In Italy, for instance, a colony of veterans, established apparently by Titus (AD 79–81), accelerated the disappearance of Greek at Naples, just as, in republican times, Sulla's colonies in the north and south had helped to bring the use of Etruscan and Oscan to an end. The emperors could not have been unaware of the Roman tradition, preserved by Livy, that the very first Roman colony to be planted, by no less a person than Romulus himself, had been a means for spreading the knowledge of Latin; and they must also have been aware of the conviction of their great predecessor, Augustus, that the colonies were the repositories of the authentic Roman spirit.[295] Romanization, therefore, may have been the conscious aim of some of their foundations, especially in the western provinces, the *provinciae togatae*, or latinized areas, par excellence.

It is most unlikely that an emperor like Claudius, who withheld Roman citizenship from those who could not speak Latin,[296] ignored the usefulness of *coloniae militares* as romanizing foci; his preference for planting them in the newer provinces indicates that he expected them to help spread the Latin language and Roman customs. Conversely it may also be the case that one of the reasons for the comparative paucity of *coloniae* and the total absence of *municipia* in the east, until after AD 193 at any rate, was the realization by the emperors that colonies were unlikely to succeed in any such role in a region where Greek speech and civilization were so firmly entrenched.[297]

The imperial colonies, however, had another important purpose besides that of absorbing veterans or possibly expediting romanization. They were also intended, if the necessity should arise, to supplement the efforts of that great latinizing instrument, the imperial Roman army. Rome no longer needed to rely, to the same degree as formerly, on colonies for the defence of Roman soil. The legions and auxiliary units, which composed the standing army of the Empire, were now stationed in permanent stone camps or powerful forts, and the function once performed by colonies could be discharged by them. Nevertheless the ex-legionaries, or in some cases ex-praetorians, peopling the colonies were guardians of the Empire in whose armed forces they had so long served, and they could help the standing army either to repel invaders from without or to repress insurgents from within.[298] This helps to explain why the early emperors followed Augustus' example and planted colonies of veterans in key positions in newly annexed border regions: Claudius in Britain and in Mauretania, the Flavians (AD 69–96) along the middle Danube, Trajan (AD 98–117) along the lower Danube and in Dacia.

In one respect the colonies strengthened the army considerably. They were exceptionally valuable sources of recruits, since the sons of soldiers were somewhat less reluctant than Roman citizens in general to serve in the imperial army. Living in colonies as the offspring of veterans, they enjoyed the twin advantages of familiarity with the army and of favour with the administration, and they could expect preferment when they enlisted. They formed local aristocracies throughout the Empire, and they were a large component in the officer class of the imperial Roman army.

As beneficiaries of provincial soil and as the permanently privileged local upper class, the colonists were often objects of hatred and suspicion to the natives in whose midst they lived. According to Tacitus, the Britons regarded Claudius' colony of veterans at Camulodunum (Colchester) as the very citadel of their permanent subjugation and the seat of their enslavement. Elsewhere Tacitus describes the walls of a colony as 'bulwarks of slavery'[299] (*Pl. 58*; Fig. 13).

The situation, however, was not everywhere the same. If there were some places where the natives were despised and inferior, there were also 'double communities' where the two groups were on much more equal terms: at Apulum in Dacia, at Dyrrhachium in Macedonia, at Patrae in Achaea and at Thamugadi in Numidia each part of the double community seems to have had full autonomy.[300]

Fig. 13 Plan of Colchester

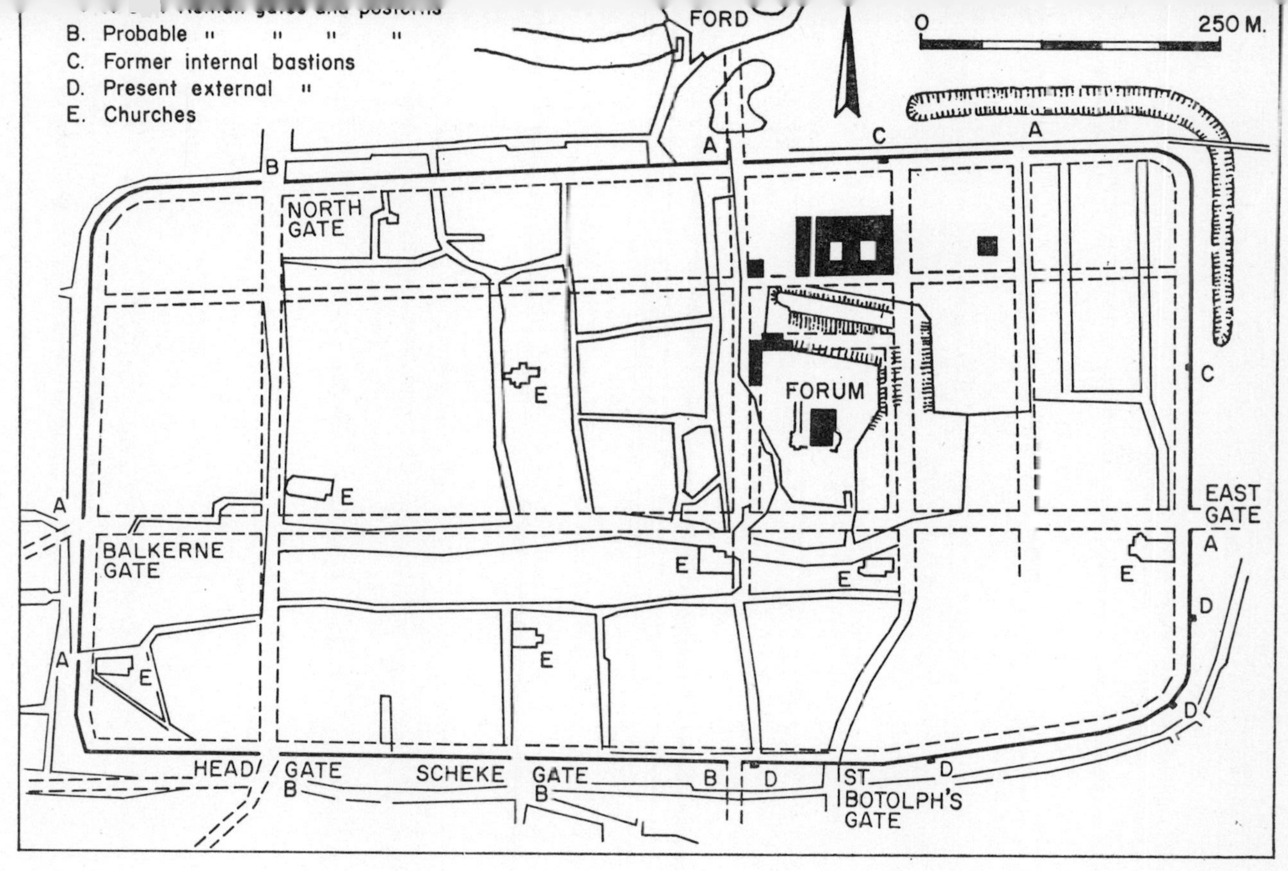
B. Probable " " " "
C. Former internal bastions
D. Present external "
E. Churches
FORD
0
250 M.
NORTH GATE
BALKERNE GATE
FORUM
EAST GATE
HEAD/ GATE
SCHEKE GATE
ST BOTOLPH'S GATE
A
B
C
D
E

Some colonies may even have been positively welcomed as centres of law and order, sources of prosperity and city-life, and defenders of what the Elder Pliny calls 'the boundless majesty of the Roman peace',[301] affording protection against bandits and foreign foes. This would be particularly true of those colonies, of which Caesarea Stratonis in Syria is an example,[302] into which natives, in the tradition of the earliest Citizen colony at Antium, were admitted as full citizens, if not at the actual time of the colonization, then very shortly afterwards;[303] and there were more than a few such foundations, especially in a province like Pannonia, where a number of colonies were created out of the civilian settlements (*canabae*) that had sprung up around the military camps.

As ex-legionaries, the *coloni* must have been themselves increasingly sons of the provinces, since that is where, more and more, Rome found her soldiers. This meant that the romanization brought about by the colonies was largely the work of men who were not themselves Roman by origin, and this, as Tacitus noted,[304] affected its Roman quality. Under the Republic the colonies in Italy represented almost the quintessence of the Roman spirit and tradition, and because of this Augustus had made them a principal recruiting area for his original Praetorian Guard. But in the *coloniae militares* of the Empire, the Roman flavour must have been to some degree diluted and the general Roman culture subtly changed in its transmission through alien media: local usages persisted or grew,[305] and differentiated one 'Roman' region from another, a state of affairs that ultimately contributed to the disintegration of the Roman Empire. This, however, came much later, and there can be no doubt that, during the heyday of the great organism in the first two centuries AD, the colonies served it magnificently. This was the period when the municipality as an instrument of government came into its own; and, as the Gromatici Veteres repeatedly emphasize, of all the municipalities the colonies were easily first. They were one of the most important factors in knitting the Empire together then and in promoting its political unity.

The status and prestige of the *colonia* grew ever higher, understandably, since it was regarded as the authentic representative of Rome abroad, a provincial fragment, so to speak, of the imperial city herself. Romantically nostalgic though this view may have been, it had very real force and the ambition of all cities was to be styled *colonia*: the title was a badge, an irrefutable proof of their loyalty. 'They are eager to become colonies because that condition, despite certain theoretical disadvantages, carries with it very great prestige, owing to the grandeur and majesty of the Roman People: the colonies convey the impression of being miniatures and reproductions of Rome herself.'[306] Even towns, that were Roman *municipia* and as such indistinguishable for all practical purposes from *coloniae*, thirsted after the title, whereas we never hear of the reverse, of provincial *coloniae* asking to be styled *municipia*.[307] The emperors, down to and including Constantine (AD 313–337), recognized the aspiration and bestowed the title of *colonia* upon those cities which in their view deserved it, even if they were cities that had never been formally 'colonized' with an organized group of settlers.[308] Such titular colonies, of course, rarely had any strategic or military purpose, although we can well believe that the emperors counted on them being centres of strong pro-Roman sentiment.

As noted above, the first such titular colonies may possibly be as early as Julius Caesar, although it seems to have been Claudius who first made them a part of normal policy. Gradually more and more of them were created. In Italy every town of any consequence was sooner or later designated a colony, and in the provinces too they became quite numerous, some of them developing into places of more importance and influence than many a genuine foundation, as for instance Vienna (Vienne) and Nemausus (Nîmes) in the Gallic province of Narbonensis.[309] From the time of Hadrian (AD 117–138) on, titular colonies were the normal type of *coloniae*, even though the scene of the ritual ploughing is still found on colonial coinage issues as late as the reign of Commodus (AD 180–192). Actual colonizations, however, were very rare after Hadrian, except possibly in the reign of Septimius Severus (AD 193–211). By Hadrian's time, too, the time lag had been reduced and a community often did not have long to wait for the honour: once it had received the title of *municipium*, that of *colonia* was not far behind.[310]

Inevitably the emperors' ideas of what should qualify a town for the distinction had evolved. Even in the first century AD a town might become a *colonia* for reasons that do not always seem especially cogent;[311] but by the second century they sometimes appear downright trivial, as for example when Marcus Aurelius made a mere hamlet a *colonia* simply because his wife had happened to die there.[312] Even places that were not really cities at all in the true sense of the word, such as the tribal administrative centres of the imperial Gallic provinces, became *coloniae*.[313]

Needless to say, it was another kind of colony that emerged from all this, different in its nature as well as in its origin. The worthiness of a community, however defined, and above all the emperor's favour were the generative agents; and, even though it is true that it was the emperor who decided which province should be studded with colonies and who proclaimed which towns in that province were to be elevated, it was usually the towns themselves that petitioned for the honour. Thus the initiative that had belonged successively to the Latin League, the Roman Senate, the plebeian tribunes and the military despots, now very largely passed to communities that were already in existence.

Titular colonies of this kind could hardly have counteracted the growth of local diversity to anything like the same extent as the regular colonies that had been brought into being for the actual settlement of romanized settlers. It is difficult, for instance, to visualize some of Septimius Severus' titular colonies as promoters of Roman customs or propagators of the Roman spirit: a place like Nisibis in Mesopotamia was not only not latinized, it was not even hellenized, but was an essentially semitic community. Perhaps there was some hope that such cities might somehow grow more Roman once they became titular colonies. Be that as it may, estrangement between the different parts of the Empire gradually developed.

Except in designation, a *colonia* could not have differed much from the other kind of Roman town to be found in the provinces, the *municipium*.[314] Good evidence of this is the frequency, and indeed after AD 100 the normalcy with which the inhabitants of colonies were referred to as *municipes* by everybody, including themselves: the very *colonia* itself was sometimes called a *municipium*, even apparently in official documents.[315] The usual view, that a *colonia* was different from a *municipium* in having the traditional duoviri instead of quattuorviri as its chief officials, while in general correct, is not invariably so: examples of exactly the opposite of this occur.[316] But even if it were a hard and fast rule, it might not mean very much more than a mere difference in nomenclature. The officials in both types of town seem to have discharged very similar functions. It is noteworthy that the magistrates who conducted the local census every fifth year, that is who in effect revised the roll of the local senate (*ordo*), were described as quinquennales in both. The titles of the junior officials (quaestors, aediles) were also likely to be the same in both; and such lower offices, the prerequisites to the highest local dignity, seem to have been held in much the same order, insofar as that was fixed. The same kinds of priests and religious officials, flamines, sacerdotes, and, on a lower social plane, seviri Augustales are encountered; and officials of a non-Roman type are likewise liable to be found in both: even in the west, colonies with agonothetae are not unknown.[317] In either type of town the expenses attached to office-holding were high. In addition to being required to pay a substantial fee on election into the *ordo*, the officials were expected to confer benefits on their town, by providing it with splendid buildings, endowments, gladiatorial shows, beast-baitings and other forms of entertainment.

It is often said that the *coloniae*, by being officially of Roman origin, were obliged to use Latin and to follow Roman law in cases heard by their local magistrates, whereas the *municipia*, being officially non-Roman in origin, were free to use their original vernaculars and retain their own traditional legal procedures. But, however true this may once have been, by the second century AD it was no longer the case: by then all Roman *municipia* spoke Latin and used Roman law.

Hadrian, if Aulus Gellius reports him correctly, was of the

opinion that it was pure snobbery on the part of his official birthplace, the *municipium* Italica (near Seville) in the Spanish province of Baetica, to petition for the rank of *colonia*, and it is unquestionably true that this kind of snobbery was common in the Roman Empire. Dio Chrysostom reveals how in the east cities quarrelled bitterly even over such a title as *metropolis* (or first city) of their province, and a *metropolis* was not even Roman. One can imagine, then, with what fierce eagerness the title of *colonia*, with its implication of the very highest Roman status, was likely to be coveted.[318] Hadrian himself realized that this was the state of affairs, and it is difficult to believe that only snobbery was involved.

There seem to have been two ways in which the *colonia* had the advantage of the *municipium*, and it would not have been prudent of Hadrian to draw attention to either of them. In the first place its leading men stood a better chance than did the leading men of a *municipium* of being appointed to the Roman Senate and thereby fulfilling the universal ambition of the upper class throughout the Roman world: a very high proportion of the so-called *viri militares*, the real careerists of the Roman Empire, came from colonies. In the second place, a provincial *colonia* might hope to escape the taxes to which all provincial communities were liable, by being pronounced the equivalent of an Italian community through the grant of Ius Italicum. A colony that received this stroke of good fortune customarily erected a statue of Marsyas in its forum as a symbolic gesture, since a similar statue stood in the forum at Rome.[319] Some provincial colonies had obtained this valuable privilege from Augustus, as we have seen, but they did not constitute a large proportion of the total. Indeed, during the first two centuries AD, comparatively few provincial communities enjoyed Ius Italicum. Later, especially under the Severan dynasty (AD 193–235), which systematically ironed out many of the differences between Italy and the provinces, their number grew very much larger and the statue of Marsyas must have become a not uncommon sight in provincial colonies.[320] As it was almost impossible for any other type of provincial city to win this favour,[321] the superiority of the *colonia* becomes manifest: it opened up wider opportunities for its wealthiest burgesses and the hope of an escape from certain forms of taxation (*Pl. 60*).

Otherwise it is not easy to see how a titular colony differed from a *municipium*. Certainly after Hadrian's time the distinction must have been recognized as largely nominal, even though the title of *colonia* continued to enjoy great prestige, to such an extent indeed that Commodus even tried to change the name of Rome to Colonia Lucia Antoniniana Commodiana.[322]

By AD 212, when all provincial cities became Roman, the *colonia* no longer had much meaningful independent role to play, although the title was still being given to cities as a mark of honour and favour in the reign of Constantine and even later.

For well over half a millennium of changing vicissitudes the *coloniae* had done yeoman service. Through all their changes of purpose, size and constitution they had made their vigorous and fruitful contribution to the growth and government of Rome. The colonies had defended her soil and helped her to win and digest an empire. They had provided lands and homes for her proletariat and her soldiers. They had served the needs of her commerce and promoted the spread of her language and her ways. They had been the sinews of her civilizing power, helping her to maintain law, order and the Pax Romana. Their history, it has been aptly said, 'is the history of the Roman state'.[323]

APPENDIX

List of Roman colonies

Certainty about a town's status in the Roman Empire is not always possible. Notices in the Gromatici Veteres and the use of words such as *coloni* or *municipes* to describe the inhabitants are not necessarily reliable or conclusive evidence; and sometimes only the title of its chief officials indicates that a place may have been a *colonia*. For that reason this, like any other list of Roman colonies, cannot claim to be definitive: it may include some places that never were *coloniae*, while omitting others that did attain that grade of dignity. It will be noted that some names are given with a question mark.

It is likewise often impossible, even in the case of indubitable colonies, to decide whether they were merely titular or genuine foundations, and consequently no attempt has been made to distinguish them. In this matter, however, chronology can be of considerable help. Down to and slightly beyond the reign of Augustus (27 BC–AD 14) colonies were nearly always actually founded; from Claudius (AD 41–54) on the increasing tendency was for them to be titular; and beginning with Hadrian (AD 117–138) they were almost invariably of the latter type.

An asterisk means that the place had been a Latin colony before the Social War.

Places colonized more than once are shown with more than one notation after them. The colonies of the first of the emperors, except when their dates seem reasonably certain, are attributed to Augustus even though some of them were probably founded by him while he was still Octavian.

ACHAEA

Buthrotum	Julius Caesar
Corinth	44/43 BC; Domitian
Dyme	44–27 BC
Patrae	16 BC

AFRICA including NUMIDIA

Ammaedara (=Heidra)	Flavians (AD 69–96)
Anonymous (a *municipium* transformed into a *colonia*)	unknown
Aphrodisium	2nd century AD
Assuras	Augustus
Bisica Lucana	3rd–4th century AD
Bulla Regia?	Hadrian
Calama	3rd century AD
Capsa	3rd century AD
Carpis	Julius Caesar
Carthage	Julius Caesar; Augustus; Septimius Severus
Cast . . . colonia	Severus Alexander?
Chullu	Augustus; Trajan; 3rd century AD
Cillium	Trajan
Cirta (=Constantina)	Augustus; Trajan
Cuicul	Nerva; 3rd century AD
Clupea	Julius Caesar
Culcua (or some similar name)	2nd century AD
Curubis	Julius Caesar
Hadrumetum	Julius Caesar; Trajan
Hippo Diarrhytus	Julius Caesar
Hippo Regius	unknown
Lambaesis	Gordian III
Lares	Hadrian or Antoninus Pius
Lepcis Magna	Trajan; Septimius Severus
Mactar	Marcus Aurelius
Madauros	Flavians (AD 69–96)
Maxula	Augustus
Milev	Augustus; Trajan; 3rd century AD
Neapolis	Julius Caesar
Oea	Trajan
Pupput	Commodus
Rusicade	Augustus; Trajan; 3rd century AD
Sabrata	Trajan?
Sicca Veneria	Augustus
Simitthu	Augustus
Sufes	Marcus Aurelius
Sufetula	2nd century AD
Tacapae	3rd century AD
Thabraca	Augustus; 2nd century AD
Thaenae	Hadrian
Thamugadi	Trajan
Thapsus	Julius Caesar
Thelepte	Trajan
Theveste	2nd century AD
Thibiuca	2nd century AD
Thigiba	2nd century AD
Thuburbo Maius	Augustus; Commodus
Thuburbo Minus	Augustus
Thuburnica	Augustus; 2nd century AD
Thubursicum Bure	Gallienus
Thubursicum Numidarum	3rd century AD
Thugga	Gallienus
Thunudromum	2nd century AD
Thunusuda	Julius Caesar or Augustus
Thysdrus	2nd century AD
Tutcensium colonia	Julius Caesar; 2nd century AD
Uchi Maius	Severus Alexander
Uppenna	3rd–4th century AD
Uthina	Augustus
Utica	Hadrian; Septimius Severus
Uzalis	unknown
Vaga	Septimius Severus
Vallis	3rd century AD
Zama Minor	2nd century AD
Zama Regia	Hadrian

AQUITANIA: *see* GAUL

ARABIA

Bostra	Severus Alexander
Philippopolis	Philippus Arabs

ARMENIA: *see* ASIA MINOR

ASIA: *see* ASIA MINOR

ASIA MINOR including ARMENIA MINOR, ASIA, BITHYNIA, CAPPADOCIA, CILICIA, GALATIA, MYSIA, PAMPHYLIA, PAPHLAGONIA, PISIDIA, PONTUS

Alexandria Troas	Augustus
Antiochia	Julius Caesar; Augustus
Apamea	Julius Caesar; Augustus; Septimius Severus
Archelais	Claudius
Attaleia?	3rd century AD
Comama	Augustus
Cremna	Augustus
Faustinopolis (=Halala)	Marcus Aurelius
Germa	Augustus
Heraclea Pontica	45 BC?
Iconium	Claudius; Hadrian?
Lampsacus	Julius Caesar
Lystra	Augustus
Mallus	Elagabalus
Nicomedia	Diocletian
Ninica	Augustus
Olba	3rd century AD
Olbasa	Augustus
Parium	Augustus; Hadrian
Parlais	Augustus
Satala	2nd century AD?
Selinus	Hadrian
Sinis	Claudius
Sinope	45 BC
Trebenna	3rd century AD
Tyana	Caracalla

BAETICA: *see* SPAIN

BELGICA: *see* GAUL

BITHYNIA: *see* ASIA MINOR

BRITAIN

Camulodunum	Claudius
Eburacum	unknown
Glevum	Nerva
Lindum	unknown

CAESARIENSIS: *see* MAURETANIA

CAPPADOCIA: *see* ASIA MINOR

CILICIA: *see* ASIA MINOR

CORSICA

Aleria	Sulla; Julius Caesar?
Mariana	Marius; Julius Caesar

CRETE

Cnossus	Augustus

CYRENAICA

Cyrene?	unknown
Tauchira?	unknown

DACIA

Apulum	Marcus Aurelius
Drobetae	*c.* AD 200
Malu . . . colonia	unknown
Napoca	Marcus Aurelius
Potaissa	Septimius Severus
Romula	unknown
Sarmizegethusa	Trajan
Zerna (=Dierna)	Septimius Severus

DALMATIA

Claudia Aequum	Claudius?
Epidaurus?	unknown
Iader	33 BC?
Narona	Augustus
Salonae	33 BC?
Scodra	Augustus

GALATIA: *see* ASIA MINOR

GAUL including AQUITANIA, BELGICA, GERMANIA INFERIOR, GERMANIA SUPERIOR, LUGDUNENSIS, NARBONENSIS

Apollinaris Reiorum	Augustus
Apta	Augustus?
Aquae Sextiae	Augustus
Arausio	35/33 BC
Arelate	45 BC
Augustodunum?	Augustus?
Auscorum Augusta?	unknown
Avenio	Hadrian

Aventicum (=Helvetiorum colonia)	Vespasian
Baeterrae	36–27 BC
Cabellio	Augustus
Colonia Agrippinensis	Claudius
Cugernorum colonia (=Ulpia Traiana Colonia)	Trajan
Elusatium colonia	Severus Alexander
Forum Julii	30 BC
Lingonum colonia	Otho
Lug(u)dunum	43 BC
Morinorum colonia	Flavians (AD 69–96)
Narbo Martius	*c.* 114 BC; 45 BC
Nemausus	unknown
Noviodunum (=Colonia Equestris) (=Suessionum Augusta?)	Triumvirs (43–32 BC)
Noviomagus Nemetum	Vespasian
Rauricorum Augusta	43 BC
Segusiavorum Forum	Vespasian
Senonum colonia?	Severus Alexander?
Sequanorum colonia	Galba
Treverorum colonia	Claudius
Tricastinorum colonia?	Flavians (AD 69–96)?
Valentia	Julius Caesar or Augustus
Vellavorum colonia	3rd century AD
Veromanduorum Augusta?	3rd century AD
Vienna	Gaius (Caligula) or Claudius
Vocontiorum colonia?	unknown

GERMANIA: *see* GAUL

ITALY

Abella	Sulla?
Abellinum	Sulla; Augustus; Severus Alexander
Aecae	2nd century AD
Aeclanum	Hadrian
Aesis	2nd century AD?
Allifae	Sulla?
Alsium	247 BC
Ancona	Triumvirs (43–32 BC)
Antium	338 BC; Nero
*Aquileia?	Augustus?
Aquinum	Triumvirs (43–32 BC)?
*Ardea	Sulla?
*Ariminum	Triumvirs (43–32 BC); Augustus
Arretium	Sulla
Asculum Picenum	Triumvirs (43–32 BC), or Augustus
Atella	Augustus
Ateste	Augustus
Augusta Praetoria	25 BC
Ausculum	Sulla?
Auximum	128 BC?
*Beneventum	Triumvirs (43–32 BC); Augustus
*Bononia	Augustus
Bovianum	Augustus?; Vespasian
Bovianum Vetus	Triumvirs (43–32 BC)
Brixellum	Augustus
Brixia	Augustus
Buxentum	194 BC
Calatia	59 BC
*Cales	2nd century AD
Canusium	Antoninus Pius or Marcus Aurelius
Capua	59 BC; 36 BC; Augustus; Nero; Diocletian
*Carseoli	2nd century AD
Casilinum	59 BC
Casinum?	Triumvirs (43–32 BC)?
Castrum Novum (Etruria)	264 BC; Julius Caesar?

Concordia	Julius Caesar or Augustus
Consentia?	Augustus
*Cremona	Triumvirs (43–32 BC)
Croton	194 BC
Cumae?	1st century AD
Cupra Maritima?	Augustus
Dertona	*c.* 109 BC; Julius Caesar or Augustus
Eporedia	100 BC
Fabrateria Nova	124 BC
Faesulae	Sulla
Falerii	Gallienus
Falerio	Augustus
Fanum Fortunae	Augustus?
*Firmum	Triumvirs (43–32 BC)
Florentia	Augustus?
Formiae	Hadrian
Fregenae	245 BC
Frusino	unknown
Graviscae	181 BC
Grumentum	Sulla?
*Hadria	Sulla or Triumvirs or Augustus
Heba	128 BC?
Hispellum	Julius Caesar or Augustus
Interamnia Praetuttianorum	Sulla?
Julium Carnicum	Claudius
Libarna	unknown
Liternum	194 BC
Luca	Augustus?
*Luceria	Triumvirs (43–32 BC)?
Lucus Feroniae	Julius Caesar or Augustus
Luna	177 BC
Lupiae	unknown
Mediolanum	Hadrian?; Gallienus
Minturnae	295; Augustus
Misenum	Claudius
Mutina	183 BC; Augustus?
Neapolis	Titus?; Septimius Severus or Caracalla
Nola	Sulla; Augustus
Nuceria Alfaterna	Triumvirs (43–32 BC) Augustus?; Nero
Ocriculum	unknown
Opitergium	Claudius
Ostia	*c.* 338 BC
*Paestum	Sulla?
Parentium?	Augustus?
Parma	183 BC; Augustus
Perusia	Trebonianus Gallus
Pisae	Julius Caesar or Augustus
Pisaurum	184 BC; Julius Caesar or Augustus
*Placentia	Triumvirs or Augustus
Pola	33 BC?
Pompeii	Sulla; Nero
Potentia	184 BC
Praeneste	Sulla; 1st century AD
Privernum	unknown
Puteoli	194 BC; Augustus?; Nero
Pyrgi	247 BC?
Regium Lepidum	2nd century AD
Ricina	Pertinax or Septimius Severus
Rome	Commodus
Rusellae	Triumvirs or Augustus
Saena?	Augustus?
Saepinum?	AD 2
Salernum	194 BC
Salvia	Trajan
Saturnia	183 BC
Scolacium	122 BC; Nerva
Sena Gallica	289–283 BC
Septempeda	unknown
Sinuessa	295 BC; Flavians (AD 69–96)
Sipontum	194 BC
*Sora?	Triumvirs (43–32 BC)?
*Suessa Aurunca	Augustus?
Suessula	Sulla?
*Sutrium	Julius Caesar or Augustus
Tarentum	122 BC; Nero
Tarracina	329 BC
Taurinorum Augusta	*c.* 27 BC
Teanum Sidicinum	Augustus?; Claudius
Teate	unknown
Tegeanum	Nero

Telesia	Sulla?; Triumvirs (43–32 BC)
Tempsa	194 BC
Tergeste	33 BC
Trea	unknown
Tridentum	2nd century AD
Tuder	Augustus?
Ulubrae?	Triumvirs (43–32 BC)
Urbana	Sulla
Venafrum	Augustus
*Venusia	43 BC
Verona	Gallienus
Volturnum	194 BC

LUGDUNENSIS: *see* GAUL

LUSITANIA: *see* SPAIN

MACEDONIA

Byllis	Julius Caesar or Augustus
Cassandrea	Triumvirs or Augustus
Dium	Triumvirs or Augustus
Dyrrhachium	30 BC
Pella	30 BC
Philippi	42 BC; 30 BC
Stobi	3rd century AD
Thessalonica	Valerian

MAURETANIA including CAESARIENSIS, TINGITANA

Aquae Calidae	Augustus; 2nd century AD
Arsennaria	2nd century AD
Auzia	Septimius Severus or Caracalla
Babba	Augustus
Banasa	Augustus; Aurelian?
Bida	2nd century AD
Cartenna	Augustus
Equizetium	3rd century AD
Gilva	unknown
Gunugu	Augustus
Icosium	Diocletian?
Igilgili	Augustus
Iol Caesarea	Claudius
Lixus	Claudius
Oppidum Novum	Claudius
Quiza?	2nd century AD
Rusadder	unknown
Rusazu	Augustus
Rusguniae	Augustus
Rusucurru	unknown
Sala?	unknown
Saldae	Augustus
Siga	2nd century AD
Sitifis	Nerva
Th . . . colonia	unknown
Tingi	Claudius
Tipasa	Claudius; 2nd century AD
Tupusuptu	Augustus
Volubilis	unknown
Zucchabar	Augustus
Zulil	Augustus

MESOPOTAMIA

Carrhae	Marcus Aurelius
Dura?	Septimius Severus
Edessa	Marcus Aurelius
Maiozamalcha	Trajan
Nisibis	Septimius Severus
Rhesaena	Septimius Severus
Singara	Marcus Aurelius
Zaytha	Septimius Severus

MOESIA

Oescus	Trajan
Ratiaria	Trajan
Scupi	Vespasian
Singidunum	Gordian III
Viminacium	3rd century AD

MYSIA: *see* ASIA MINOR

NARBONENSIS: *see* GAUL

NORICUM including RAETIA

Flavia Solva	Hadrian?
Ovilava	Marcus Aurelius
Virunum	unknown

NUMIDIA: *see* AFRICA

PALESTINE: *see* SYRIA

PAMPHYLIA: *see* ASIA MINOR

PANNONIA

Aquincum	3rd century AD
Bassiana colonia	Caracalla
Brigetio	3rd century AD

Carnuntum	3rd century AD
Emona	34 BC
Mursa	Hadrian
Poetovio	Trajan
Pra . . . colonia	3rd century AD
Savaria	Claudius
Sirmium	Flavians (AD 69–96)
Siscia	Augustus?; Vespasian

PAPHLAGONIA: *see* ASIA MINOR

PISIDIA: *see* ASIA MINOR

PONTUS: *see* ASIA MINOR

RAETIA: *see* NORICUM

SARDINIA

Turris Libisonis	before 27 BC
Uselia	Hadrian

SICILY

Catana	21 BC
Lilybaeum	Pertinax or Septimius Severus
Panormus	Augustus
Syracuse	21 BC
Tauromenium	36 BC
Thermae Himeraeae	21 BC
Tyndaris	21 BC

SPAIN including BAETICA, LUSITANIA, TARRACONENSIS

Acci Gemella	Triumvirs (43–32 BC)
Asido Caesariana	Julius Caesar or Augustus
Astigi	Augustus
Barcino	Augustus
Bilbilis	Augustus?
Caesaraugusta (=Salduba)	Augustus
Carthago Nova	45 BC
Celsa	45 BC
Clunia Sulpicia	Nerva
Corduba	46/45 BC?; Augustus
Dertosa	Augustus
Emerita	25 BC
Flaviobriga (=Amanum Portus)	Flavians (AD 69–96)
Hasta Regia	Julius Caesar
Hispalis	45 BC; Otho
Ilici	Augustus
Italica	Hadrian
Itucci	unknown
Libisosa	Augustus
Metellinum	Julius Caesar
Norba	Julius Caesar
Pax Julia	Augustus
Salaria	Augustus
Scallabis (=Praesidium Julium)	Julius Caesar
Tarraco	45 BC
Traducta	Augustus
Tucci	Augustus
Ucubi	Julius Caesar
Urso	44 BC
Valentia	60 BC?; Augustus

SYRIA including PALESTINE

Antioch	Caracalla
Ascalon	unknown
Berytus	14 BC
Caesarea ad Libanum	Caracalla
Caesarea Stratonis	Vespasian
Damascus	Severus Alexander
Eakkaia	unknown
Emesa	Caracalla
Gaza	unknown
Heliopolis	Augustus
Jerusalem (=Aelia Capitolina)	Hadrian
Laodicea	Septimius Severus
Neapolis	Philippus Arabs
Palmyra	Septimius Severus
Ptolemais	Claudius
Samaria (=Sebaste)	Septimius Severus
Sidon	Elagabalus
Tyre	Septimius Severus

TARRACONENSIS: *see* SPAIN

THRACE

Apri	Claudius
Develtus	Flavians (AD 69–96)
Flaviopolis	Flavians (AD 69–96)
Philippopolis	Philippus Arabs

TINGITANA: *see* MAURETANIA

NOTES

ABBREVIATIONS

AJA	*American Journal of Archaeology*
AJP	*American Journal of Philology*
Ann. Epigr.	*Année Epigraphique*
CAH	*Cambridge Ancient History*
CIL	*Corpus Inscriptionum Latinarum*
CQ	*Classical Quarterly*
FIRA	Riccobono, *Fontes Iuris Romani Antejustiniani*
G. & R.	*Greece and Rome*
ILLRP	*Inscriptiones Latinae Liberae Rei Publicae*
ILS	Dessau, *Inscriptiones Latinae Selectae*
JRS	*Journal of Roman Studies*
Mem. dei Linc.	*Memorie dell' Accademia dei Lincei*
MRR	T.R.S. Broughton, *Magistrates of the Roman Republic*
Nuova Riv. Stor.	*Nuova Rivista Storica*
R. E.	Pauly-Wissowa-Kroll, *Realencyclopädie der classischen Altertumswissenschaft*
SC	*Senatus Consultum*
SHA	*Scriptores Historiae Augustae*
SIG	W. Dittenberger, *Sylloge Inscriptionum Graecarum*

CHAPTER I

1 *Provincia* was the Latin word for a big subject territory overseas. The Romans normally used *colonia* in the technical sense that is the subject of this study; but they sometimes used it more informally, as for instance when referring to non-Roman and even non-Italian peoples, such as Gauls (Caes., *B.G.*, VI. 24) or Germans (Tac., *Germ.*, 41)

2 The Romans often seized one-third of the defeated enemy's land, but sometimes more (as in the Ager Bruttius or Ager Gallicus) and sometimes less (as in the Paeligni country)

Often it was the well-to-do who exploited the *ager publicus*, but Italians could also lease it, and frequently its original owners remained on it, perhaps for many years, until the Roman authorities decided what to do with it

3 Viritane settlers resemble American homesteaders to some extent. Examples of such land settlement are numerous: viritane distributions followed Camillus' conquest of Veii (396), the Latin War (338), Dentatus' defeat of the Sabini (290), the expulsion of the Senones (283), the victory over Hannibal (202), etc.

4 This study deals only with Roman colonization in this technical sense. It does not treat of forcible transfers of population, such as those of Picentes or Ligures to southern Italy, important though these were in their effects. Much less does it deal with private ventures of the kind attempted by Sittius at Cirta in Numidia, which was clearly the work of an outlaw (Caes., *B. Afr.*, 25, 96; App., *B.C.*, IV. 54). No doubt private migration occurred in ancient Italy, as well as in modern America or Australia, and with similar consequences: but it is beyond the scope of this book

5 There are obvious resemblances between the colonies of the Romans and those of the Greeks: the Locrian colony at Naupactus *c.* 460, for instance, is in some respects almost startlingly like a Latin colony (*SIG* I^4. 47 [=p. 59]), and the similarity between a Citizen colony and an Athenian cleruchy has often been noted (see, for instance, B. Levick, *Roman Colonies in Southern Asia Minor* [1967], 1). But Greek colonies were different in purpose, and were more a matter of private enterprise, and were much less closely bound to their founding state

6 The description 'urban commonwealth' does not entirely suit the earliest Citizen colonies: nevertheless they were organized communities in a way that the settlements resulting from a viritane distribution (*fora*, *conciliabula*) were not

7 References to Roman colonies on Corsica and Sardinia in the fourth century (Theophr., *H.P.*, V. 8. 1; Diod., XV. 27. 4) must be in error

8 App., *B.C.*, I. 7; the statement was written in the second century AD, but it is confirmed by other writers both before and after that date. *Cf.*, for example, Serv., *ad Aen.* I. 12: *colonia dicta est a colendo*, etc.

9 The quotation is from Siculus Flaccus, *de cond. agr.*, p. 135, 20. Before *c.* 107 paupers did not serve in the Roman army. Colonists are usually described in military terms: *pedites*, *equites*, *centuriones*, *supplementum*, *ascribere* (Livy XXVI. 36. 12; XXVII. 50. 6; XXXI. 49. 6; XXXIV. 56. 8; XXXVI. 2. 9; XXXVII. 47. 2; Ascon., *in Pis.* p. 3 Cl.)

10 Livy XXXIX. 55. 5; Ascon., *in Pis.*, p. 3 Cl. (*duo porro genera coloniarum*). Mommsen, *St. R.*, III. 793, conjectured that there was a third type (*coloniae peregrinorum*), but this view is not accepted

11 The source for the list of colonies in Velleius I. 14, 15 is unknown: it does not distinguish Latin colonies from Citizen and its inadequacies are not entirely due to the fact that Velleius' is 'one of the most corrupt among the surviving texts of classical authors' (F. W. Shipley, *Velleius Paterculus*, LCL, xix); to give one example, it prefers 177 to Livy's 194 as the date for

Puteoli: yet epigraphy confirms Livy (*ILS* 5317). Livy was obviously interested in colonization, possibly because of the large amount of it carried out in his own lifetime by Julius Caesar and Augustus, and his information is generally trustworthy: *cf.* A. N. Sherwin-White, *Rom. Citizenship* (1939), 3 'Livy often describes events in phraseology which seems to have changed little from the first recording—oral or written—of the matter in question'; and note the remarks of G. Tibiletti in *Athenaeum* XXVIII (1950), 185. Cicero's immediate concern, of course, was with the colonies of his own day; but he says much incidentally about earlier foundations and it has the ring of truth (P. L. MacKendrick in *Athenaeum* XXXII [1954], 201–249, especially 223). Strabo and Pliny had Agrippa's famous map available as a source. Augustus' activity also takes up much of the space in the Liber Coloniarum portion of the Gromatici Veteres (this latter name derived, obviously, from *groma* [='the surveyor's plane-table']). New light from inscriptions is always possible and not merely for colonies of the Empire: in 1935 evidence was found of a late republican colony near Ausculum in southern Italy (A. Degrassi, *ILLRP*, II 592 [=p. 85]). Ptolemy and the Itineraries also give occasional help for identifying colonies. E. Kornemann in *R.E.* IV (1901) s.v. 'Coloniae', 514–560 lists the known *coloniae*. But a definitive catalogue is impossible

12 Aul. Gell. XVI. 13. 9

13 Under the Empire a *territorium* of 500 square miles seems to have been by no means unusual and it may even have been smaller than the average

14 For the *lex coloniae* see Livy VIII. 16. 14; XXXII. 29. 3; Cic., *Phil.*, XIII. 31; *de leg. agr.*, II. 17; *ILS* 6087 (=*CIL* II. 5439), the only surviving colonial charter, from Urso in Spain; Mommsen, *St. R.*, II³. 626

15 That the Senate really decided on colonization throughout most of the Republic is indicated by Livy VIII. 16. 14; IX. 26. 3; 28. 8; XXXVII. 46. 10; XLIII. 17. 1; Vell. I. 14. 1

16 For the election of commissioners and for their *imperium* see Livy IX. 28. 8; X. 21. 9; XXXIV. 53. 2; XXXVII. 46. 10; Cic., *de leg. agr.*, II. 31. It seems to have been exceptional for a consul, such as Sempronius Longus or Gaius Marius, to act as commissioner (Livy XXXIV. 45. 2; Cic., *pro Balbo*, 48) or for plebeian tribunes to preside at the election of the commissioners (Cic., *de leg. agr.*, II. 17). For the head commissioner see Cic., *de div.*, 102; J. Carcopino, *Autour des Gracques* (1925), 125f, who uses a passage in App., *B.C.*, I. 9 to argue that the commissioners took it in turns to be head, each serving in that capacity for one year

17 Many names of founding commissioners (*tresviri coloniae deducendae* [*agroque dividundo*]) are recorded by Livy, Festus, Asconius, and inscriptions. They come from a very large number of *gentes* (forty-seven, according to P. L. MacKendrick in *Athenaeum* XXXII 1954, 225). Sometimes they numbered more than three, as for example at Venafrum in imperial times, where there were five (Lib. Colon. p. 239, 7); but usually the larger

commissions (*viri agris iudicandis adsignandis*) were employed for viritane distributions (*cf.* Cic., *de leg. agr.*, II. 17)

18 Polyb. III. 40. 8f; Livy XXI. 25. 3–7; XXVII. 21. 10; XXX. 19. 9

19 By Augustus' day (27 BC–AD 14) *coloniae* were regularly Roman (i.e. Citizen): hence what is known of foundation procedures really applies to Citizen colonies. But archaeological evidence, at Cosa for instance, implies that the foundation of a Latin colony was similar; and Livy's description of the colonization of Ardea in 442 (IV. 11. 5) indicates that in his opinion even a *Prisca Latina Colonia* was planted in the same way

20 For the *centuria* see Varro, *L.L.*, V. 35; Festus p. 46, 47 L.; each side measured 20 *actus* (=2,400 Roman feet). The Gromatici Veteres regard it as the standard section in a Roman survey

21 A *iugerum* was the amount of land that a yoke of two oxen could plough in one day (Pliny, *N.H.*, XVIII. 9). For two *iugera* as the *heredium* of a Roman citizen see Varro, *R.R.*, I. 10: Pliny, *N.H.*, XVIII. 7; Juv. 14. 163; Sic. Flaccus, *de cond. agr.*, p. 153, 26; *cf.* Cic., *de re pub.*, II. 26; Dion. Hal. II. 74; Plut., *Numa* 16; E. De Ruggiero in *Diz. Epigr.* s.v. 'Colonia', 435–437

22 Ideally the principal *decumanus* might be forty feet wide: Hyginus Grom., *de mun. cast.*, p. 76, 77 L

23 On centuriation see further F. Castagnoli, *Ricerche sui Resti delle Centuriazione* (1958); O. A. W. Dilke in *G. &R.*, ser. 2, IX (1962), 170–180

24 Suet., *Dom.*, 9. 3

25 At Luceria it seems to belong to the Gracchan period: J. S. P. Bradford in *Antiquity* XXIV (1950), 84–95. There is a good specimen of centuriation at Zara (=Iader, where Augustus was *parens coloniae* [*CIL* III. 2907]) in Yugoslavia. Comparatively little of it has been found in Britain

26 Cicero, *pro Caecina* 98, says that Roman citizens joined Latin colonies either of their own free will or to escape a penalty imposed by law. By this, Cicero does not mean that Roman citizens were fined if they were told to join a Latin colony and refused to go, but that Roman citizens already threatened with a sentence for some other offence could escape it by joining a Latin colony and availing themselves of its *ius exilii*

27 The use of the *cinctus Gabinus* and the observance of Etruscan religious practices emphasize the solemnity of the occasion. In fact the ceremonies were identical with those used by the Roman censors when they were formally bringing the five-year period known as a lustrum to a close, and they were believed to have been instituted by Romulus when he founded Rome. Undoubtedly the ritual prescribed by the *Etrusca disciplina* was very old: it was said to have been laid down by the mythical Vegoia. See Varro, *L.L.*, V. 143; Cic., *de leg. agr.*, II. 85; *Phil.*, II. 102; Verg., *Aen.*, V. 755; Ovid, *Fasti* IV. 819–836; Festus p. 270, 310 L.; Plut., *Rom.*, 11; Grom. Vett. p. 350 L.; Hyginus Grom., *de lim.*, p. 113, 176, 199; Sic. Flaccus p. 156, 10f.

When assigning the allotments the commissioners started at the outside and worked towards the centre

28 Note how the Ligures, forcibly removed from the region of the Apuan Alps to Samnium, were assisted during their awkward period of adjustment by Rome (Livy XL. 38). *Cf.*, too, App., *Syr.* I (Antiochus providing colonists at Lysimachia with oxen, sheep and tools)

29 See in general Tac., *Ann.*, XI. 24; *ILS* 212; and in particular: for natives as *coloni*, Livy VIII. 14. 8 (Antium), Dig. 50, 15, 8, 7 (Caesarea Stratonis), Paus. VII. 18. 7 and *CIL* III. 2756 (Patrae); for natives as *incolae*, *ILS* 6753 (Augusta Praetoria); for 'double communities', J. Johnson, *Exc. at Minturnae*, I, 2 (Minturnae), *CIL* X, p. 182 and Livy XXIV. 7. 10 (Puteoli), Cic., *pro Sulla* 62 (Pompeii), Livy XXXIV. 9. 1 (Emporiae)

30 F. Castagnoli in *Mem. dei Linc.*, ser. 7, IV (1943), 83–118; I. A. Richmond and C. E. Stevens in *JRS* XXXII (1942), 65f. A linen copy of the *forma* was apparently kept in the *tabularium* at Rome

31 Known birthdays of colonies: Brundisium, 5 August 244 (Cic., *ad Att.*, IV. 1. 4); Placentia, 31 May 218 (Ascon., *in Pis.* p. 3 Cl.); Bononia, 30 December 189 (Livy XXXVII. 57. 7)

32 Antium seems to have had a turf rampart rather than a stone wall, and this would heighten its resemblance to a Roman military camp. Military camps, however, were normally square rather than rectangular

33 *Cf.* the quotation from Aul. Gellius, p. 18

34 B. D. Meritt in *AJA* XXXI (1927), 452; J. Johnson, *Exc. at Minturnae* I, 41; B. Levick, *Roman Colonies in Southern Asia Minor*, 76f

35 Livy XXII. 14. 3

Appendix to Chapter I

36 How the site acquired the name Ansedonia is not known. It has had several changes of ownership since late antiquity; the Sienese, the Saracens, the Abbey delle Tre Fontane have been masters of the place for longer or shorter periods; and there has been sporadic occupation of the hill from time to time (a community of monks, for instance, lived there for a while and transformed the Capitolium into a Christian church). See F. E. Brown in *Mem. Amer. Acad. Rome*, XX (1951), 16–113 and XXVI (1960), 10–14; F. Castagnoli *ibid.* XXIV (1956), 149–165 and in *Studies Presented to D. M. Robinson*, I. 389–391: P. L. MacKendrick, *The Mute Stones Speak* (1960), 98–115

37 Rutilius, *de reditu suo* I. 285f; Pliny, *N.H.* III. 51; Fasti Triumph. *ad an.* 280; Strabo V. 2. 8, p. 225; Tac., *Ann.*, II. 39; Verg., *Aen.*, X. 168; H. H. Scullard, *The Etruscan Cities and Rome* (1967), 276

The port, which has long since become completely filled with earth, was protected from the open sea immediately to the south of it by a line of petrified dunes stretching from west to east. Ships could get into the port by going north around the western end of these dunes where there was a channel hugging the cliffs of the hill of Cosa immediately to the west. In origin the channel was probably a natural cleft through the dunes, but the

Romans had scarped and straightened its sides to a height of over 75 feet. To prevent the channel from silting up the Romans constructed two long stone jetties that ran out to sea for about 100 yards parallel with the line of petrified dunes; the jetties were on either side of the entrance to the channel and served as breakwaters. More important were two sluiceways, each with an intake immediately south of the entrance to the channel and with another intake (or outlet) at the open sea still further south. The sea tides could be made to race through these sluiceways and scour away any silt that, despite the breakwaters, had managed to accumulate at the channel entrance. The one sluiceway, the Spacco della Regina, was a natural but narrow cleft through the rocks: the Romans gouged it out to a uniform depth and made its sides straight and vertical; it is almost 300 yards long and about 2 yards wide on the average. The other sluiceway, the Tagliata Etrusca, was wholly artificial. It was a narrow canal, part trench, part tunnel, which the Romans had laboriously cut through the rocks: it is about 75 yards long and 4 yards wide on the average. The seaward end of either sluiceway is in deep water well beyond the region of silting, and sluicegates controlled the rush of the waters. Fallen masonry blocked the sluiceways centuries ago, so that today the silting up is pretty complete. Nevertheless the ship channel and its entrance are still clearly discernible, and excavation is gradually disclosing the port installations

38 The battlements that crowned the wall at Cosa have not survived. One of the towers, in the north-eastern section of the wall, is now circular: it had, however, been square originally. Santa Maria di Fálleri has towers but is not really analogous, since its walls are of ashlar type and in tufa: Telesia, with wall and round towers in *opus incertum*, resembles Cosa more closely, but it is much later (time of Sulla: *CIL* IX. 2235). The polygonal wall at Saturnia is of travertine instead of the normal limestone

39 Strabo V. 2. 6, p. 223

40 According to Servius (*ad. Aen.* I. 422), an Italic *iusta urbs* was one *in qua tres portae erant dedicatae et tot viae et tot templa*. Cosa had three principal streets (two *decumani* and one *kardo*) and three principal temples (the Capitolium on the citadel, temple A near the north-west gateway, and one at the eastern extremity of the town). Besides the three gateways it also had a small postern, at the western end of the citadel: Alba Fucens had one too

41 Cosa displays none of the brick, concrete, *opus reticulatum*, or marble that a town of the Empire almost invariably shows in abundance: the materials and the structural methods used there remind one of the Citizen colony of Tarracina. Nor did Cosa have a theatre or amphitheatre or even a monumental baths (the bath at the centre of the town was quite small)

42 Later, at Placentia and Cremona (218) for example, square blocks rather than rectangular became the rule, inside the town wall as well as in the centuriated *territorium*

43 The long side of the basilica regularly faced the forum: so at Rome, Ardea,

Alba Fucens and elsewhere. The Vitruvius reference is I. 6. 1. On the forums in early colonies see J. Russell in *Phoenix* XXIII (1968), 304–336

44 The precinct wall was an integral part of the whole layout: it had been planned and built simultaneously with the town wall

45 Signia had a large circular reservoir, it too lined with *opus signinum*, immediately behind its Capitolium. At Cosa the rainwater, which the cisterns and reservoirs were designed to catch, has left archaeological evidence of its presence: in the rock at the base of the Capitolium one can see a groove cut by the run-off of water from the wide overhang of the temple roof. The quotation is from Vitruvius I. 7. 1

46 Thucyd., I. 10

47 Only *decumani* can be discerned, and the grid of streets in the town is not aligned with them, although the axis of the Capitolium is (which means that at Cosa, as in other colonies, the centuriation of the *territorium* is in some way related to the town proper)

48 It is true that Placentia and Cremona, when reinforced in 190, received fifty per cent of their original complement. But they were a very special case. They had been particularly exposed to Gallic and Ligurian assault ever since 218 and had lost many settlers through enemy action, flight and (in the case of Placentia) capture. Proportionately both these places must have needed strengthening much more badly than Cosa

49 Cic., *pro Font.*, 13

CHAPTER II

50 See Livy I. 3. 7; 14. 11; 27. 3; IV. 37. 2; 49. 7; V. 33. 8; VII. 27. 2; Strabo V. 2. 10, p. 227; [Aur. Vict.], *Orig.*, 17. According to Dionysius of Halicarnassus (II. 16. 1–3), the *colonia* was invented by Romulus. From their earliest days the Romans must have been familiar with the Sacred Spring (*ver sacrum*), a colonizing usage of the Italic peoples; all the animals, including the human ones, born in a certain year, might be dedicated to a god; the human babies thus dedicated were obliged to migrate on reaching manhood and seek new homes elsewhere (E. T. Salmon, *Samnium and the Samnites* [1967], 35f)

51 In the very early Republic Rome seems to have had separate treaties with Gabii, Lavinium and the Hernici, all of whom participated presumably in the liberation of Latium

52 In imperial times Latin rights (Ius Latii) were customarily extended to those who gave promise of becoming latinized: this was one of the principal ways of promoting romanization and its importance can hardly be overstressed

53 The relevant texts are: for *Priscae Latinae Coloniae*, Festus p. 276 L. (*cf.* Livy I. 3. 7); for *Coloniae Romanae*, Livy I. 27. 3; 56. 3; II. 31. 4; 34. 6; III. 1. 5; IV. 17. 1; V. 24. 4; 29. 3; VI. 16. 6; 21. 4; 22. 8; 30. 9; VII. 42. 8;

VIII. 3. 9. Add Diod. XII. 34. 5; XIV. 34. 7; 102. 4; Dion. Hal. IV. 63. 1; VI. 43. 1; IX. 59. 2; Velleius I. 14. 2; Suet., *Vit.*, 1. 3. Suessa Pometia is not listed as one of the fourteen since Livy's mention of a Latin colony there (II. 16. 8) is an error, arising out of confusion with Suessa Aurunca (colonized after 338).

In recording these colonizations Livy does not mention the previous owners of the territory in the way that he regularly does later when describing genuinely Roman foundations. He also does not seem to have found any certain Roman record concerning the colonization in this period of Setia (he appears doubtful whether to assign it to 383 or 379: VI. 21. 4; 30. 9) or of Sutrium (he does not record its foundation and later calls it an 'ally': IX. 32. 1, with which contrast Diod. XX. 35. 1). Note, too, that at Ardea the settlers included more Rutuli (=Latini) than Romans (Livy IV. 11. 4) and that in the Latin War Circeii and Setia led the opposition to Rome (Livy VIII. 3. 9). All this suggests that these colonizations resulted from Latin rather than Roman decision, especially in regions threatened by the Volsci

54 These colonies were intended to be protections for the city, as Livy (I. 56. 3) says of Signia and Circeii: Cicero (*de leg. agr.* II. 73) similarly calls the early colonies 'bulwarks of empire rather than towns of Italy'. Cicero adds that the abiding habit of the Romans was to place their colonies on suitable sites: in pre-Gracchan times this usually meant a hill or mountain-top, although less defensible sites would be used if strategically useful; Interamna, Paestum, Ariminum and Brundisium are examples. Actually two of the *Priscae Latinae Coloniae* were on relatively low-lying sites, Vitellia and Satricum: both had been destroyed well before 338

55 Circeii and Setia: see Livy VIII. 3–6

56 By Campani the people of Capua and her immediate dependencies, such as Calatia and Atella, are meant

57 Latium Antiquum (Old Latium) stretched from the Tiber to the headland of Circeii; Latium Adjectum (Enlarged Latium) was the area south-east of this as far as the River Savo (Pliny, *N.H.*, III. 56–59). For the sake of simplicity the region north-west of the Tiber, as far as Sutrium and Nepet, is here spoken of as if it, too, were part of Latium Adjectum

58 For an excellent, up-to-date account of the settlement at the end of the Latin War see A. J. Toynbee, *Hannibal's Legacy* (1965), I, 115–258

59 For the dual citizenship of the inhabitants of *municipia* see Cic., *de legg.*, II. 5; Festus p. 126 L.; Aul. Gell. XVI. 13. 6. Perhaps the early incorporation of Tusculum explains why a number of its native sons won the consulship at Rome. The view that Caere was the first *municipium sine suffragio* has now been exploded (see M. Sordi, *I Rapporti Romano-Ceriti* [1960], *passim*). References to the Campani in Diodorus (XIX. 76. 5) and Livy (IX. 6. 4; XXII. 13. 2 and many other passages) as 'allies' are not proof that Capua was not a *municipium sine suffragio*

60 On this view one of these three towns, rather than Neapolis (Naples), was the earliest *civitas foederata*. Tibur and Praeneste both had dependencies of their own (Livy VI. 29. 6; VII. 18. 2; 19. 1). The allied status of Cora is established by *CIL* I². 2. 1513 and by its coins: after 338 it was not a Latin colony (Mommsen in *CIL* X, p. 645)

61 Livy (XXXII. 2. 6f and XLIII. 17. 1) shows that Roman authorization was needed for additional settlers.

There is general agreement today that the Roman ban on social and commercial intercourse between the Latin states was of short duration (A. N. Sherwin-White, *Roman Citizenship*, 31f, 107), but there is no evidence when it was lifted. Nor is there certain information about the number of troops a Latin colony supplied to the army *ex formula togatorum*: G. Vitucci (in *Riv. di Fil.*, XXXI, 1953, 49f) guessed five hundred in the case of one founded in 244. In any event, the troops supplied by the Latini served in their own formations and under their own officers, just like *socii* from the *civitates foederatae*. But Cicero (*de har. res.*, 19), Livy (XXXVIII. 44. 4; XL. 42. 4) and official Roman documents (*SC de Bacch.* 7, 8; *Lex Agr.* 29, 31) make it clear that technically the Latini were not regular *socii*, even though in law they were *peregrini* (Gaius I. 79).

That the word Latini could be used non-technically with the meaning of 'inhabitants of Latium' is shown by Livy (XXXIV. 42. 5) who uses it of Hernici and by Florus (I. 5. 11) who uses it of Aequi and Volsci

62 Livy (XXVII. 9) implies that only Latin colonists were technically Latini. Polybius (VI. 14. 8) regards Tibur and Praeneste as *civitates foederatae*. Cicero (*pro Balbo* 53) mentions two Tiburtines who acquired Roman citizenship by successfully prosecuting Romans: had they been Latini they would have been Roman citizens already as ex-local magistrates (*cf.* L. R. Taylor, *Voting Districts of the Roman Republic*, [1960], 107, n. 19). Livy (XXIII. 17. 8; XXVI. 8. 10; XLII. 1. 6) and Appian (*B.C.*, I. 62) clearly distinguish Praenestines from Latini (*cf.*, too, *CIL* I. 1116, 1118); but then their speech had always set them apart (Plaut., *Truc.* 691; Varro, *L.L.* VI. 4; Quint. I. 5. 56). The Roman attitude towards Tibur and Praeneste (about Cora we have no information) was harsher than towards the Latin colonies: compare, for instance the courteous treatment of Aquileia (Livy XLIII. 1. 5 and 17. 1) with the arrogance of senatorial behaviour towards Tibur (*ILS* 19) or with the repeated Roman bullying of Praeneste (Livy IX. 16. 17; Val. Max. I. 3. 1; App., *B.C.*, I. 94)

63 Ardea is the only apparent exception and may not really be one: the establishment of the seven Latin colonies may have coincided with the planning of an eighth, Cales (founded, unpaired, in 334).

The pair were normally in the same region of Italy and sometimes even conterminous: Minturnae, Sinuessa (295); Placentia, Cremona (218); Potentia, Pisaurum (184). But the pair occasionally might be widely separated: Cosa, Paestum (273); Ariminum, Beneventum (268);

Sipontum, Buxentum (194). Mixed pairs, one Citizen and one Latin, were rare

64 See A. J. Toynbee, *Hannibal's Legacy*, I, 209, 140; P. Fraccaro in *Enciclopedia Italiana* s.v. 'Colonizzazione', 834; *cf.* A. N. Sherwin-White, *Roman Citizenship*, 94

CHAPTER III

65 For the foundation of Cales see Livy VIII. 16; Velleius I. 14. 3. Livy (IX. 24. 15; 26. 4; X. 1. 2; XXVII. 9. 11) implies that the overwhelming majority of the settlers for Latin colonies came from the Roman citizen body, before 200 at least: after that date the situation probably changed radically: see p. 96. For their loss of Roman citizenship see Cic., *de domo* 78; *pro Caec.*, 98; Gaius I. 31; III. 56. That the non-Roman settlers could include others besides ethnic Latini is shown by the persons with Oscan names at Paestum (A. Degrassi, *Scritti Vari* [1967], III. 338), by Dasius the native Brundisine (Polyb., III. 69. 1; Livy XXI. 48. 9), by the Gallic character of the population of Placentia (Cic., *in Pis.*, 53), and by the reinforcements at Cosa in 197 who came from anywhere in Italy (Livy XXXIII. 24. 8). Of course, after 338 the Roman citizen body was not composed exclusively of ethnic Romans or even of speakers of Latin

66 The expression Ius Latii for the Latin status first occurs in Asconius; under the Empire it was often called, simply, *Latium*; the expression *Latinitas*, on the other hand, is very rare, found only in Cic., *ad Att.*, XIV. 12. 1 and Suet., *Aug.*, 47. 1

67 It is also possible that Cales was meant to round out the number of Latin colonies to eight, that is four pairs (see note 63). There are, however, other instances of colonies being planted singly when they were distant: for example, Luceria, Venusia, Brundisium

68 Cic., *de leg. agr.*, II. 73. Undoubtedly the colonies were often offensive bases (as, for example, Placentia against the Ligures: Livy XXXIX. 2. 10); some of them, however, were founded on territory that had long been under Roman domination but that was not colonized until an enemy demonstrated its vulnerability: Suessa Aurunca, Sora, Minturnae, Sinuessa, Brundisium, Alsium, Fregenae, and perhaps Spoletium are examples. Saturnia and Auximum are cases where the territory had been Roman an exceptionally long period before its colonization. Note, too, the words of Horace, *Sat.*, II. 1. 35–37: 'As the ancient story has it, after the Samnites had been expelled, colonists were sent for this purpose: to prevent an enemy from ever attacking the Romans across an undefended boundary.'

For the efficacy of the colonies see A. J. Toynbee, *Hannibal's Legacy*, I, 157

69 Livy VIII. 19. 1; 22. 2: the number of settlers is unrecorded but was prob-

ably the same as at Cales immediately preceding and at Luceria immediately succeeding, namely 2,500

70 Livy VIII. 21. 11; Velleius I. 14. 4. Tarracina was a Citizen colony; but there seems to be at least one other example of a Latin colony being paired with a Citizen: Hadria and Sena Gallica (note also Firmum and Castrum, which, however, may not have been intended as a pair)

71 There were three Samnite Wars: 343–341, 326–304 (with a five-year armistice, 321–316), 298–290; and the Pyrrhic War (284–270) virtually makes a fourth. The four Samnite tribes were leagued together in a confederation which the Romans ultimately encircled and dismembered by means of colonies

72 Livy IX. 26. 1; Diod. XIX. 72. 8; Cic., *ad Att.*, VII. 20; VIII. 1; 11a. Velleius' date for Luceria, 323 (I. 14. 4), is wrong. The colony dated officially from the moment when the foundation was complete, which was in 314 according to Livy

73 Festus p. 458 L.; Livy IX. 28. 7–8; Diod. XIX. 101. 3; 105. 5; Velleius I. 14. 4 (date inaccurate). The colonies also kept a watchful eye on Aurunci and others who had rebelled after Lautulae

74 King Philip V of Macedon was convinced that freedmen were enrolled in the Roman colonies: Dittenberger, *SIG* 2⁴. 543, 26 (=p. 20)

75 The expression is copied from the famous saying of Philip of Macedon (Polyb. XVII [XVIII]. 11. 5)

76 For these four colonies see Livy X. 1. 1; 3. 2; 9. 8; Velleius I. 14. 5 (Livy IX. 24. 5 seems to suggest 315 as the date for Sora; but at that time the place was garrisoned, not colonized: Diod. XIX. 72. 3). The Fabian *gens* may have been strongly in favour of these colonies, but even without Fabian urging, the military need was self-evident, and it called for a prodigious effort.

The Via Salaria dated from prehistoric times; the Via Valeria from 306 (Livy IX. 43. 25)

77 To the Romans Nequinum sounded too much like *nequam*, their word for 'worthless'. Their habit of bestowing new names upon the places that they colonized later assumed extravagant forms. They called their colonies after personified abstractions (Copia, Virtus, etc.) or by names formed from fair-sounding adjectives (Firmum, Placentia, etc.) or from deities (Saturnia, Neptunia, etc.) or from colony founders (Mariana, Julia, etc.), and under the Empire the official title of a colony might consist of a combination of such names. See pp. 119, 122, 130, 145

78 Livy X. 3. 2; 13. 1

79 The expression is that of A. J. Toynbee, *Hannibal's Legacy* I, 151

80 Velleius I. 14. 6; Dion. Hal. XVII/XVIII. 5, who says that 20,000 settlers were sent to Venusia, an impossibly high number. Venusia probably got the same number as Alba Fucens, 6,000. So far as is known, it was not one of a pair of colonies

81 The name, no doubt originally unaspirated, appears as Hatria on its coins, but inscriptions show that Hadria became the accepted Roman spelling. Whether it was this town or the Atria much further north that gave its name to the sea has been much discussed. The date of the colony is quite uncertain. Curius Dentatus, according to Florus (I. 15. 2), marched like Sherman all the way to the sea in 290, and Livy (*Epit*. XI) places the colonization immediately afterwards, coupling it with that of Castrum and Sena. Polyb. II. 19. 12, however, seems to assign Sena to 283, and Castrum may belong to 264 (see p. 79). The number of settlers at Hadria may well have been 4,000 (A. Bernardi in *Nuova Riv. Stor.* XXX [1946], 278)

82 If, however, Hadria belonged to 289 and Sena to 283 (see note 81), they obviously did not form a pair. The difficulty is to decide whether one or both these colonies came before or after the Roman defeat at Arretium, *c.* 284

83 *de leg. agr.*, II. 73

84 Livy, *Epit*. XIV; Velleius I. 14. 7. The town wall at Cosa extended for about 1,500 yards, that at Paestum more than three times that distance.

85 Beneventum: Livy, *Epit*. XV; cf. IX. 27. 14; Velleius I. 14. 7; Eutrop. II. 16. Aesernia: Livy, *Epit*. XVI; Velleius I. 14. 8

86 Livy, *Epit*. XV; Velleius I. 14. 7; Eutrop. II. 16. It is to be noted that the next *tumultus Gallicus* took place on the Tyrrhenian and not on the Adriatic side of Italy

87 But Velleius (I. 14. 8), our only authority for the foundation of Firmum, couples it with Castrum rather than with Aesernia. The colony could have had 4,000 settlers (A. Afzelius, *Die röm. Eroberung Italiens* [Copenhagen, 1942] 124f). Nearby Falerio always resented Firmum, down even to the days of the Empire (*CIL* X. 5420 [=p. 517]): but boundary disputes between colonies and their neighbours were not unusual: Livy XLV. 13. 10; Frontinus Grom. II p. 46 L

88 Brundisium was founded on 5 August (Cic., *ad Att.*, IV. 1. 4) in the consulship of Torquatus and Sempronius, 244 (Velleius I. 14. 8). Livy, *Epit*. XIX seems to assign it to 246, but agrees with Velleius that it came immediately after Fregenae.

The Via Appia had been built from Rome to Capua *c.* 312, and was probably extended to Brundisium some time after 267 when the Romans captured the seaport (Zonaras VIII. 7)

89 The 4,000 Oscan-speaking naval allies recorded by Zonaras (VIII. 11) and Orosius (IV. 7. 12)

90 Velleius I. 14. 8; Livy, *Epit*. XX; *cf.* Cic., *pro Balbo*, 48. The territory had evidently been acquired by Rome half a century earlier: K. J. Beloch, *Röm. Geschichte* (1926), 443, 604

91 Polyb. I. 65; Livy, *Epit*. XIX; Zonaras VIII. 18; Eutrop. II. 28; Orosius IV. 11. Livy appears to have placed the colonization of Spoletium after the revolt of Falerii

92 Polyb. III. 90. 7; Livy XXIII. 42. 3

93 Admittedly Flaminius crossed the Po; but Julius Caesar also crossed the Rhine long before there was any serious Roman intention of permanent conquest there

94 Polyb. III. 40; Livy, *Epit.* XX; XXI. 52. 2; Velleius I. 14. 8. Polybius calls Mutina a colony on this occasion, but must be in error: Mutina was a Roman garrison town at this time.

Ascon. p. 3 Cl. and Tac., *Hist.* III. 34 agree with Livy XXXI. 47. 6 that the purpose of Placentia and Cremona was to oppose the Gauls

Appendix to Chapter III

95 *JRS* IX (1919), 205f

96 Ascon. p. 3 Cl.; Mommsen, *Röm. Münzw.*, 860. For the colonial commissioners see Broughton, *MRR* I. 240–242, 359

97 Cic., *Phil.*, II. 102

98 Livy XXXI. 49. 6; XXXII. 2. 6f; XXXIII. 24. 8f; XXXVII. 46. 10f

99 See p. 97

100 In somewhat the same way his master Cicero mistook the second consulship of Fabius Cunctator in 228 for his first in 233 (*Cato Maior* 11)

101 Dittenberger, *SIG* II⁴. 543, 26 (=p. 20)

102 *Hermes* XVII (1882), 479f

103 Livy I. 43. 2; *Epit.* XX

CHAPTER IV

104 That is, if one can assume that an early Citizen colony was a self-administering body: Livy XXVII. 38. 4 regards them as *populi*

105 Aul. Gell. XVI. 13. 6f: '*Municipes* accordingly are Roman citizens from *municipia*: they enjoy their own laws and their own rights and merely share a special privilege with the Roman People (it is from this *munus*, so it would seem, that they derive their name); they are bound by no restrictions and by no law of the Roman People other than what their own community has formally ratified . . . (8) But the relationship of the *coloniae* is different. They do not come into the Roman citizenship from outside, nor do they sprout from roots of their own; but they are, so to speak, generated out of the citizen body and they have all the laws and institutions of the Roman People, and not those of their own choosing'

106 Cic., *de domo* 75; *pro Sest.* 32; *in Pis.* 51; *Phil.* II. 58; IV. 7

107 Siculus Flaccus p. 135 L.: 'Accordingly the Romans placed settlers on these shores to guard the coasts of Italy, . . . and they called them all *coloniae maritimae*.' Similarly Livy (XXVII. 38. 3; XXXVI. 3. 4) refers to the settlers as *coloni maritimi*

108 Livy I. 33. 9; Dion. Hal. III. 44. 4; it is the secondary writers like Florus (I. 4. 2) who call Ancus' settlement a *colonia*. Terracotta fragments of *c.* 425

have been found at Ostia. See R. Meiggs, *Ostia* (1960), 16–27. Fortification of Ostia seemed indicated when a group of Etrusci and Falisci menaced it in 355 (Livy VII. 17. 6) and when Greek ships cruised off it in 348 (Livy VII. 25. 4). Probably the Romans were more concerned to protect the salt-pans on the right bank than the anchorage at the river mouth: the latter did not become important until the late Republic (Cic., *de re pub.* II. 10; Strabo V. 3. 5, p. 231) and it was in the early Empire under Augustus and Claudius that harbour installations were built

109 The *castra* at Pyrgi and Minturnae were of about the same size as the one at Ostia. It may be just a coincidence that the Senate in early Rome also seems to have numbered 300

110 G. Tibiletti in *Athenaeum* XXVIII (1950), 223. Two *iugera* are also recorded for the *Prisca Latina Colonia* at Labici (Livy IV. 17. 7) and two and a half *iugera* for the one at Satricum (Livy VI. 16. 6; *cf.*, too, Livy VI. 36. 11; VIII. 11. 4). S. V. Pearson, *Growth and Distribution of Population* (1935), 144f, estimates that 4½ acres (=roughly 6½ *iugera*) are needed to support an average family at subsistence level. (The allotments in viritane distributions were larger than those in the maritime colonies.) For *compascua* in Citizen colonies see Siculus Flaccus, *de cond. agr.*, p. 157, 7. But even with them it is hard to visualize the maritime colonists in an agrarian role: their coast-guard function may have included supervision of harbour dues, prevention of smuggling and draining of marshes (at places like Ostia, Liternum and Sipontum)

111 For example, one fortieth (5 *iugera*) at Mutina and Graviscae; *c.* one thirtieth (6½ *iugera*) at Luna; one twenty-fifth (8 *iugera*) at Parma; one twentieth (10 *iugera*) at Saturnia. Only at Potentia and Pisaurum, probably the first and therefore perhaps the most experimental of the large Citizen colonies, was the fraction intractable: *c.* one thirty-third (6 *iugera*), and even there the allotment was exactly three times the size hitherto prevailing.

A 'miniature' of Tarracina (*Pl. 3*) may give a true picture of what a centuriation was like: F. Castagnoli in *Mem. dei Linc.* ser. 7, IV (1943), 108

The *territorium* of a Latin colony was not technically *centuriatus ager* (Festus p. 47 L.) and therefore its allotments did not need to be suitable fractions of a *centuria*

112 Cic., *pro Balbo* 28, 29, says flatly that if a Roman citizen left Rome and acquired the citizenship of the place to which he migrated, he lost his Roman citizenship (and the Roman who joined a Latin colony is, of course, the classic example of this). How the *municipium* was reconciled with this provision of the civil law Cicero does not precisely explain: presumably the argument was that the burgesses of a *municipium* had not left Rome, but in a manner of speaking had come to it: Cicero points out that there were states which allowed their burgesses to acquire Roman citizenship while still retaining their own. At any rate, it is certain that in the fourth century the Romans allowed a large self-governing community living elsewhere

than at Rome to enjoy the Roman citizenship, provided that its members had not gone thither from Rome itself. By the second century the principle was extended to large communities that had emigrated from Rome itself.

113 That the Latin colonies on the coast were expected to discharge some maritime function is evident: the settlers at Paestum were *socii navales* (Livy XXVI. 39. 5), and the coins of Ariminum and Cosa, as well as the seaward-facing towers of the latter, suggest that their business was at least to some extent with the sea

114 H. Rudolph, *Stadt und Staat im röm. Italien* (1935), 130. It is to be noted that for practically every *colonia maritima* there was a Latin colony reasonably near, to lend it aid in time of trouble; and such aid was forthcoming (as, for example, when Tarracina needed help to defend the Lautulae pass in 217; Livy XXII. 15. 11)

115 For the foundation of Antium in 338 see Livy VIII. 14. 8: the details given for the *Prisca Latina Colonia* there in 467 (Livy III. 1. 7; Dion. Hal. IX. 59. 2) almost certainly belong to the later colonization. Antium was not only contemporary with Ostia, but may also have supplied the constitutional model for it (A. J. Toynbee, *Hannibal's Legacy*, I. 391). The reluctance of Roman citizens to go there is understandable. Even paupers would not find a *colonia maritima* attractive. It has sometimes been argued (for example, by E. Kornemann in *R.E.* IV [1901], s.v. 'coloniae', 572) that *proletarii* could not join the Citizen colonies since they did not form part of the *exercitus centuriatus*. If this was the case, then the reluctance of Roman citizens to join a *colonia maritima* is even more understandable. But it probably was not the case. It seems likely that the *coloni* were normally found among the landless poor, who would not have been eligible for the levy and whose subsequent exemption from legionary service did not represent a real loss for the Roman army. In the case of non-Romans who joined the colony, how could the Roman authorities know whether they were paupers or not?

116 At Minturnae, too, there was a 'double community'. The native Aurunci were physically separated from the Roman colony by a wall: J. Johnson, *Exc. at Minturnae*, I, 2

117 Polyb. III. 22. 11

118 Livy's lists are: (i) Ostia, Alsium, Antium, Anxur (=Tarracina), Minturnae, Sinuessa, Sena (XXVII. 38. 4); and (ii) Ostia, Fregenae, Castrum Novum, Pyrgi, Antium, Tarracina, Minturnae, Sinuessa (XXXVI. 3. 6). It will be noted that the first list lacks Castrum Novum, Pyrgi and Fregenae and the second lacks Alsium and Sena.

The duoviri of the colony must have taken charge in times of crisis. The colonists were not normally concerned with the fleet: Mommsen, *St. R.* III. 677 n. 1

119 Polyb. II. 19. 13; Livy, *Epit.* XI. It was suggested on pp. 62 & 78 that Sena may have been intended to form a pair with Hadria (a Latin colony).

Others have conjectured that its partner was not Hadria, but Aesis (for which see note 120). It is impossible to say whether it was founded after the end of the Third Samnite War (290) or after the Battle of Arretium (*c.* 284).

A single *colonia maritima* on the Adriatic coast is implied by Livy (XXVII. 38. 4). but has seemed inadequate to some scholars, despite the number of Latin colonies ultimately there (Hadria 289?, Ariminum 268, Firmum 264, Brundisium 244). Accordingly they argue that Castrum Novum in Picenum, the modern Giulianova, was one. Now it is true that Livy, Epit. XI, records the foundation of a Castrum [*sic*] at the same time as Sena and Hadria; and Velleius I. 14. 8 also records the foundation of a Castrum [*sic*], but he couples it with Firmum. Both authors might be referring to Castrum Novum, the *colonia maritima* at Santa Marinella in Etruria (Livy XXXVI. 3. 6). (The simultaneous mention of Castrum with Sena and Hadria or with Firmum does not necessarily mean that it was near these places any more than the coupling of Cosa with Paestum, or of Ariminum with Beneventum, means that they were neighbours.) Castrum Novum in Etruria was most certainly a colony. Castrum Novum in Picenum probably was not, in republican times at least: it could not have been a Latin colony, since it is missing from Livy's list of the Latin colonies existing at the time of the Second Punic War (Livy XXVII. 9, 10); and apparently it was not a Citizen colony either, since its chief official was a praetor (*CIL* IX. 5143 and perhaps 5073), and officials with that title are unknown in Citizen colonies before Gracchan times

120 Velleius specifically pairs Firmum with Castrum (see note 119). Pyrgi was certainly founded before 191 (Livy XXXVI. 3. 6), and probably before the Second Punic War, to judge from the activities of the rascally M. Postumius from there during that struggle (Livy XXV. 3, 4). According to Velleius I. 14. 8 an otherwise unknown Aefulum was colonized in 247. Mommsen, *Röm. Münzw.*, 332, 113, emended this to the equally unknown Aesium (the Aision of Strabo V. 2. 19, p. 227 is an error for Asision), and then argued that Aesium was the same as Aesis (Jesi), which is known to have been a *colonia* under the Empire. The emendation does not seem very likely, nor does the suggestion that Aesis was a Citizen colony in the third century at a time when all Citizen colonies were maritime: Aesis is not on the coast and is nowhere mentioned as a colony in Livy.

Possibly Velleius' text, a notoriously corrupt one, is concealing under Aefulum an allusion to Pyrgi, which as the port of Caere (*Greek* Agylla) may have been described by some such expression as Agyllanum, either with or without the word Castrum added: *cf.* Castrum Portorium (or Castrum Salerni) and Castrum Frentinum as the names respectively of the colonies at Salernum and Thurii (Livy XXXII. 7. 3; 29. 3; XXXV. 9. 7). Undoubtedly 247 would be a very suitable date for the foundation of Pyrgi

121 Livy obviously cannot work up great enthusiasm about Citizen colonies: G. Tibiletti in *Athenaeum* XXVIII (1950), 187, 198. Livy X. 21. 10 says that they were unpopular because they were 'virtually permanent outposts in enemy territory'. The tradition that they were undesirable places in which to settle persisted down to Cicero's day (*de leg.. agr.* II. 71). The difficulty of finding recruits for them in itself tells against the prevailing view that only Roman citizens were enrolled for them; non-Romans were certainly recruited for Antium in 338, for the eight Citizen colonies founded in 194, and for the two in 184

122 For the competence of the duoviri see A. N. Sherwin-White, *Roman Citizenship*, 78. It was obviously limited: the Roman consuls, praetors and censors could exercise their authority directly over Citizen colonists and the latter could invoke the aid of the plebeian tribunes (Cic., *de orat.* II. 287; Livy XXVI. 38. 3; XXXVI. 3. 5)

123 In the last century burgesses of Citizen colonies clearly must have frequented the Roman assemblies, since there is evidence that their votes were worth canvassing: Q. Cic., *Comment. Petit.*, 30; Cic., *Phil.* II. 76, 100. But by then they were no longer 'permanent outposts in enemy territory', and the participation of the colonists in meetings of the People had perhaps been made more feasible in 179. Moreover from 128 on military motives for their foundation were secondary.

On Pyrgi notables see Livy XXV. 3, 4; Cic., *de orat.* II. 287

124 *Vacatio militiae* was regarded as a privilege: *FIRA* I². 7, 70f

125 Livy XXVII. 38. 3; XXXVI. 3. 4

CHAPTER V

126 Livy XXVII. 9, 10, 38; XXXVI. 3. Livy calls the thirty Latin states *coloniae populi Romani* (XXVII. 9. 7): this does not mean that they were Citizen colonies but that they had been founded by the decision and on the authority of the Roman People

127 Varro, *R.R.* II. 4. 17; Verg., *Aen.* III. 389; VIII. 83f; *cf.* Timaeus in F. Jacoby, *Fr. Gr. Hist.* IIIb, Commentary 532. The story that there were exactly thirty communities in prehistoric Latium gained universal currency: Lycophron, *Alex.* 1255; Livy II. 18. 3; Dion. Hal. III. 31. 4; V. 61 (where, however, only twenty-nine are named)

128 A. Alföldi, *Early Rome and the Latins*, 16

129 As Latium had varied in size from time to time, variation in the membership of its leagues was inevitable. The relevant texts are Dion. Hal. IV. 49. 2; Pliny *N.H.* III. 70; Cato fr. 58 P.

For the sow and piglets, see *Pl. 19*

130 E. Pais in *Mem. dei Linc.*, ser. 5, XVII (1924), 338

131 Polyb. II. 24

132 Livy IX. 43. 25

133 H. Nissen, *Ital. Landesk.*, II. 299f., 310f.; G. Radke in *Gymnasium* XVII (1964), 204–235

134 Livy XXI. 59. 10

135 It is sometimes argued, from Livy XXV. 3. 16, that this voting privilege dates precisely from the Second Punic War, but Dion. Hal. VIII. 72. 4 thought otherwise. Years ago it was pointed out by A. H. J. Greenidge, *Roman Public Life*, 308 that the Latin states 'combined the anomalies of sovereignty and a partial Roman citizenship'

136 Cales, Suessa, Alba Fucens, Cosa, Paestum

137 The evidence for the magistrates in Latin colonies is collected by K. J. Beloch, *Röm. Gesch.*, 489–492. For a while Ariminum and Beneventum called their chief officials consuls, and occasionally the title duoviri, more usually to be found in Citizen colonies, occurs (at Paestum, Ariminum, Aesernia, Aquileia), but perhaps not always to indicate the chief local magistrates. There was also provision for a dictator in at least some Latin towns (*CIL* XI. 3257: Sutrium). The evidence for the lower officials is all later than the Social War, but it probably reflects the situation prevailing before the colonies were transformed into Roman *municipia*; it is conveniently set forth in A. N. Sherwin-White, *Roman Citizenship*, 110

138 Note how the quaestors at Paestum and at Firmum constructed buildings with money obtained from fines (*CIL* IX. 5351,=*ILS* 6132; A .Degrassi, *Scritti Vari* III. 337–343). For the powers of officials in colonies, in imperial times admittedly and therefore in Citizen colonies, see A. N. Sherwin-White, *Roman Society and Roman Law in the New Testament* (1963), 74

139 See the Appendix to this chapter, pp. 92–4

140 K. J. Beloch, *Röm. Gesch.*, 492. For the officials of a Citizen colony see A. N. Sherwin-White, *Roman Citizenship*, 84–90

141 H. Rudolph, *Stadt und Staat im röm. Italien*, 141; J. Johnson, *Exc. at Minturnae*, II. 123f. The title 'praetor' was used at Auximum in Gracchan times and praetores duoviri were serving at Narbo Martius, Abellinum, Grumentum and Telesia shortly afterwards. These titles reflect the growing assimilation of Citizen colonies to Latin which began with the foundation of large Citizen colonies in 184. 'Praetor' would be a natural title to give to a Citizen colony official who had by now acquired jurisdictional powers similar to those of his counterpart in a Latin colony, and it was certainly a much coveted title (Cic., *de leg. agr.* II. 92). But there was a very real risk that the praetor at Auximum might be confused with the praetor at Rome, and this probably explains why the immediately succeeding colonies distinguished their officials by calling them praetores duoviri. From this it was a short and swift step back to the original title of duoviri

142 *ILS* 5317 (=*CIL* X. 1781): Puteoli, a colony that certainly enjoyed a very high degree of autonomy (Cic., *de leg. agr.* II. 86). The quorum at senate meetings was 20, which presupposes a full senate of 30 (that is, at the time

of the colony's foundation one out of every ten settlers was a decurion). Two lists of decurions from Roman colonies survive, but they belong to imperial times when Citizen colonies were large establishments: *CIL* IX. 338 (Canusium in AD 223), *CIL* VIII. 2403 (Thamugadi *c.* AD 367)

143 They cannot be documented before the Social War, but this does not prove that they did not exist (contra H. Rudolph, *Stadt und Staat in röm. Italien*, 134f)

144 Capua may have taken offence when at least some Sabini obtained the full citizenship before she did; but it is more probable that Capua was more interested in disputing Rome's leadership than in acquiring Rome's citizenship: she was a large city with a history and traditions of her own and was not prepared, in the third century, to accept the inevitability of Roman domination

145 See Livy XXIII. 32. 19; XXV. 5. 6: and possibly XXIV. 18. 7. These passages suggest that the Roman authorities had serious difficulties in finding recruits in the *fora* and *conciliabula*

146 It was near Venusia that Marcellus finally met his end: Polyb. X. 32; Livy XXVII. 28; Plut., *Marc.* 29; App., *Hann.* 50; Zonaras IX. 7; Val. Max. III. 8. 1

147 Pliny, *N.H.* VII. 104f

148 It cannot be proved that the quotas of the Latini had been increased after Cannae, but note the implication of Livy XXVII. 10. 4 (Latin colonies ready to provide additional troops as needed)

149 Livy XXVI. 34. 10 makes it clear that Sutrium and Nepet were greatly depopulated by 209. It is also possible that the soldiers hitherto supplied by the recalcitrant twelve had been brigaded with the disgraced and permanently mobilized legions made up of the survivors from Cannae (Livy XXVII. 9. 1f seems to imply this). In that case their reluctance to supply any more men is understandable (A. J. Toynbee, *Hannibal's Legacy* II. 91)

150 Most modern scholars agree that the Romans fielded 25 legions in 212 and 21 in 210: see, for example, G. De Sanctis, *Storia dei Romani* III. 2. 248f

151 The magistrates of the colonies were held as hostages to ensure that the terms were carried out (Livy XXIX. 14. 5f). The terms show that Rome recognized that it might be impossible for some of these colonies to find 120 troopers. The annual tax levy was one *as* per thousand (of assessed capital?) (Livy XXIX. 15. 9), which was apparently the rate at which Roman citizens were then taxed (A. J. Toynbee, *Hannibal's Legacy*, II. 116). Hitherto no Latin colony had paid tribute to Rome: how long the twelve were obliged to go on paying it is unknown

Appendix to Chapter V

152 Cic., *pro Caec.* 102. Cicero is saying in effect that some Latin colonies might have a more favoured status than others. The punishment of the recusant twelve of 209 proves that this could indeed be the case

153 F. von Savigny, *Verm. Schriften* (1850), I. 24f; K. J. Beloch, *Ital. Bund* (1880), 155

154 *St. R.*, III. 623f

155 A. Bernardi in *Studia Ghisleriana* (1948), 237–259

156 *JRS* XXVI (1936), 58–61. A. N. Sherwin-White, *Roman Citizenship*, 98f points to other shortcomings of the theory

157 Cic., *pro Balbo* 21

158 A. J. Toynbee, *Hannibal's Legacy*, I. 404. The last communities to get *civitas sine suffragio* may have been certain Samnite towns after the Pyrrhic War: Allifae, Atina, Aufidena, Casinum and Venafrum

CHAPTER VI

159 Livy XXXII. 29. 4 says that 'families' were envisaged for the Citizen colonies authorized in 197, and it has been suggested that this means that provision was being made for veterans: B. Levick, *Roman Colonies in Southern Asia Minor*, 1. This may be reading too much into Livy: it was standard practice for *coloni* to have their families with them

160 Livy XXXI. 49. 6. Many of its inhabitants had Sabellian names: A. Degrassi, *ILLRP* II. 690–692

161 Livy XXXII. 29. 3, who makes it clear that the number of projected colonies began to be enlarged immediately, Buxentum being added. The Castrum of Livy XXXII. 7. 3 is Salernum: V. Panebianco in *Rass. Stor. Salernitana* VI (1945), 18.

For Citizen colonies as customs stations see T. Frank, *Econ. Survey of Anc. Rome*, I, 151; F. Cassola, *I Gruppi Politici Romani* (1962), 72, 389

162 Livy XXXVIII. 50–56. It was the Plebeian Assembly that formally made the decision to found the colonies, but in response to a suggestion from the Senate (Livy XXXII. 29. 3; XXXIV. 53. 1). The actual founding took place when Scipio Africanus was consul for the second time. But it should be pointed out that one of the principal founding commissioners, M. Servilius Geminus, may have belonged to the anti-Scipio faction in the Senate: F. Münzer, *Röm. Adelsparteien* (1920), 146

163 Livy XXXIV. 45. 1f; Strabo V. 4. 13, p. 251. In view of the aftermath Roman fear of the Hellenistic monarchs seems ridiculously exaggerated: yet an echo of these fears can be heard as late as Tacitus (*Ann.* IV. 56). Hannibal's destruction of places like Tempsa (Strabo VI. 1. 5, p. 256) may have caused the Romans to think that the coast was defenceless at some points

164 Livy XXXII. 29. 3

165 Livy XXXIV. 42. 5f says that among the accepted recruits for Puteoli, Salernum and Buxentum were men from Ferentinum, in other words Hernici, although he calls them Latini (meaning presumably 'inhabitants of

Latium'), and he adds that in 195 'as a result of this they began to pass themselves off as Roman citizens, whereupon the Senate ruled that they were not'. This passage has often been adduced as evidence that non-Romans were inadmissible to Citizen colonies (see, for example, A. N. Sherwin-White, *Rom. Citizenship*, 92). The true explanation is that the Ferentinates were claiming to be Roman citizens from the moment that their offer to join a Citizen colony was accepted, even though they had not yet gone to the colony or been registered by the Roman censors: the Senate ruled that they could not anticipate matters in this way (R. E. Smith in *JRS* XLIV [1954], 18–20). In 195 the Ferentinates may have been hoping that, as the colonies had been authorized in 197 and had not yet been founded, they might never have to go to them; they were looking for a short cut to the Roman citizenship

166 Liternum was a forlorn and forgotten marsh: Val. Max., V. 3. 2

167 Livy XXXII. 23. 3f: the deserters from Buxentum no doubt included the Ferentinates mentioned in note 165. The unattractiveness of Sipontum is stressed by Cic., *de leg. agr.* II. 71: one might have expected it to be the port for Arpi but marshes and silting impeded its development and contributed to its almost total disappearance later (recently it has been drained and made healthy and is consequently now becoming a fashionable seaside resort)

168 Livy XXXIV. 53. 1; XXXV. 9. 7; 40. 5; Strabo VI. 1. 13, p. 263. Velleius I. 14. 8, more than usually inaccurate, assigns Valentia to 239. The place was known as Monteleone in mediaeval times, but was renamed Vibo Valentia in 1928

169 As self-governing and independent commonwealths the Latin colonies had their own armed forces which were probably organized along timocratic lines in imitation of the Roman (G. Tibiletti in *Athenaeum* XXVIII [1950], 222). The Citizen colonies were still such small communities at this time that the question of a governing class for them could hardly arise: hence there is as yet no mention of equites or centurions getting abnormally large allotments in them. Under the Empire, by which time the colonies of citizens were also big and therefore in need of far more officials, centurions did get larger land grants than the ordinary colonists

170 As Velleius I. 15. 1 puts it, after the Second Punic War Rome needed to husband her strength rather than to disperse it. The census statistics also indicate this: in 173 there were fewer Roman citizens than there had been in 234 (269,015 as against 270,212: Livy, *Epit.* XX; XLII. 10. 3). Note, too, that the complement of a Latin colony drops from the 6,000 or 4,000 norm of the third century to 3,000 at a time when there was land available for many more (at Vibo, Thurii and Bononia: G. Tibiletti in *Athenaeum* XXVIII [1950], 220). Land intended for viritane distribution also went begging (Livy XLII. 22. 5). The Romans prevented some of this land from lying idle by assigning it to Ligures

171 Many of the colonists had run away from Cremona and Placentia during the Second Punic War (Livy XXVIII. 11. 10) and after the war both places had been under heavy assault from the Gauls (Livy XXXI. 10. 2); for good measure, the Ligures had carried their devastations up to the very walls of Placentia (Livy XXXIV. 56. 10), a town which seemed to Plautus a typical example of the dangerously exposed outpost (*Captivi* 162). The advocates of the Latin colonies in Cisalpine Gaul were more probably the Valerii than Cato the Censor: they dominate the founding commissions for Placentia, Cremona and Bononia. Later the influence of the Aemilii Lepidi in the region was immense: one wonders whether they won this by sponsoring Citizen colonies instead of Latin

172 Any Italian who had not sided with Hannibal was eligible to join the group of new colonists for Cosa (Livy XXXIII. 24. 8). Some of the Italians who had immigrated unofficially into Narnia before 199 (Livy XXXII. 2. 6) must have had their status regularized into that of *coloni*

173 Livy XXXVII. 47. 2; 57. 7

174 Livy XXXIX. 3. 4–6

175 *Inscr. Italiae* XIII. 3, 70a (= *CIL* VI. 1283, or I². 1. xxxii, p. 200)

176 Cic., *Brutus* 170

177 Livy XLI. 8 and 9. The Romans were certainly prepared to recruit Latini for a viritane distribution (Livy XLII. 4. 4); hence they were also likely to accept them for colonies

178 Livy XXXIX. 2. 7, 10

179 Five *iugera* were sufficient to entice settlers to Mutina, a Citizen colony so exposed that Ligures overran it just six years after its foundation (Livy XLI. 16. 7), whereas it took ten times that amount to attract settlers to a Latin colony (Bononia) that was closer to Rome and very much safer

180 The proposer of a colony had no doubt always derived some benefit: Plut., *Tit. Flam.* 1, 4, reveals that Flamininus' bid for the consulship of 198 was aided by colonies where he had been commissioner (although Plutarch seems to be in error about the names of the colonies: E. Badian, *Foreign Clientelae* [1958], 162 n. 6). But so long as strategic need was urgent, colonization did not depend on the whim of a single *gens*

181 The military need for the colonies at Saturnia (183) and Graviscae (181) is not very evident; and it may be that the activity of a Roman censor at Potentia and Pisaurum in 174 (Livy XLI. 27. 11) was in an attempt to build up a following of clients (H. H. Scullard, *Roman Politics* [1950], 192)

182 Livy, *Epitt.* XXXIV ('several colonies', 194), XXXVII, XXXIX, XL; Velleius I. 15. 1–3.

On the basis of *CIL* IX. 5793 it has been argued that, when first founded, Potentia had praetors rather than duoviri (K. J. Beloch, *Röm. Gesch.*, 492). If true, this would strengthen the case for its being large and like a Latin colony (note how, in imperial times, a *municipium* when elevated to a *colonia* was sometimes uncertain whether to call its officials quattuorviri or duoviri and compromised by styling them quattuorviri duoviri; so, for example, at Placentia: *CIL* XI. 1217, =p. 242). The evidence, however, is very dubious, since the inscription in question may not belong to Potentia (it was found some distance away at Pausulae [Montolmo]) and may not mean a praetor anyway (the abbreviation PR could stand for praefectus)

183 Cic., *Brutus* 79; *cf. pro Arch.* 22; *de orat.* III. 168

184 Saturnia: Livy XXXIX. 55. 6f; five roads came together there. Graviscae, the port for Tarquinii: Livy XL. 29. 1. Its allotments were smaller than those at Saturnia (10 *iugera*) or at Parma (8 *iugera*), perhaps deliberately so. The Roman authorities may have been trying to make Graviscae compare very unfavourably with Aquileia, the Latin colony that was being founded at exactly the same moment. This may also be the reason why they did not change the ill-sounding name of Graviscae (derived from the oppressive air [*gravis aer*] of the place, according to Cato, a contemporary: Servius, *ad Aen.* X. 184: *cf.* Rutilius, *de red. suo* I. 282)

185 Bononia controlled the Futa pass, Mutina the Abetone and Parma the Cisa

186 In somewhat the same way provincial districts close to Italy later enjoyed Roman *ius commercii*: E. De Ruggiero in *Diz. Epigr.* s.v. 'Ius Italicum'

187 Livy XL. 51. 9. It is usually thought that the changes of 179 mainly dealt with the registration of freedmen (L. Lange, *Röm. Altert.* II³. 235f, 354f; G. W. Botsford, *Rom. Assemblies*, 85 n. 3; L. R. Taylor, *Voting Districts of the Rom. Republic*, 139). But the date, immediately after the institution of large Citizen colonies, suggests that one purpose of the change may have been to favour colonists in some way. After this date, at any rate, Citizen colonists are mentioned as influential voters

188 Livy XXXIX. 22. 6; 54; 55; XL. 34. 2

189 The reference is to Carteia (171). It was peopled with the emancipated offspring of Spanish (slave?) women by Roman soldiers serving in the Iberian peninsula (Livy XLIII. 3. 1–4). Its purpose was probably to spare Rome the necessity of recognizing these children as Roman citizens.

The Roman notion of the appropriate distance for a Latin colony to be from Rome had obviously changed with the years: in 315 they had hesitated about sending a Latin colony to Luceria because it was so far away (Livy IX. 26. 4)

190 Livy XL. 34. 2; 53. 3; XLIII. 17. 1

191 There were titular Latin colonies later, but these were not founded. Carteia (see note 189) is an apparent exception, but it, too, was not a colonization in the technical sense; it seems to have resembled Scipio's establishment at Italica

192 On the Ligures see Cic., *Brutus* 255 and contrast Livy XXXIX. 1. 2 (see, however, XL. 59. 1); Strabo IV. 6. 3, p. 203

193 On the colonization of Luna see E. T. Salmon in *CQ* XXVII (1933), 30–35. The ancient texts are Livy XL. 43. 1; XLI. 13. 4; XLV. 13. 10; Velleius I. 15. 2 (where Luca is to be emended to Luna). The land the Pisans offered

was doubtless that which the Ligures had taken from the Etrusci in the vicinity of the R. Macra. Livy XLI. 13. 14 says that the *coloni* received $51\frac{1}{2}$ *iugera* apiece, an impossible figure for a Citizen colony at this time: the LIS of Livy is to be emended to VIS (=$6\frac{1}{2}$ *iugera*, *c.* one-thirtieth of a *centuria*)

CHAPTER VII

194 Velleius I. 15. 3 assigns Auximum to 157, but his text is more than usually disordered at this point and his numerals have got attached to the wrong names, as H. Kasten demonstrated long ago (*Berliner Phil. Wochenschrift* LIV [1934], 671): the CLVII that is given for Fabrateria really belongs to Auximum, whose date thus becomes 128 (E. T. Salmon in *Athenaeum* XLI [1963], 10f). A colony in 157 would be an isolated and aberrant phenomenon; even scholars who accept this date for Auximum are surprised by it (see, for example, J. Carcopino, *Autour des Gracques*, 239)

195 Cimbri and Teutoni were hardly contiguous in 128

196 The quotation is from Sall., *Jug.* 41

197 Two different commissions were appointed on the occasion of the Pisan offer of land for a colony in 180; and it has been noted in note 171 that Valerii and Aemilii both seem to have been striving for influence in Cisalpine Gaul. See further A. J. Toynbee, *Hannibal's Legacy*, II, 633–635

198 The charter of Urso, Julius Caesar's colony in Spain, provides for a levy en masse of all the colonists in an emergency: *ILS* 6087, 103. Auximum served some military purpose if it did nothing more than convert some *proletarii* into *adsidui*. The extent to which the Roman authorities were vigilant against Asculum in 128 is uncertain. One ancient source (*De vir. ill.* 65. 2) says that the town supported the revolt of Fregellae in 125: but few scholars believe this

199 The consul, App. Claudius Pulcher, had thought it necessary to attack the Salassi in 143, but the evidence is clear that they were not threatening Roman soil (Livy, *Epit.* LIII; Strabo IV. 6. 7; Dio XXII fr. 74; Oros. V. 4). In any case Auximum was much too far away to have any connection with them

200 The number of settlers and the size of their allotments are not recorded, but the use at Auximum of the title praetor for the chief officials, besides being evidence for their jurisdictional authority and for the increasing complexity of the constitution of a Citizen colony, suggests that the place was very much like one of the old Latin colonies

201 H. Last in *CAH* IX, 42

202 On Heba see A. Minto in *Not. degli Scavi* 1919, 199–206; K. J. Beloch. *Röm. Gesch.* 608. The only references to it in ancient writers are Ptol, III. 1. 43 and, doubtfully, Pliny, *N.H.* III. 52 (where *Herbanum* has to be emended). Like Cosa, Saturnia and the rest of the Ager Caletranus it had

been Roman territory since 280. Livy's failure to mention its colonization is not conclusive, since he similarly fails to record the reinforcement of Cales, *c.* 184. For the suggestion that Heba and Auximum may belong to the same period see G. Tibiletti in *Athenaeum* XXVIII (1950), 233 and F. E. Brown in *Mem. Amer. Acad. Rome* XX (1951), 18. The failure of the Gracchan land commission to settle small farmers in Etruria is indicated by the find-spots of its terminal stones, southern Italy and the Adriatic coast

203 Livy III. 1. 4; IV. 47–49; VI. 11. 8; 16. 6; VIII. 16 .13; Dion. Hal. IX. 59. In fact the older colonies were so obviously needed on military grounds that it is improbable that political disputes arose about the desirability of founding them

204 The *tabulae* proper as distinct from the Annales Maximi, a later and very much expanded version of the contents of the *tabulae*

205 See pp. 97, 103

206 During the Second Punic War Roman infringement of the autonomy of Latini and Italians could be justified, and tolerated, since it was dictated by overriding military necessity. But after the war the exasperation of the non-Romans grew steadily greater: Sall., *Hist.* I. 14 M.; Diod. XXXVII. 15; Velleius II. 15. 2; App., *B.C.* I. 35, 99

207 The Romans ceased extending their citizenship in 188, when Arpinum, Formiae and Fundi received it *optimo iure*; and the grant of it to these three places was opposed (Livy XXXVIII. 36. 8)

208 Cic., *de re pub.* III. 41; *cf.* I. 31

209 One indication of their more favoured status is that they were chosen, presumably because of the confidence reposed in them, to be places of detention for Roman state prisoners: Livy XXVI. 16. 6; XXX. 17. 2; 45. 4; XXXII. 2. 4; 26. 5; XXXIX. 19. 2. But they could decline to act in this capacity: in 167 Spoletium refused to serve as a prison for the Illyrian King Gentius and his family (Livy XLV. 43. 9)

210 Livy XXXVIII. 44. 4; XLII. 4. 4

211 For Venusia see p. 96. For Fregellae: Livy XLI. 8. 8. Fregellae had evidently not sought Roman permission to increase its population in this way, which no doubt exacerbated Roman opinion. In 125 the town seems to have been betrayed to Rome, probably by the Latin-speaking part of its population, led by a certain Q. Numitorius Pullus (Cic., *de invent.* II. 105; *Phil.* III. 17)

212 Mommsen, *CIL* X. 5584, p. 547, argues that Fabrateria was a Latin colony since it appears as a *municipium* after the Social War and is not called a colony by Pliny. The argument is not conclusive: there are other examples of Roman colonies being called, carelessly, *municipia* or overlooked by Pliny. Fabrateria had duoviri immediately after the Social War, whereas quattuorviri might have been expected had it been a Latin colony. In fact the political climate at Rome excludes the possibility of a Latin colony in 124: in the Gracchan age only Citizen colonies were founded (E. De

Ruggiero in *Diz. Epigr.* s.v. 'Colonia', 451). It may be suspected that the settlers at Fabrateria included the Latin-speaking elements from Fregellae. It seems certain that it was Fabrateria Nova that replaced Fregellae: Fabrateria Vetus, at Ceccano probably, was too far away

213 For the date see G. Tibiletti in *Rend. dell'Istituto Lomb.* LXVI (1953), 45–63, especially 57f. Thereby a new type of citizenship was created, the *civitas per magistratum*

214 Velleius II. 7. 7; Plut., *G. Gracchus* 8. 3; 9. 2. Admittedly, however, there is no positive evidence that he was responsible for Scolacium. At about the same time the proconsul C. Sextius Calvinus, according to Livy, *Epit.* LXI, founded a colony, named Aquae Sextiae after him, in Transalpine Gaul, but this seems to have been a Roman garrison, not a true *colonia* (Pliny, *N.H.* III. 36 says that its status was Latin, not Roman, even in Augustus' day). The same is probably true of the 'two cities' which, according to Strabo III. 5. 1, p. 167, were established, also at about this time, on the Balearic Is. with 3,000 settlers

215 Wolves were said to have appeared at Carthage (Plut., *G. Gracchus* 10. 1). In Africa these would indeed be an ominous phenomenon. For the number of colonists see App., *B.C.* I. 24; Solinus 27. 11

216 Some individuals, however, were settled there on a viritane basis. In somewhat the same way some of Marius' veterans later kept the allotments assigned to them in Africa even though Saturninus' colonies of which they were to have formed part never materialized. See notes 246, 247

217 Plut., *G. Gracchus*, 9. 1

218 Cic., *de leg. agr.* I. 21; II. 10; 76; 81, regards this new kind of colonization as political bribery, its object being to promote the despotism of demagogues. Paupers had, of course, been enrolled in colonies in earlier days, but for military reasons, not political

219 The Liber Coloniarum lists at least seven colonies as Sempronian, not including Neptunia, Minervia and Junonia. K. J. Beloch, *Röm. Gesch.*, 493f would also regard Abellinum, Grumentum and Telesia as colonies of the Gracchan period, since their chief officials were called praetores duoviri, like those of Narbo Martius, founded a few years after Gracchus; in fact the adjective Livia seems to have formed part of the title of Abellinum (*CIL* X. 1117)—from Livius Drusus?

220 Cic., ad Att. I. 19. 4

221 Narbo: E. Badian in *Mélanges Piganiol* (1966), 903f. Velleius I. 15. 5 assigns it to 118, but his text is very disordered at this point. The recent attempt by H. B. Mattingly (in *Mélanges Grenier* [1962], 1159f) to date it from coins has not proved successful (C. A. Hersh in *Num. Chron.*, ser. 7, VI [1966], 71–93). Exactly which branch of the Volcae it was to watch is uncertain, but it was evidently successful since by Augustus' day the Volcae were very much romanized (Strabo IV. 1. 2, p. 186), a result to which Julius Caesar had also no doubt contributed.

Dertona: Strabo V. 6. 7, p. 205. Velleius (I. 15. 5) says that there is uncertainty about Dertona, which has generally been interpreted to mean uncertainty about its date: but Velleius may mean that it is uncertain whether it was a colony at all before 43 (U. Ewins in *Pap. Brit. Sch. Rome* VII [1952], 68f).

Eporedia: Velleius places this town *in Bagiennis* (I. 15. 5): in fact it was *in Salassis*. Apart from this careless reference in Velleius there is no evidence for a colony there at this time

222 Cic., *pro Cluent.* 140; *pro Font.* 13, 46. C. H. Benedict, *History of Narbo* (1941), *passim*, seems to exaggerate the commercial importance of the place. At the time of its foundation southern Gaul had probably not been organized as a separate province, a fact that would have provided its opponents with ammunition

223 Livy, *Oxy. Frag.*, line 176f; Strabo V. 1. 11, p. 217

224 Pliny, *N.H.* III. 123, who, however, calls it an *oppidum*, not a *colonia*. See P. Fraccaro in *Annali dei Lavori Pubblici* LXXIX (1941), 6, 719. The Cimbri and Teutoni may have made a colony seem necessary there

225 *Cf.* Cic., *de leg. agr.* II. 10

226 F. T. Hinrichs in *Historia* XVI (1967), 162–176

227 Cic., *pro Balbo* 48, rejecting the emendation *trecentos*

228 One of the thirty Latin colonies of 218 had been destroyed, and four new ones planted

229 Diod. XXXVII. 2. 1; Florus II. 6. 11

230 For writers of the first century AD, particularly Tacitus, the expression *municipia et coloniae* means *tota Italia*

231 Bruns, *Fontes*[7], 27, p. 120

232 Rejecting H. Rudolph, *Stadt und Staat im röm. Italien*, 134–153

233 Cic., *de leg. agr.* II. 93 shows that a Roman colony was usually headed by duoviri. But there were exceptions to prove the rule: Napoca in Dacia apparently had only aediles and praefecti (*CIL* III. 827, 858, 867). See, too, note 316

234 Cic., *de leg. agr.* II. 86, 96. According to Cicero, Puteoli was independent and enjoyed liberty and its own jurisdiction

235 This did not, of course, prevent many of them from becoming Roman colonies later

236 Note Cic., *ad Att.* V. 2. 3: 'the Transpadani were instructed to institute quattuorviri.' Some towns that had been *municipia* before 91 retained their earlier non-quattuorviral constitutions.

237 Ascon. p. 3 Cl. Carteia in Spain may have suggested the idea to Pompeius Strabo: see note 189. The only surviving charters of Latin communities are from towns of this type, Salpensa and Malaca in Spain (*ILS* 6088, 6089). They are of Flavian date and suggest that Latin towns of the Empire resembled their prototypes of the Republic so far as their relations with

Rome were concerned. Neither charter, however, actually calls its town Latin, much less a Latin colony

Appendix to Chapter VII

238 But Vienna became a Roman colony very early in the Roman Empire (*ILS* 212; Pliny, *N.H.* III. 36; Tac., *Hist.* I. 66)

239 H. Braunert in *Corolla Memoriae Erich Swoboda Dedicata* (1966), 68–83. For Latini *coloniarii* see Gaius I. 22. 9. 79; III. 56. A town whose inhabitants enjoyed Latin status was likely to erect a symbolical statue of the sow and thirty piglets (*CIL* II. 2126, Obulco in the Spanish province of Baetica), just as a Roman colony that enjoyed Ius Italicum would erect a symbolical statue of Marsyas (see notes 320, 321)

240 T. R. S. Broughton, *Romanization of Africa Proconsularis* (1929), 138; A. N. Sherwin-White, *Rom. Citizenship*, 110

241 At Gigthis, for instance: *CIL* VIII. 22737

CHAPTER VIII

242 Velleius I. 15. 5. For colonization in the period covered by this chapter see F. Hampl in *Rhein. Museum* XCV (1952), 52–78

243 See note 159

244 Of course the state domain was likely to be put to use at all times. But some portions of it were 'possessed' *precario*, that is, occupied on sufferance by squatters who could be instructed to vacate at a moment's notice; and it was these portions that were normally used for colonies. By 100 there was not much of it 'possessed' in this way

245 It proposed allotments of 100 *iugera*: De Vir. Ill. 73, and see E. Badian, *Foreign Clientelae* 199. Saturninus also carried an agrarian law in 100, but, according to Cicero, *pro Balbo* 48, no colonies resulted from it. T. R. S. Broughton, however, in *AJA* LII (1948), 324–330, suggests that Julius Caesar's father founded one at Cercina (Lesser Syrtis) in 100, adducing the fragmentary evidence of *Inscr. Italiae* XIII. iii. no. 7: [C Iul]ius [C. f. Caesar] pater di[vi Iulii p]r(aetor) q(uaestor) tr(ibunus [mil(itum) . . . c]olonos Cerce[nam? deduxit]

246 Pliny *N.H.* III. 80 (but Mariana may have been founded, not by Marius himself, but by his party after his death on 13 January 86: E. Gabba in *Athenaeum* XXIX [1951], 20). An inscription of *c.* AD 100 describes Marius as *conditor coloniae* at Thuburnica (*Comptes rendus de l'Académie des Inscriptions* 1950, 332–336; *Ann. Epigr.* 1951, no. 81). But this is municipal vanity and is not to be taken literally. Marius' veterans got land grants on a viritane basis at Thuburnica, just as they did at Uchi Maius and Thibaris, and formed an *oppidum civium Romanorum* there (Pliny, *N.H.* V. 29). Only in this sense could Marius be described as 'founder' of the place. See notes 216, 247

247 *CIL*. VIII. 15450, 15454, 15455, 26181, 26270, 26275, 26281 (all apparently of the 3rd C. AD, from Uchi Maius and Thibaris); Val. Max. IX. 15. 1; T. Frank in *AJP* XLVII (1926), 56f

248 This was Aleria (Pliny, *N.H.* III. 81)

249 According to Cicero, *de leg. agr.* II. 63–67, the first person to propose that land for colonies should be bought was Rullus in 63

250 Cic. *ad Fam.* XIII. 4. 1

251 Velleius I. 14.1

252 R. Syme, *The Roman Revolution* (1939), 88, estimates that Sulla settled 100,000 veterans on the lands of his enemies. For Sulla's colonization see E. Gabba in *Athenaeum* XXIX (1951), 270f

253 See note 307 and *Pl. 54*

254 Cic., *pro Sulla* 62. For another 'double community' see *CIL* X. 6087

255 Cic., *de leg. agr.* III. 5; Plut. *Sulla* 33; App. *B.C.* I. 98–99

256 His brother was founding commissioner at Pompeii: Cic., *pro Sulla* 62

257 Corduba in Baetica, according to Strabo III. 2. 1, p. 141, was founded by M. Claudius Marcellus, consul in 152: it was certainly a veterans' colony under Augustus.

Valentia in Tarraconensis, founded apparently by D. Junius Brutus, consul in 138, is a puzzle: it was an *oppidum* in the second century (Livy, Epit. LV) and an *urbs* in the first (Sall. Hist. II, fr. 96, 6 M.), yet the consul for 60 regarded it as a *colonia* (*ILS* 878, =*CIL* IX. 5275). It undoubtedly had the rank of *colonia* later and the adjectives Julia and Augusta do not appear in its title.

It seems impossible that either place could have been regarded officially as a *colonia* at the time of its foundation: the furore over Carthago-Junonia confirms the statement of Velleius (II. 7. 8) that it was the first transmarine colony

258 *CIL* XI. p. 530f

259 Suet. *Iul.* 38. 1; App., *B.C.* II. 94; Dio XXXVIII. 1

260 Pliny, *ad Trai.* 47, 48

261 Suet., *Iul.* 44. 2; 79. 3. The rumour is reflected in Hor., *Odes* III. 3. 57f

262 Velleius II. 7. 7. Velleius' attitude is revealed by his gross exaggeration that Gaius 'sought to fill the provinces with new colonies' (II. 6. 3)

263 Sometimes a place that had been a *municipium Julium* and subsequently made a *colonia* by someone other than Julius Caesar or Augustus is also styled Julia

264 Suet., *Iul.* 42. 1. 80,000 might be equivalent to one-tenth of the population of the city of Rome. F. Vittinghoff, *Röm. Kolonisation unter Caesar und Augustus* (1952), *passim*, calculates that Caesar founded thirty-one colonies and Augustus seventy-five, the overwhelming majority of them in the western provinces

265 *ILS* 6087, =*CIL* II. 5439

266 *CIL* VIII. 977; X. 6104

267 Strabo VIII. 6. 23, p. 381

268 Strabo XVII. 3, 15, p. 833; Plut. *Caes.* 57; Paus. II. 1. 2; Dio XLIII. 50; App., *Lib.* 136. The colony at Carthage and the native town there formed a 'double community': *CIL* VIII. p. 133

269 Cic., *ad Att.* XVI. 16a

270 Strabo III. 2. 1, p. 141; Dio XLIII. 39. 5

271 *CIL* VI. 1006; XII. 4344–4349

272 *CIL* II. pp. 500f, 538f. Admittedly the first titular Roman colony of real importance seems to have been Vienna (Vienne) in the Gallic province of Narbonensis, under Claudius or possibly Gaius: *CIL* XII. 2327

273 It was from the colonies of Caesar and Augustus that the Empire obtained many of its officials during the first two centuries AD, in the west at any rate

274 Antony, for example, planted his colonies to safeguard his lines of communication between Rome and Cisalpine Gaul: E. Gabba in *Parola del Passato* VIII (1953), 105

275 Dio LI. 4. 6

276 App., *B.C.* V. 3; Hyginus, *de lim. cast.*, p. 177, 8 L

277 *Res. Gestae* 16; cf. Velleius II. 81. 2; Dio XLIX. 14. 5

278 *Res Gestae* 15. 3; 28. 2

279 *CIL* V. 4212

280 *Res Gestae* 16; Dio LI. 4. 6

281 Dio XLIII. 39. 5. Apparently he also granted a less valuable degree of immunity to a few colonies in Baetica and Mauretania

282 From now on *coloniae* precede *municipia* in documents (see *ILS* 212)

283 The Gallic province of Narbonensis well illustrates this: Arausio, Baeterrae and Forum Julii were colonized with veterans from Legions II, VII and VIII respectively (*CIL* XII. 1242; 4227 etc.; 3203). Even when civilians were admitted, as at Patrae in Achaea (Paus. VII. 18. 7), veterans (from Legions X and XII) predominated (Strabo VIII. 7. 5, p. 387)

284 Tac., *Ann.* I. 17

285 *Res Gestae* 28. It is appropriate that Africa should head the list, since Augustus founded colonies there on approximately the same scale as Julius Caesar. Pisidia, however, was not a province in his day, but only part of one. Obviously it is singled out, and the fact that it is named last indicates the same thing. Augustus may have wished to draw attention to his great feat in establishing as many colonies in this difficult terrain as in Africa, six. For his Pisidian colonies see B. Levick, *Roman Colonies in Southern Asia Minor*, *passim*

286 The Mauretanian colonies seem to have been under the general supervision of the governors of the neighbouring provinces of Baetica and Africa: P. Romanelli, *Province Romane dell' Africa*, 205

287 Suet., *Aug.* 40. 3

288 G. W. Bowersock, *Augustus and the Greek World* (1965), 66f argues strongly

that the nineteen certainly identifiable Augustan colonies in the east were not founded with romanization in mind (*cf.*, too, B. Levick, *Rom. Colonies in S. Asia Minor*, 162). But it is worth noting that Augustus does pride himself on his successful diffusion or revival of genuine Roman customs (see, for example, *Res Gestae* 8)

CHAPTER IX

289 The cited examples show that both the emperor's *gentilicium* and his cognomen might be employed to form the name of the colony. The titulature could be expanded, in the event of a place being 'colonized' a second time, and thus reveal more than one founding emperor. Equally the titulature could be changed in the event of the founding emperor suffering *damnatio memoriae*. Personified abstractions (Virtus, Laus and the like) were sometimes used as the names for colonies (note 77)

290 Augustus boasts in the *Res Gestae* 28. 2 that his twenty-eight colonies in Italy were already *celeberrimae et frequentissimae* in his own lifetime. His successors variously call themselves *conditor coloniae* (*CIL* III. 374, 1443, 3279; VIII. 17841, 17842; IX. 5247), *parens coloniae* (*CIL* III. 2907; XI. 720), or *restitutor coloniae* (*CIL* III. 7282). Note, too, the expression *colonia beneficiis aucta* (*CIL* VIII. 12517; XIV. 95). For the inscription recording Trajan's foundation of Thamugadi in Numidia see *CIL* VIII. 2355 (=17842) (=*ILS* 6841)

291 Lib. Colon. I p. 201, 3 L.; Rudorff, *Grom. veteres* II. 367

292 *CIL* XII. 218

293 Roman colonies began issuing their own coins under Julius Caesar

294 Consider, for example, the situation in Numidia. There, *c.* AD 100, four colonies—Cirta, Rusicade, Milev, Chullu—were banded together to form one huge colonial federation, to which a fifth settlement, Cuicul, was subsequently added. This arrangement, which was due to the unorthodox origin of Cirta (see note 4), endured for over a century and must have been very instrumental in diffusing Roman practices and customs. See *CIL* VIII p. 618f

295 Livy I. 27. 9: 'a large number of the Fidenates knew Latin inasmuch as Roman colonists had been settled amongst them.' Augustus restricted recruitment of his Praetorian Guard to Latium, Etruria, Umbria and the old colonies: Tac., *Ann.* IV. 5

296 Suet., *Claud.* 25. 3; Dio LX. 17. 4f

297 There were no *municipia* in Asia Minor or the Levant. There were some *coloniae*, possibly because these, being closed communities, stood a better chance of preserving their Roman character. The Roman authorities were interested in promoting the use of Latin beyond the Aegean (Val. Max. II.

2. 2), but 'Roman colonies in the east did little to spread the Latin language there': B. Levick, *Rom. Colonies in S. Asia Minor*, 162

298 According to Tac., *Ann.* XII. 32, a colony was a *subsidium contra rebelles.* Already in the pseudo-Sallustian letter to Caesar (*ad Caes.* II. 5. 8) the point is made that colonies can enrich the armed services

299 Tac., *Ann.* XIV. 31; *Agric.* 16. 1; *Hist.* IV. 64

300 *CIL* III. 975, 986, 1132 (Apulum); Strabo X. 2. 21, p. 460 (Patrae); *CIL* III. 611 (Dyrrhachium); *CIL* VIII. 2392 (Thamugadi)

301 Pliny, *N.H.*, XXVII. 3

302 Caesarea Stratonis was particularly favoured by Vespasian (AD 69–79), since it was there that his army had first proclaimed him emperor: Pliny, *N.H.*, V. 69

303 The Ubii must have welcomed Colonia Agrippinensis (Cologne), Claudius' colony on the Rhine, which he named after his wife rather than himself, since it gave them citizen rights in the highest type of Roman city: Tac., *Germ.* 28; *Hist.* IV. 65; *Ann.* XII. 27; Strabo IV. 3. 4, p. 194

304 Tac., *Ann.* XIV. 27

305 This is illustrated by the use, even if temporary, of the title 'sufetes' for the duoviri at Carthago and at Lepcis Magna in Africa (L. Müller, *Numism. de l'ancienne Afrique* II. 149; *Inscriptions of Roman Tripolitania,* 412). Lepcis Magna, however, may well have been a titular colony

306 Aul. Gell. XVI. 13. 9; immediately before this (§3) Gellius had said, 'the general opinion is that the status of the *coloniae* is superior to that of the *municipia*'

307 It is true that Praeneste successfully petitioned the Emperor Tiberius (AD 14–37) for permission to revert from *colonia* to *municipium*: it hated being a *colonia* since it had been made one by Sulla (Aul. Gell. XVI. 13. 5). But Praeneste was not a provincial *colonia*; moreover it soon reacquired the title of *colonia* and kept it (*CIL* XIV. p. 289f)

308 Conversely the emperors might have been expected to deprive of the title any cities that they wished to punish. In fact Elagabalus (AD 218–222) may have done precisely this: A. W. Zumpt, *Commentationes Epigraphicae* (1850) I. 143f

309 R. Syme, *Tacitus* (1958), 590, 620

310 E. Kornemann in *R.E.* IV (1901), s.v. 'Coloniae', 566

311 Vespasian, for instance, made Aventicum in Switzerland a *colonia*, apparently because his father had made a fortune there in banking operations (Suet., *Vesp.*, 1. 3). Here, however, an actual *deductio* probably took place

312 SHA, *Marcus* 26. 9

313 Some provinces were not thought ready for *coloniae* apparently. Britain never had more than four: Camulodunum (Colchester), Eburacum (York), Glevum (Gloucester) and Lindum (Lincoln). By contrast, the Severan dynasty greatly increased the number of colonies in Africa (birthplace of Septimius) and in Syria (homeland of his wife)

314 Aul. Gell. XVI. 13. 3 avers that most people could not see much difference between a *municipium* and a *colonia*. *Cf.*, too, Dig. 50. 15. 1. 3 (on Ptolemais): *nihil praeter nomen coloniae habet*

315 Aul. Gell. XVI. 13. 2. Some of the inscriptions which seem to give the title of a *municipium* to a *colonia* may in fact be referring to the *municipium* half of a 'double community', but not *CIL* IX. 5825, which calls Auximum a *municipium*

316 Examples: Salvia (when a colony) had quattuorviri (*CIL* IX. p. 526), whereas Ricina (when a *municipium*) had duoviri (*CIL* IX. p. 547). See, further, W. Liebenam, *Städteverw. im röm. Kaiserreiche*, 255; A. Degrassi, *Scritti Vari* (1962), I. 99–177

317 Examples: Massilia, Nicaea, Tarraco (*CIL* XII. 410; V. 7914; *ILS* 1399)

318 Aul. Gell. XVI. 13. 4f. V. Chapot, *La province proconsulaire d'Asie* (1904), 449. The inter-city rivalries of the Roman Empire are, of course, notorious: examples—Pompeii and Nuceria (Tac., *Ann.* XIV. 17), Lugudunum and Vienna (Tac., *Hist.* I. 65), Lepcis Magna and Oea (Tac., *Hist.* IV. 50)

319 Actually, to judge from representations on coins, the statue showed Marsyas as a naked Silenus carrying a sack (or a wine skin?) over his shoulder. *Cf.*, too, *CIL* VIII. 17841 (Thamugadi)

320 According to Serv., *ad Aen.* III. 20 (cf. IV. 58), Marsyas symbolized *libertas*, which may not be completely accurate. Possibly, too, his statue was not equated exactly with Ius Italicum.

Under the Severan dynasty the difference in taxation between Italy and the provinces began to disappear: this may help to account for the greater readiness of Septimius and his successors to grant Ius Italicum to such colonies as Tyre, Laodicea, Emesa, Palmyra and Heliopolis

321 It was not absolutely impossible. At least three provincial communities, which apparently were not colonies, display Marsyas: Coela in the Thracian Chersonese (coins), Verecunda in Numidia (*CIL* VIII. 4219) and another town in Numidia whose name is not known (*CIL* VIII. 16417). A fourth, Stobi in Macedonia, issued Marsyas coins, perhaps before it became a *colonia* (Dig. 50. 15. 8. 8). Antipolis in Narbonese Gaul (Strabo IV. 1. 9, p. 184) is also sometimes cited, but without conclusive evidence

322 Dio LXXII (LXXIII). 15. 2; SHA, *Commodus* 8. 6. Some of Commodus' coins show the name

323 E. Kornemann in *R.E.* IV (1901), s.v. 'Coloniae', 560

SOURCES OF ILLUSTRATIONS

The author and publishers are grateful to the many official bodies and individuals who have supplied illustrations. Pictures not otherwise credited are from Thames and Hudson's archives.

Biblioteca Apostolica Vaticana (Pal. Lat. 1564), 1–5; Stato Maggiore Aeronautica, 7, 13, 34, 35, 36, 37; Brompton Studios (from coins in the British Museum), 8, 9, 10, 40, 41, 57, 59, 60, 61; Museo Arqueológico Nacional, Madrid, 11; Musée des Antiquités Nationales, St Germain-en-Laye, 12; Ministero della Pubblica Istruzione, 14, 39, 52, 54; Fototeca Unione, 15, 16, 17, 28, 29, 30, 31, 32, 33, 43, 44, 45, 48, 49, 50, 51, 55; Ray-Delvert, 18; Mansell Collection, 19, 42; Avenches Museum (photo R. Bersier, Fribourg), 20; Alinari, 23, 26, 38, 46, 47, 56; Professor H. H. Scullard, 25, 27; Narodni Museum, Prague, 53; Colchester and Essex Museum, 58; Dr A. La Regina, 21, 22; the author, 24.

Miss Lucinda Rodd drew the 13 figures.

INDEX

'he numbers refer to pages of the text unless italicized (in which case they refer to plates) r unless preceded by the letter 'n' (in which case they refer to notes). Names are listed ı the form commonly used in English (e.g. Gracchi, not Sempronii). Only those authors re included whose names occur in the text: those cited in the notes will not be found in ıe index. Nor does the index list colonies which appear only on pp. 159–164 = Appendix ɔ Chapter IX). 'Italy', 'Italians', 'Rome' and 'Romans' are too ubiquitous to be indexed.

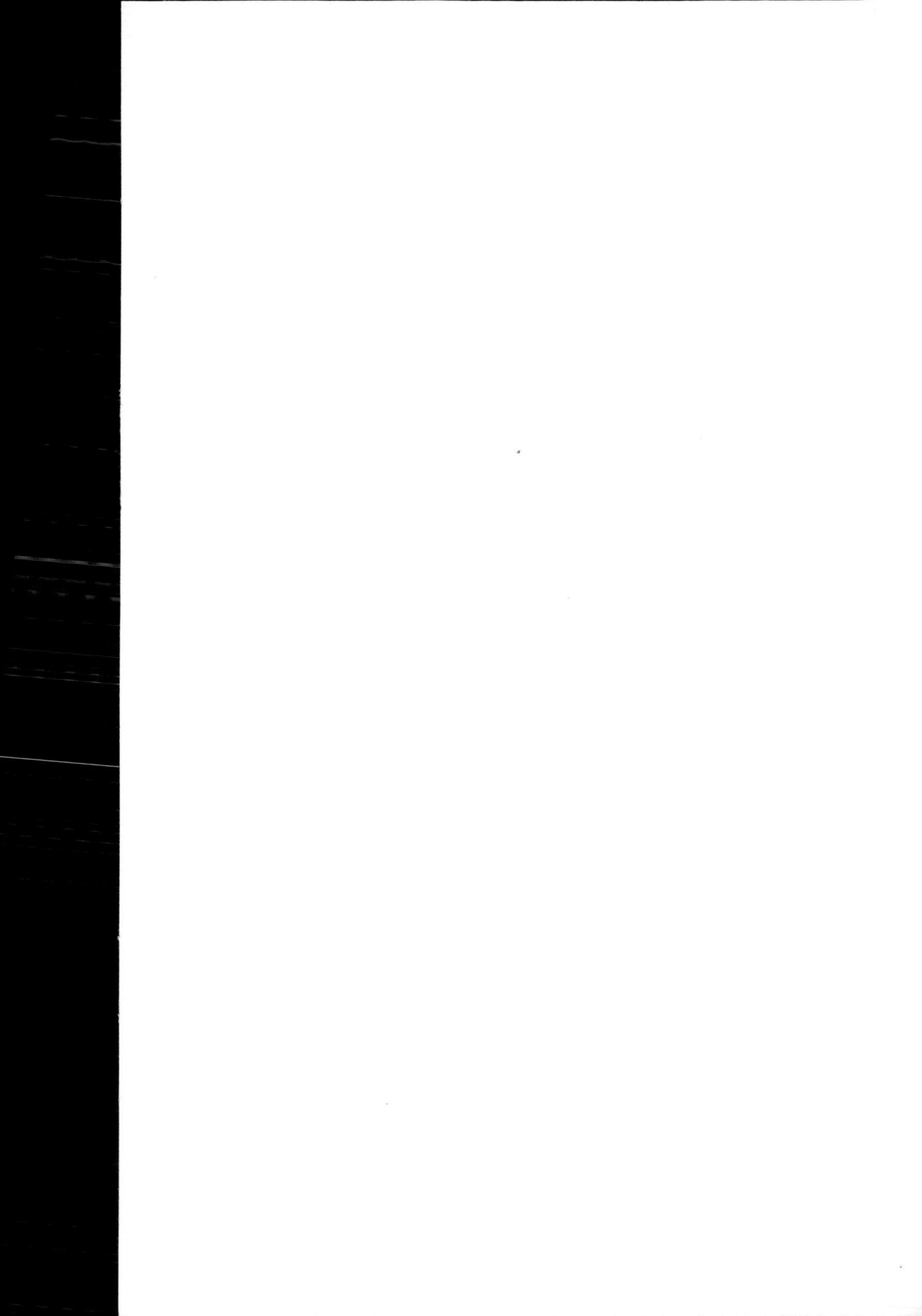